Painting the Soul: The Tarot Art of David Palladini

by

David Palladini and Anastasia Haysler

Painting the Soul: The Tarot Art of David Palladini
by David Palladini and Anastasia Haysler
ISBN 978-0-9833024-0-7

Published by Black Swan Press,
A Cigno E Gallo, Inc. Company
San Francisco, California USA
www.BlackSwanPress.net

Book design by Chris Lowrance, Chris Lowrance Illustation + Design.
Typefaces used: Palatino Linotype

For more information about David Palladini, his life, and his art, please visit the artist's website at
www.DavidPalladini.com

For more information about Anastasia Haysler and her work, please visit the author's website at www.TarotPathways.com

Special thanks to Marcia McCord for her support of this book's creation. Marcia can be found at www.MarciaMcCordTarotReader.BlogSpot.com

This book is dedicated to all the lovers of the Tarot, of my Tarot decks and of my art.

To all those who have helped me, lifted me, encouraged me, and led me through the darkness and into the light.

- David

This book is dedicated to those who opened the door to Tarot for me:
Albert "Cubby" Broccoli
Jane Seymour
My father, Dave Smith

Also to those who helped me put my feet on the Tarot path:
Mary K. Greer
Rachel Pollack
Eden Gray

To my darling husband, Christophe Pettus, for being supportive and understanding while the book consumed what little extra time I had.

To my amazing friend and incomparable assistant, Rose Red, for keeping everything going at the office so I had time to write.

And to David Palladini, whose art first captured my attention and thrilled my soul all those years ago, and who now graces me with the title of "Friend".

Your art still touches my soul, David.

- Anastasia

TABLE OF CONTENTS

ARTIST'S NOTES

As the creator of *The Aquarian Tarot* and *The New Palladini Tarot*, I have tried to infuse as much magic and meaning as possible into the artwork. These subtleties will only become apparent after careful and patient introspection. Each door that opens reveals doors to be opened. Each road travelled leads to more roads. Each new piece of knowledge gleaned from the cards leads to greater knowledge.

Your personal input is very important to the successful use of the Tarot, and intuition and sensitivity are paramount. The cards are a tool for introspection, a mirror of one's own development, an occasional counsel and help. That is the spirit in which I wish my decks to be used: not as a substitute for spirituality, but as an enhancement of belief and faith.

The Tarot is not meant to predict, but rather to give insight. The knowledge suggested by a particular card in a particular position is valid and valuable only as far as one can see into oneself. You can easily dismiss a card, or even a whole reading, if you are not ready to accept it due to fear or lack of self-awareness.

The word "arcana" means "mystery," and the Major Arcana cards signify important spiritual and energetic changes. The Minor Arcana speaks of the lesser everyday mysteries through which, moment by moment, we discover ourselves.

The Tarot has suffered much through history because it requires deep insight on the part of both the reader and the subject. Any lack of faith or shallowness of purpose will reduce the deck to a mere party game. I remember, as a child, the card games my Italian parents played with their friends using a strange set of cards from northern Italy. These cards had pictures of rods, swords, coins, and cups on them, and were called *tarrochi*. So debased had the Tarot become that it was being used in Italy and France for games of wager and chance. The Tarot had gone from philosophical meditation and the hands of kings to the smoky din of the tavern.

***

"What is a Tarot card?" I asked. Little did I know how important the answer to that question would be in shaping my life as an artist.

I was 19 years old, an art student home for the summer break from Pratt Institute in New York City and working as an intern in the art department of a large Chicago advertising agency. With my shoulder-length hair and bell-bottom jeans, I stuck out in that world of three-piece suits and three-martini lunches. But that was why I had been hired: I was rebellious new blood in a rapidly changing world. It was 1965, and the agency was looking for a different slant to reach a new, young generation.

One of the agency's clients was Brown Paper Company, which produced fine art papers in many beautiful colors and textures. The agency's creative director came up with the idea of hiring four artists to draw images of the Tarot to be printed on Brown's beautiful papers. The unseen hand entered my life, as it has many times, and I was selected as one of the four.

That was when I asked the question, "What is a Tarot card?" The creative director just smiled and handed me a deck of cards. It was the Rider-Waite-Smith Tarot. My road had begun.

I resolved to make 12 cards strong and magical. I instinctively chose The Fool, The Emperor, The Empress, and the Wheel of Fortune. I also chose The Hermit because I felt myself to be a kind of hermit, too. I had always shunned people and lived inside of myself with my books and my artwork. The Hanged Man and The Devil appealed to my sense of the macabre. I also chose the Ace, King, Queen, Knight and Page of Swords. My name, Palladini, is an Italian name meaning "knight." Swords were the weapons of my ancient heritage, so the suit of Swords seemed a natural choice for me.

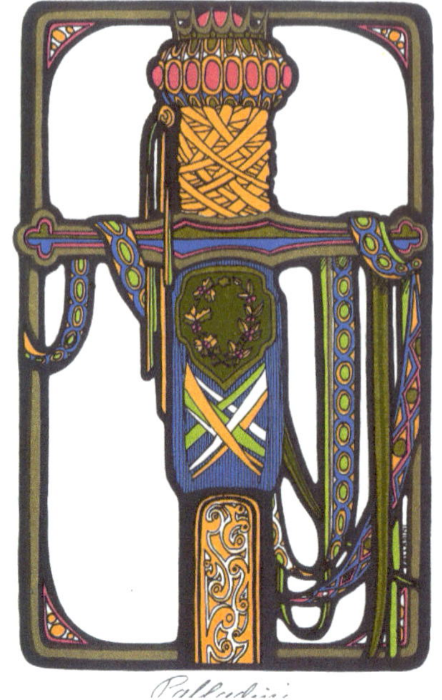
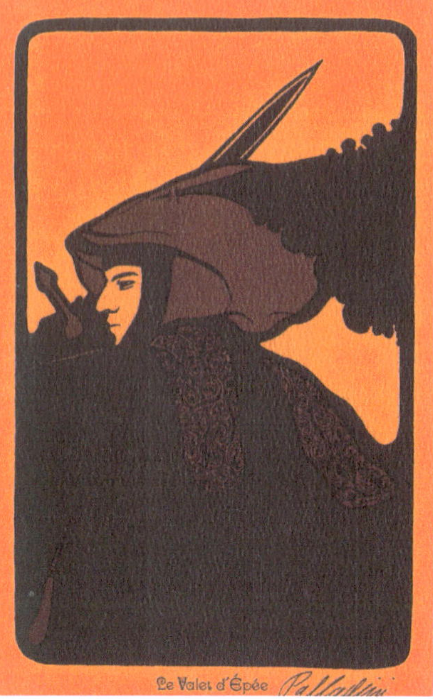
Le Valet d'Épée
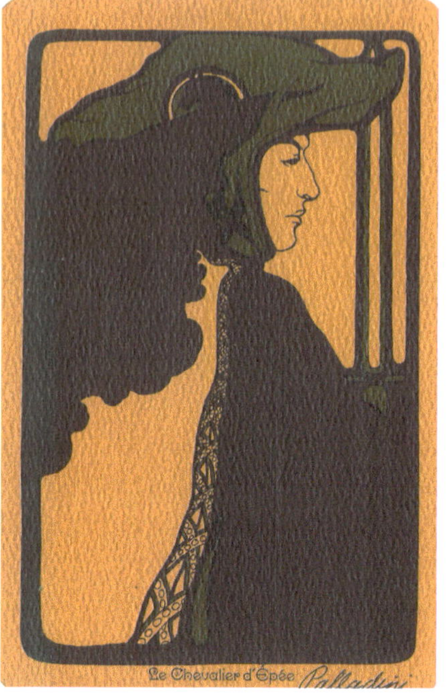
Le Chevalier d'Épée
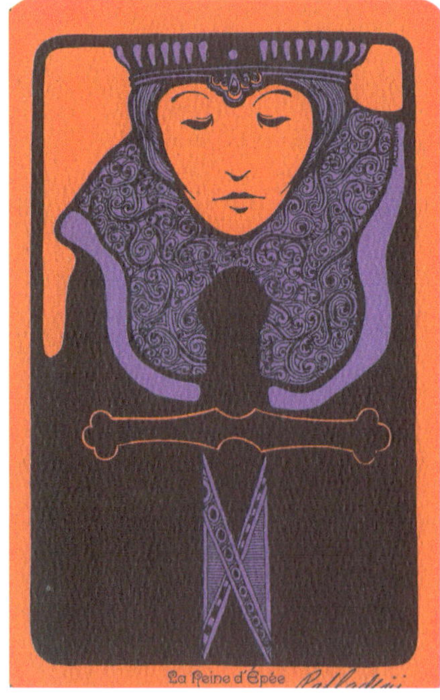
La Reine d'Épée
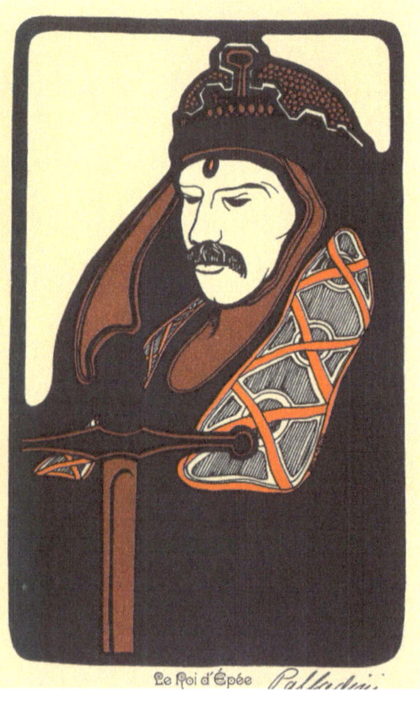
Le Roi d'Épée
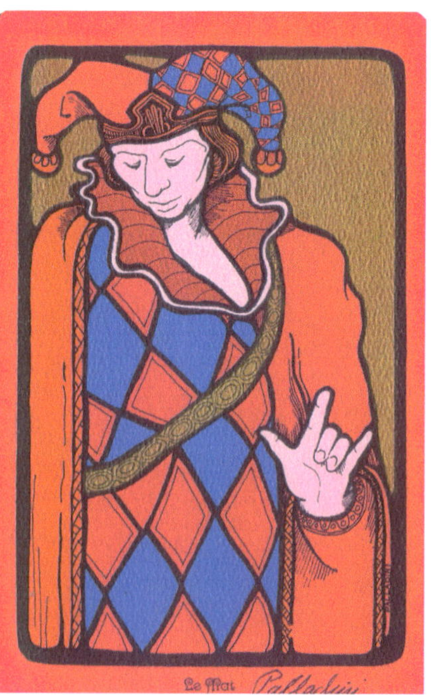
Le Mat

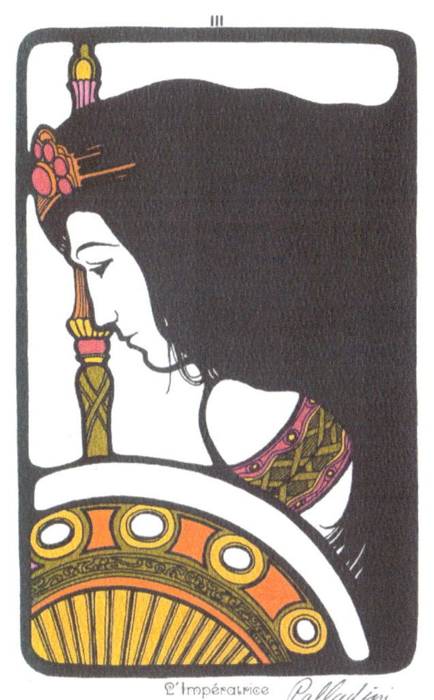
III
L'Impératrice
Palladini

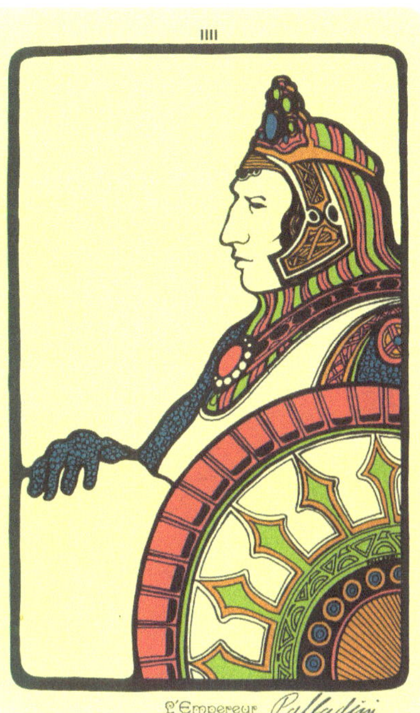
IIII
L'Empereur
Palladini

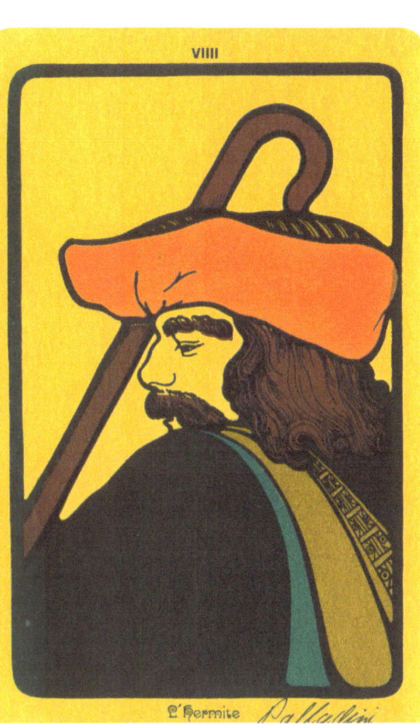
VIIII
L'Hermite
Palladini

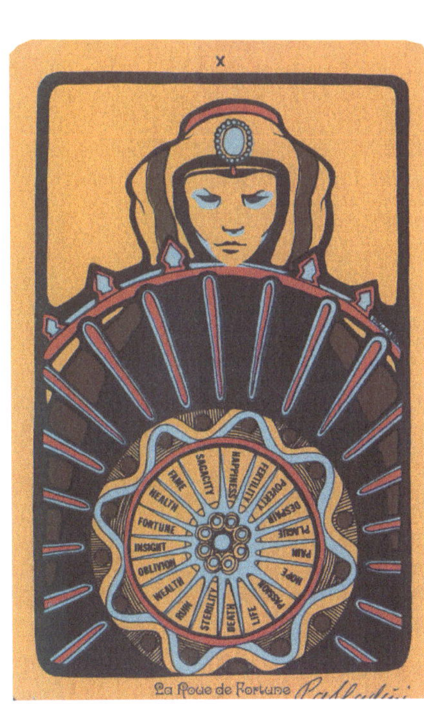
X
FAME
SAGACITY
HAPPINESS
FERTILITY
POVERTY
DESPAIR
PLAGUE
PAIN
HOPE
PASSION
LIFE
DEATH
STERILITY
RUIN
WEALTH
OBLIVION
INSIGHT
FORTUNE
HEALTH
La Roue de Fortune
Palladini

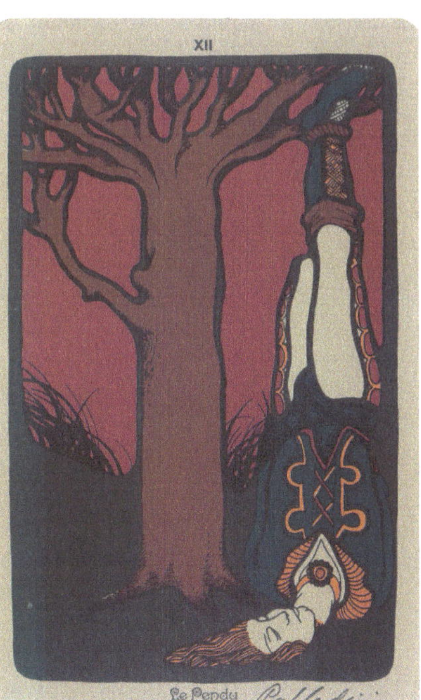
XII
Le Pendu
Palladini

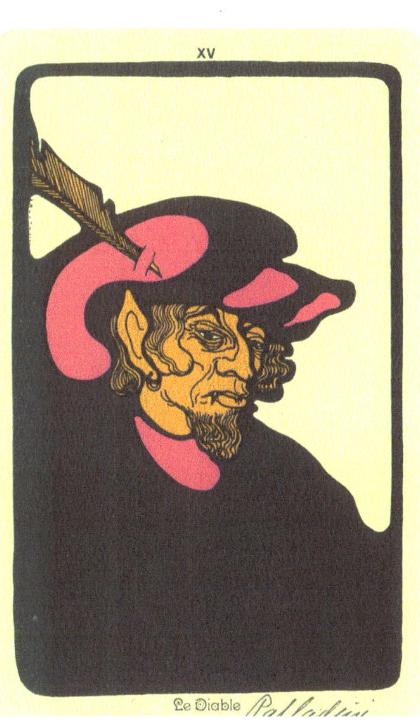
XV
Le Diable
Palladini

I drew the cards without knowledge of their meaning. I did not want to know, nor did I care. The cards were only interesting subjects to draw, and nothing more. I had only begun to learn. I did not know. Not yet.

Fast-forward six months: I was working on a large canvas in painting class at Pratt Institute when a man walked into the room. After a few words with my instructor, the man called me into the hallway. He said he was Lloyd Morgan of Morgan Press, located in a small hamlet up the Hudson River from New York City. Son of the famous modern dancer Barbara Morgan, he ran the press that was well known for beautiful graphics, rare American period typography in wood, and hand-cut fonts of oak and maple.

Morgan told me he had seen my Tarot cards for Brown Paper Company and was impressed. He said he wanted me to do a full color deck of seventy-eight Tarot cards for him. He would pay me $100 per card. Was I interested? You bet! At $100 per card, that would be $7,800: a fortune!

That kind of money would buy a lot of oil paint and brushes.
Then I made the mistake most young artists make. I shook his hand. To me, a man's handshake and his word were his bond. I still had much to learn.

After almost a year of work, I sent off seventy-eight full color drawings to Morgan. The images had come easily for me, from a place inside of me which I could not understand. The Tarot flowed out of me in an unconscious stream from another time and place.

To my disappointment, I did not hear again from Morgan. I immersed myself in my life as an artist, and did my best to focus on new opportunities. I was hired out of school to work as a photographer for the organizing committee of the 1968 Olympic Games in Mexico City.

My painful disillusionment over the Tarot contract faded as I shot photos of the beautiful country of Mexico: theatre, dance, concerts, museums, and the Olympic Games themselves.

After a year in Mexico, I returned to New York City. One day, as I walked up Madison Avenue, I happened to step into a shop named Serendipity. There, on a rack, were my Tarot cards in a handsome black box with The Fool card on the front. An electric shock ran through my body. I bought the deck and walked around the rest of the day I disbelief, holding it tightly. I still have that original deck.

In 1970, the well-known publisher and Tarot expert Stuart Kaplan of U. S. Games Systems, Inc., purchased the rights to the *Aquarian* Tarot. The rest, as they say, is history.

Now as I write these words 42 years later, *the Aquarian Tarot* is alive and well and being sold all over the world in six languages, helping people to better know themselves and their life paths, hopefully offering them beauty to illuminate their hearts and minds.

THE STYLE OF *THE AQUARIAN TAROT*

My mother wanted me to be a priest. That did not happen, but sitting in a pew of our local church throughout many years had a profound influence on me. I would gaze at the stained glass windows as the Catholic mass droned on. Those were the days when Latin was the language of the mass, so there was nothing to listen to anyway. But those glowing windows taught me much. The leaded glass was brilliantly beautiful, in bright golds, greens, blues, reds, and violets. Those jewels of color outlined in black shaped my ideas of beauty and art.

I only discovered these ideas many years later as I watched my hand do magical things that I could not understand. My style of drawing became a mélange of Art Nouveau, Art Deco, and the stained glass of my youth. Originally I had wanted to be a filmmaker, and studied film and photography at Pratt Institute. But, oh, that unseen hand. I was directed into art and illustration, which became the foundation of my life.

THE CREATION OF *THE NEW PALLADINI TAROT*

I had completed a career as one of New York's premier illustrators, having done artwork for the best publishing houses, magazines, and advertising agencies. I created movie posters; posters for Lincoln Center, Carnegie Hall, and the San Francisco Opera; covers for *Time Magazine* and *New York Magazine*; and the illustrations for Stephen King's *Eyes of the Dragon*. I had secured my place near the top of my field, but I was wearying of my task. Long hours at my drawing table working and waiting for the phone to ring was not the kind of life I was looking for.

One morning I took my easel and canvas into New York's Central Park. Painting under the trees, I had a long conversation with myself. I soon moved to Bucks County in rural Pennsylvania. The hell of Manhattan faded farther and farther away. Then I moved to the Hamptons; I bought a home in East Hampton, before it became "Hollywood East," as it is now known. I lived there when potato fields stretched right to the ocean, before multi-million dollar houses began to spring up in what used to be farmers' fields. These houses were built at such a furious pace, they wound up looking into each other's windows. They were all vacant nine months of the year.

Then a vacation to Jamaica changed everything again. I bought hillside land, built an island home, and stayed eight years.

The cell phone was not yet reality and landline phones were hard to procure. Jamaica had long waiting lists for telephones, but I had managed to find an island-wide private system. The radiotelephone I had was huge and heavy, with a tall whip antenna on top. The voice from the phone barked, "Fox-one-Fox-one. This is base." Base was a Rastafarian in a tin-roof shack in the middle of a forest near Montego Bay. I was Fox-one.

The base operator relayed a phone call to me. It was from Stuart Kaplan in Connecticut. Base would repeat Stuart's end of the conversation to me, and I would answer. Then the operator would repeat my reply to Stuart. Stuart wanted to commission me to do a second deck, because the *Aquarian* deck had been such a worldwide success. I loved the idea. Ever since I had created the *Aquarian,* I had longed to create a new Tarot deck with a different focus.

This time, I wanted to include the symbols of all the religions of the world. After all, no matter which book we're reading, we are all the creations of a greater intelligence. Wars are fought over which name is God's name, but God has no name, needs no name, never had a name, and never will. I wanted to make the wisdom and power of the Tarot open and available to everyone, a portal for growth that all could enter.

The Art Deco and Art Nouveau of *The Aquarian Tarot* were long gone. Now I drew with influences of exotic India, tropical Jamaica, ancient Egypt, and bejeweled Byzantium. I was immersed in nature, drawing sunrises on the beach surround, spending the long, hot afternoons in the cool shade of my breezy verandah. Over the next six hot, tropical months, with sweat trickling down my wrists and hurricanes pounding the shutters, I opened my mind and let the Creator do the work. Finally, it was completed: *The New Palladini Tarot!*

ABOUT THE ARTWORK

I rendered the images of the Tarot cards in ink, magic marker, and colored pencils on rag paper. Each drawing was 10" x 16.5" in the original form, and was the result of many months of execution. I combined elements of medieval, illumination, Egyptian, and modern arts in my own style. I have tried to represent in the cards all races as well as a variety of religious symbols. I believe that the Tarot must be universal in both content and power. Many writers and researchers have studied the Tarot, which has led to a multiplicity of ideas and philosophies. Consequently, many artists have created artwork for the Tarot based on this wide range of approaches. I do not profess to be any more right (or wrong) than my predecessors. I can only hope that the beauty of the art work can earn forgiveness for any inaccuracies of symbolism.

David Palladini
Corona del Mar, California
August 2013

AUTHOR'S NOTES

The Aquarian Tarot was the second Tarot deck I owned. The first was *The Tarot of the Witches*, a gift from my indulgent father after I had seen it in the James Bond film, *Live and Let Die*. I was disappointed to find that the cards did not predict the future in real life the way they did in the movie, but I was nonetheless intrigued by the images.

The *Witches* deck has plain pip cards, and I wanted something more visually engaging. So my father escorted my underage self to the local head shop, where I saw the *Aquarian* on the shelf. Being an Aquarius, I felt that a Tarot deck named after my birth sign would be a good choice, and the little black box went home with me.

The first time I opened the deck and laid out the cards, my soul lit up. I knew *this* deck was the real thing—real, living magic. I read the Little White Book, played with the cards, slept with them under my pillow, and took them everywhere with me. I had to keep them hidden in my book bag to avoid awkward conversations with people who might not understand what someone my age was doing with a Tarot deck, but at home, I could spend as much time with my cards as I wished.

I acquired other decks, played with them, read with them, and often ended up putting them on a shelf to return to my *Aquarian*. To this day, I always carry it with me.

In 2010, I received an email from Michael Yaccarino, which led to a phone call with David. I tried to calm myself for the call and be cool and professional, but *Oh my god David Palladini is going to call me oh my god oh my god* was pretty much all my brain could manage. I must have been reasonably coherent during the call, as David agreed to be a guest on our Tarot-to-Go podcast. I then managed to be coherent for almost an hour for the interview—no small feat, given that my brain was still going around in little circles over the fact that I was actually interviewing David Palladini *oh my god oh my god oh my god.*

One thing led to another, and in 2011 we published *The Journal of an Artist*, David's memoirs of the artistic life. Shortly after the release, I was at my desk when my phone rang with an unrecognized number. I almost let it go to voicemail, then picked it up at the last moment. "Hello, this is Stuart Kaplan of U.S. Games," came from the receiver. Another *oh my god oh my god* moment—I'm on the phone with *Stuart Kaplan*. Stuart was gracious and pleasant, calling to let me know that David had sent him a copy of the book. During our conversation, the idea of doing a book focused solely on David's Tarot art came up. Stuart was completely supportive of the idea of Black Swan doing the book, and the phone call ended with the new project begun.

My part of the book has been written in cafés and hotels all over the world as I've traveled hither and yon for business, and throughout late hours at my writing desk at home and the computer at my office in San Francisco. David's text and mine joined up over a long lunch at the fabulous Sherman Library and Gardens in Corona del Mar, California. Expert proofreading and copy editing by Holly Cooper, fantastic graphic design by Chris Lowrance, and the beautiful art of David Palladini are now combined in this book you hold in your hands. My hope is that it brings into your life the magic of David's art and the Tarot the way *The Aquarian Tarot* first brought magic into my life, all those years ago.

Anastasia Haysler
San Francisco, California
August 2013

NOTES ON CARD INTERPRETATIONS

The page for each card features a summary of the card, which includes David's story of the art and his thoughts on the card's meaning.

The longer analysis of each card is written by Anastasia. To understand the longer piece, it will help you to know that my reading style is eclectic, to say the least. I use the card symbols and colors, some numerology, some astrology, some Kabbala, mythologies of various cultures and eras, literary references, song lyrics, and a whole lot of intuition when I read.

I look at the numerological relationships of the cards when I'm reading. Each numbered card can be reduced to a single digit, which makes it easier to see the connections. For example, the Star is card 17. The numeral 17 is made up of 1 and 7, which add up to 8, thus linking the Star to Card 8, Strength. In the text, this idea is expressed as
17 = 1 + 7 = 8. My algebra teacher might not approve, but I think it's a simple way to show the math.

Because the cards reduce to a single digit, each Major Arcana card links to one or two other major cards, as well as to the Minor Arcana card bearing the same number. The chart below makes this easier to see than if you were to do all of that math.

1 (Aces)	Magician	Wheel of Fortune	Sun	
2	High Priestess	Justice	Judgement	
3	Empress	Hanged Man	World	
4	Emperor	Death		
5	Hierophant	Temperance		
6	Lovers	Devil		
7	Chariot	Tower		
8	Strength	Star		
9	Hermit	Moon		
10	Magician	Wheel of Fortune	Sun	Aces

I see each court character as the embodiment of an element, and each suit also associates with an element. So, for example, the Queen of Pentacles is the Water element in the Earth suit, which gives us insight into the emotional aspect of the suit.

For purposes of this book, the associations are:

SUIT	ELEMENT	COURT CARD
Pentacles	Earth	Page
Rods	Fire	Knight
Cups	Water	Queen
Swords	Air	King

Your associations may vary, but if you keep the above chart in mind as you read, the ideas within will be clearer.

There are as many ways to read a Tarot card as there are readers. The interpretations here are general; writing every possible interpretation for every card, individually and in combination, would take lifetimes. If an interpretation does not make sense for you, or does not fit with your perception of the card, do not feel compelled to use it. The important thing in a Tarot reading is that the person receiving the reading is able to understand and make sense of the meanings. If the reading does not make sense, it has no value. Use these interpretations as suggestions, take what works, and leave the rest.

The Major Arcana

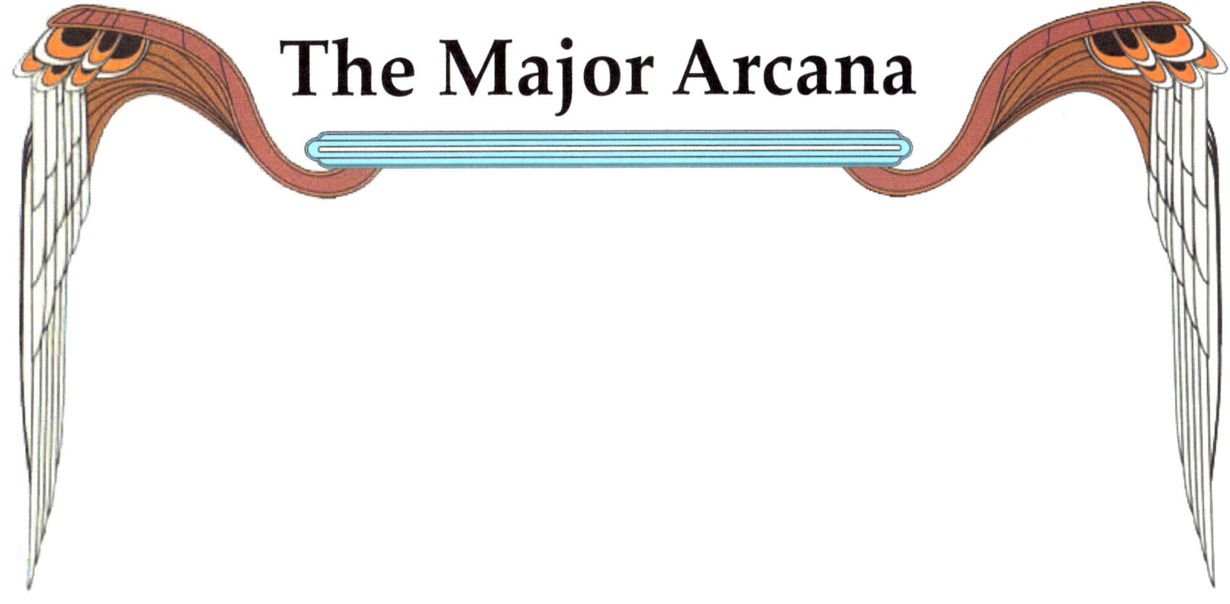

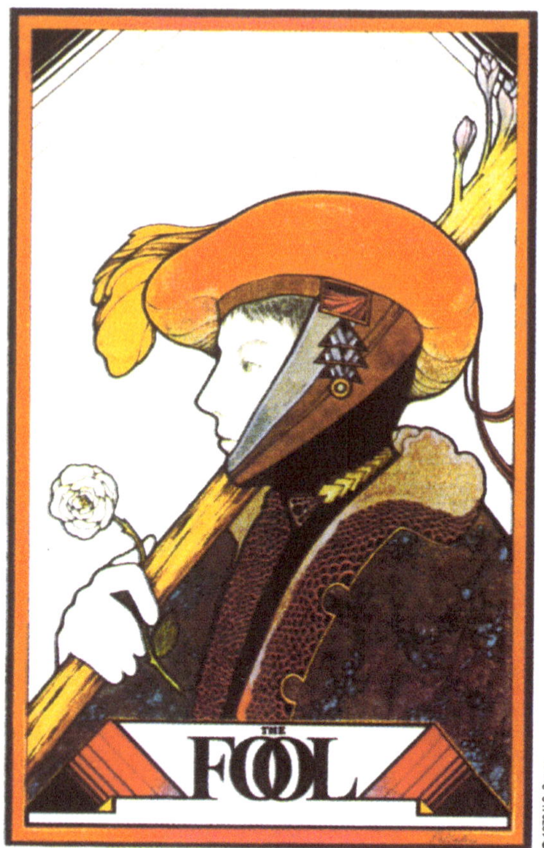

© 1970 U.S. Games

I begin with me. I am the fool. I was born on April 1, what we in the U.S. call April Fool's Day. In France, they call it Le Jour des Poissons, Fish Day. Each birthday, when I lived in France, someone always stuck a paper fish on my back, unbeknownst to me; I walked around all day advertising my birthday.

April Fool's Day in America was much worse. All my life, I was promised a birthday party, gifts, cakes, and balloons. No way, April Fool! Naturally, my birth date soured me.

But I had not yet met the Tarot Fool. Number 0, the perfect geometric shape has no beginning or end. In our capitalistic society, zero means nothing. Actually, it is the perfect number. Zero is a portal, an opening into other realities, energy entering and leaving through the doorway shaped like a 0/

The Fool wanders through the world without possessions. He carries a flowering rod, the symbol of the suit of Rods. It is a magic wand, which can transform from a tiny seed into a tall beautiful flower.

A young person, more self-absorbed than contemplative. We do not know what he is seeing; it is as though he is looking into a mirror that is not there. This could suggest looking backwards, perhaps being stuck in old ways of being or forms of identity that he has outgrown, but does not, or cannot, acknowledge.

This card looks almost like an unfinished portrait, reflecting the incomplete state of the Fool's existence. The lines are there, but the details and color must be added through actual experience of life. His heavy, padded clothing provides protection, and no sun shines upon him. The brown stalk of the rose indicates a lack of vitality. The card tells us that it is time—or more than time—to make a new start.

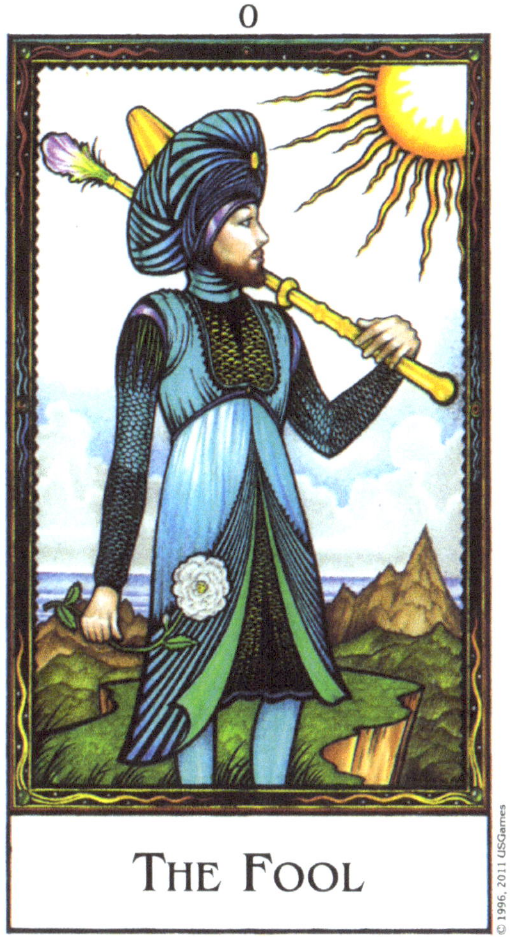

A bearded young man stands upon a high mountaintop. He wears gorgeous vestments crowned by a turban; a radiant sun warms him. He stares into the sky, rather than the chasm below. He carries the white rose of innocence and life in one hand, and a flowering staff in the other. He is a spirit in search of experience. The Fool knows everything, and nothing. He is 0, the symbol of both perfection and non-existence.

The figure here is likewise young. He is educated, although not yet wise from life experience. He has a self-awareness that seems lacking in the *Aquarian* Fool. He ponders what is outside him as separate from him; he does not yet know how he fits in with the larger world. He faces forward, looking for opportunities and possibilities.

His fitted, flowing clothing allows him ease of movement and more direct sensory experience of the world around him. He is open to the breeze of inspiration and ideas. Again, we cannot see what he is seeing, but we can see where he is, the vistas he has viewed, where he comes from. Both he and we have a better sense of who he is; he has more of a sense of self to work from. The jewel and the peak on his hat echo the gold of the sun, letting us know that he is connected to its energy and vitality. The stalk of his rose is likewise green and vital, reflecting his life energy.

I

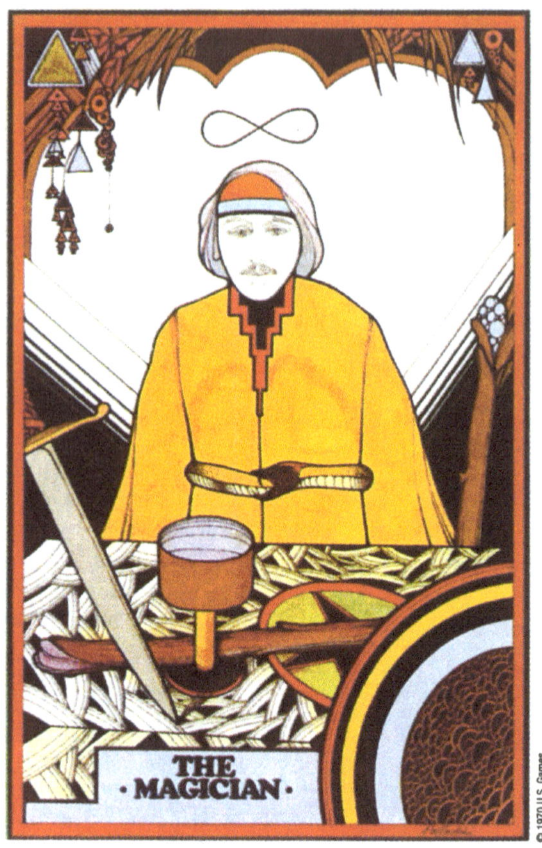

All ideas are both positive and negative. The Aquarian Magician works for good. He is self-confident and uses his skills for positive ends. Before him are arrayed his tools: the sword of justice, the flowering rod of fertility, the cup of plenty, and the pentacle of prosperity. Above his head floats the sign of infinity. He waits to use his magic in the service of humanity.

The Magician is static, and his hands are down and not visible, as though contemplating his tools rather than being in the act of creation. The ouroboros on his belt faces left, backwards towards the past. He is possibly relying too much on prior accomplishments, prior knowledge, and not moving forward in his work.

The wind chimes, as the element of Air, suggest a mental focus on the creative process rather than creating from the whole self. All his chakras are covered, including his Third Eye and Crown chakras, suggesting a strong containment of energy.

Everything in the card is highly geometric rather than flowing shapes; even the cup is more cylindrical than round.

The suit symbols on the *Aquarian* Magician card are not the same as the ones depicted on the pips, and the symbols themselves vary within the suit. The symbols on the Magician card are the ur-symbols; the pips are the diminished reflection of these ur-symbols.

The card feels enclosed; the image seems imposed upon the background, rather than coming from it. There is almost no sign of nature; everything in the card is made by human hands, reinforcing the idea of human creation and manifestation.

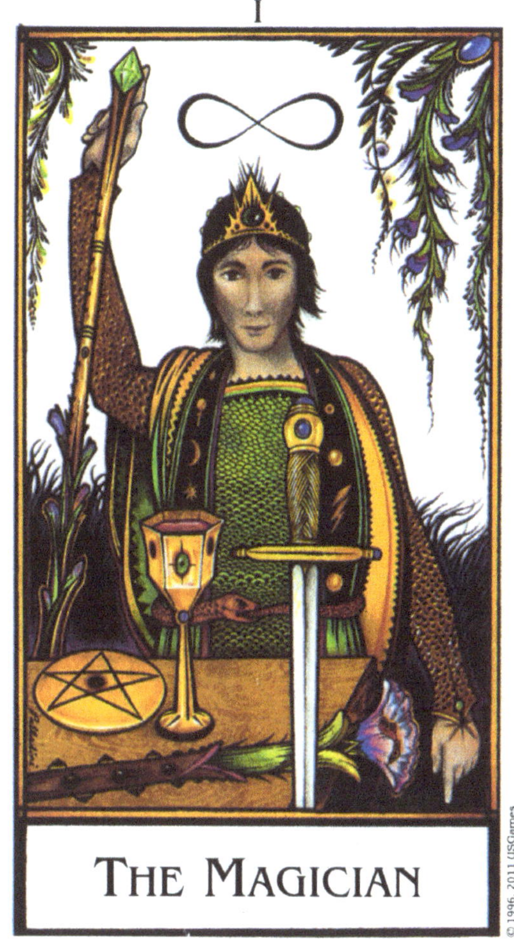

A young man stands in a garden. He wears the chain mail robes of the Magician. Upon his chest, he wears the signs of the planets and nature. He holds a flowering wand tipped with green crystal, through which energy flows. His right hand points above and his left points below. In front of him are the symbols of the four Tarot suits: Rods, Swords, Pentacles, and Cups. These are the signs by which he creates magic. Around his waist coils a snake swallowing its tail, the symbol of the circle of life. Above his head floats the symbol of infinity, for his power is everlasting. The Magician uses the power of the spirit to create magic on Earth. He represents the highest motives of man: to create, and not destroy.

This Magician is dynamic, deep in the process of creation. With his raised right arm holding the wand (the will) and his left arm pointing to the earth, he is the connection between above and below, divine and mundane, potential and manifestation.

His ouroboros belt faces forward, towards the future, towards new experience and knowledge.

The card is filled with the vital energy of living plants in addition to the human-made objects on the table. The plants grow up from the earth into the air and back again towards earth, almost a full circle and cycle of life. The gems and precious metals underscore the creative energy as human shaping of natural objects; the gems seem almost to be growing from the plants.

His top three chakras are open, allowing free flow of energy. The gem at his Third Eye looks like an actual green eye, seeing through a lens of life energy and creativity. He is guiding the staff through will rather than grasping it, showing us his incredible command of energy and will.

The geometry of the human objects offsets the curves of the natural objects. The picture feels whole rather than imposed.

II

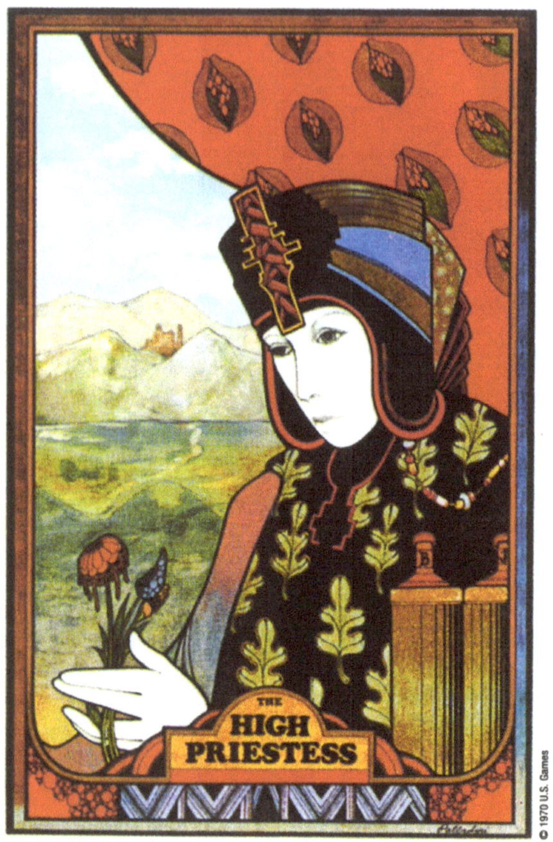

Backed by a castle on a hill overlooking a tranquil lake, the High Priestess sits, pondering the flowers she holds in her hand. The curtain behind her is pulled aside. It is covered in pomegranates on a field of red. It is said that this curtain covered the entrance to the Jewish temple in Jerusalem, which was torn asunder by a storm-wind at the moment of Christ's death on the cross. Before her are the rolls of the Torah, the Words of God which Moses transcribed atop the fiery mountain. The High Priestess knows many things. She can see the future, the past, and the present. She knows that they are one and the same. All one.

The *Aquarian* High Priestess is fully covered, except for her face; all is hidden, as is her knowledge. She contemplates the rose (consciousness) and butterfly (soul), aware of our presence; she will acknowledge us when the time is right. Meanwhile, we would do well to contemplate our own consciousness and soul.

With the curtain behind her and the landscape in the background, this card feels more organic, more natural; the High Priestess seems to be outside in a natural temple, rather than sequestered in a temple structure.

The Torah scroll by her side contains the secret wisdom which can be gained only by learning to read—knowledge that requires a special skill to acquire. We must learn to learn, and then we learn how much we have to learn.

The pomegranates and oak leaves connect her to the Empress and Emperor; she gives them the wisdom they need to fulfill their roles. She wears an abstract shape on her headdress, rather than the moon often seen on High Priestess cards. Her coif shows stars, her connection to the intuitive aspect of wisdom.

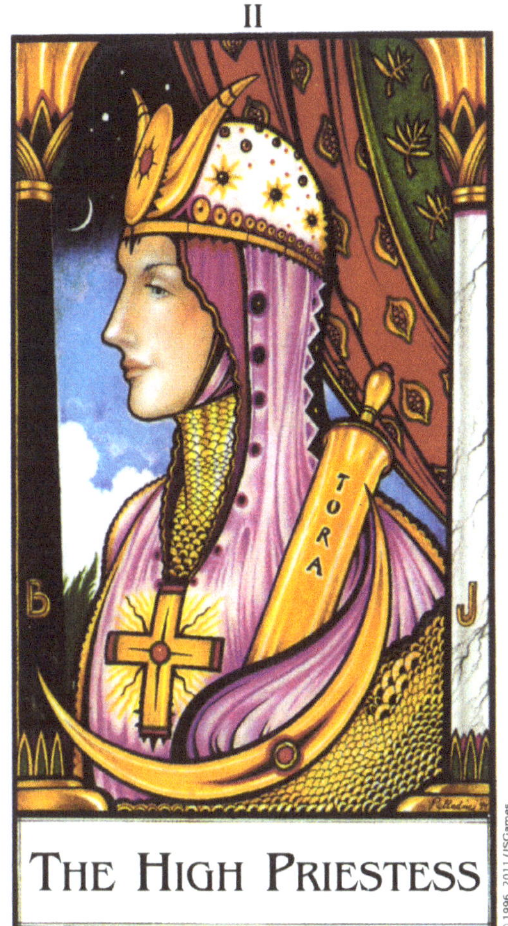

She smiles a secret smile. Below her, the crescent of Islam. In her arms she holds the Torah of Moses. On her head she wears the Horus of ancient Egypt. She is helmeted and girded with chain mail. There is a sliver of moon in a starry sky overhead. She knows the truth: We are all one.

In the *New Palladini* card, the pillars representing the temple (generally considered as Boaz and Jachin, the pillars of the original Temple in Jerusalem) frame the image and the High Priestess herself, and are as majestic as one would expect to find in a grand temple. The High Priestess seems larger than life, larger than the temple; it is a stage or shadow box for her. Indeed, she is so grand that she seems more like a Queen—the Empress of the Spirit, as compared to the material Empress in Trump 3. Set between the two pillars, she forms the Middle Pillar of the Kabbalistic Tree of Life, between the Pillar of Mercy and the Pillar of Severity. She is the wisdom that moderates between the two.

Her clothing is sumptuous, although plainer than that of the *Aquarian* High Priestess. She, too, has stars on her headdress, as well as sunbursts bringing in rational solar energy. The trim on her wimple suggest the phases of the Moon, and the headdress is crowned by the Triple Moon often associated with the High Priestess. She wears a cross with a jewel radiating light and energy from its center. The scales of mail are perhaps like fish scales, linking her to the Vesica Piscis, the symbol of the Divine Feminine. Or perhaps they are snake scales, connecting her to the wisdom of the Pythian seeresses of ancient Greece.

Pink is the diminutive of red, the color of Mars/Ares and the very masculine energy of those archetypes. In medieval and Renaissance times in Western Europe, women were typically depicted in blue capes or robes in emulation of Mary, Mother of Jesus. Choosing a purplish pink for the High Priestess reinforces the idea of her authority and strength.

Her Torah is a single-handed scroll. The crescent moon in the foreground and the Torah are like a staff and shield for her to direct and project her energy.

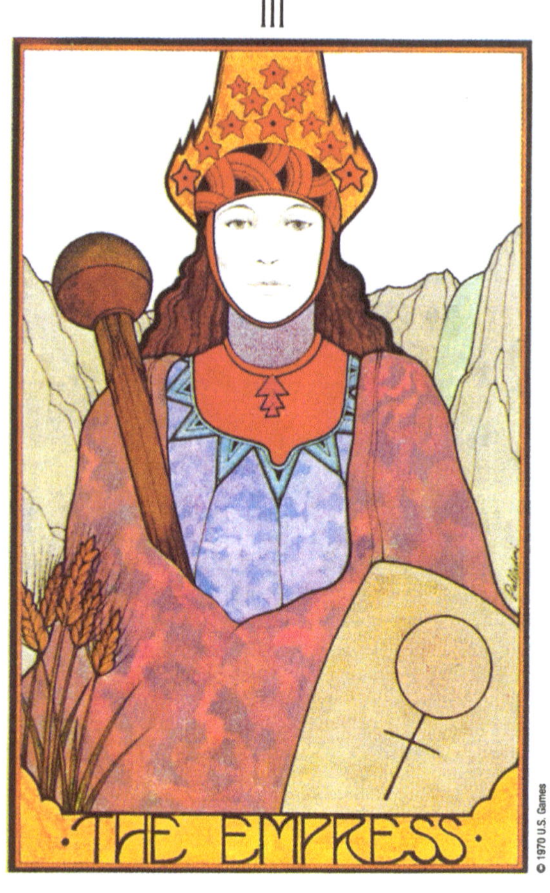

The Empress, strong and resolute, sits waiting. She bears her shield, upon which is her symbol, the sigil of Venus. She is the embodiment of fertility. Wheat stalks are before her, and behind her a waterfall plunges over the rocky cliffs. On her crown she wears 12 stars. She is good luck, a bountiful harvest, initiative, action, female power.

A woman of serious demeanor and dignity, the Empress gazes at us calmly and confidently. Her rich robes and starry crown indicate her wealth and rank. The scepter and shield remind us of her power.

The card is mostly rock, barren except for a few stalks of wheat. A waterfall in the background at first appears to be part of the cliff face, until we look again and see it for what it is. The waterfall, almost implied rather than explicit, speaks of the Empress's emotional strength and lets us know we are dealing with a woman of great emotional reserves as well as material resources. The wheat connects her to Ceres, the Great Mother, Creator, and Nurturer of life.

Her robes and scepter are unjeweled. Her shield bears a simple version of the sigil for Venus/ Aphrodite. The Empress does not need fancy trims and trappings to show herself to her best advantage; she herself is magnificent, and sufficient to impress us without showiness.

She is comfortable in her own self, comfortable in her role, and confident of her capabilities and achievements.

Holding her scepter, which bears a golden globe representing the world, the Empress contemplates life. She is surrounded by ripe corn and a fertile landscape. Fruits and flowers cover her cape. Her crown bears the stars of a secret constellation. She rules with strong, kind eyes.

She is the fruitful mother, universal fecundity. She is action, initiative, growth and development. She is loving, and ready to defend that which she loves.

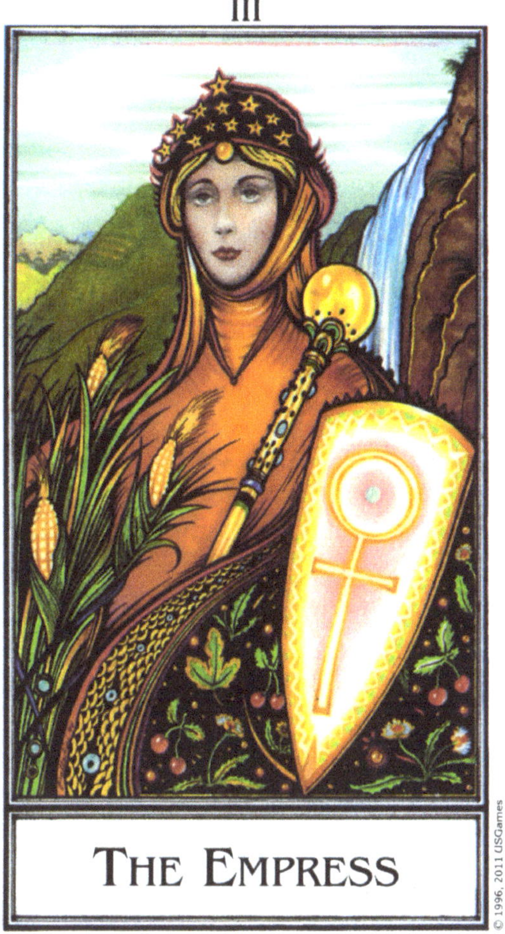

This Empress is also richly attired, set in a lush landscape with flowing water. The landscape is half green and growing, and half rock—the vitality of nature and the vigor of mental discipline joined by the watery emotions and intuition.

The waterfall here is easily seen; we are quite clear on the strength and depth of the Empress's emotional energy.

Her robe is flowered; the plants bear jewels. We are shown the inseparability of abundance on all levels. Creation is a continuous and complex cycle, intertwined in myriad ways and forms.

Her cloak is embroidered with oak leaves, cherries, and flowers. The oak leaves represent her formal duties as Empress and her responsibilities in her role. The cherries show the sweet reward for hard work. The flowers represent the beauty of the creative life. The blue jewels are like captured starlight, caught and placed on her robe to increase its magnificence.

Her headdress has the 12 stars of the zodiac as well as a golden jewel representing the sun. She draws upon both stellar and solar energies in her thinking.

Her jeweled scepter and shield are the perfected gifts of the earth, and speak to us of the Empress's own gifts of abundance and wisdom, which she shares with us.

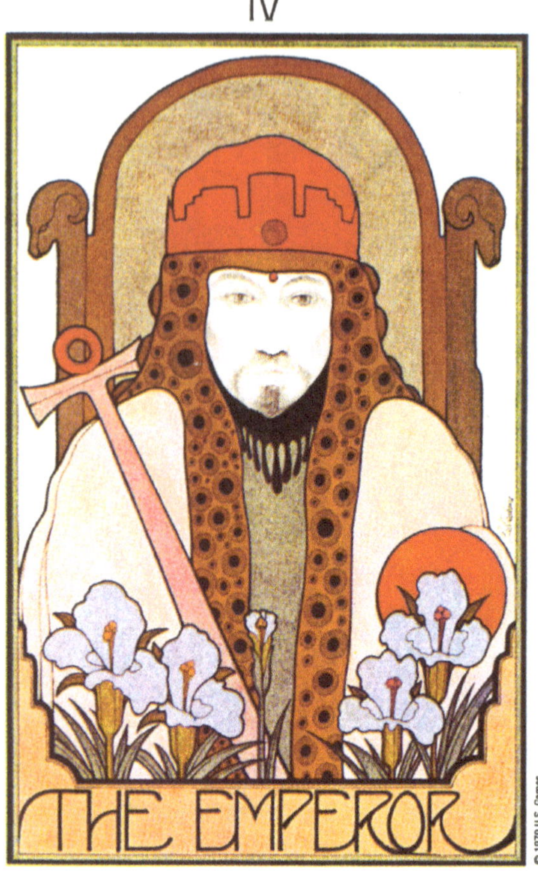

Authority, master of his emotions. Intelligent, a man of ideas. His staff is the Egyptian ankh. He is a crowned monarch seated on a throne which bears carved rams' heads. He is lost in deep thought. He holds the world in his hand. He is the protector, a wise warrior.

The Emperor sits securely on this throne, his orb and scepter resting on him, his gaze clearly upon those who view him. The orb is the orange of the sun, the star and center of the universe, as the Emperor is the star and center of his empire. His scepter is an ankh, symbol of the Pharaoh's power in ancient Egypt. His power is old and deep, and he wields it confidently.

The dark suns on his robe pair with the stars in the Empress' crown, reminding us that she is his consort and mate.

The pistils of the flowers in front of his throne are heavy with pollen, nature affirming his virility and powers of fecundity. We do not see any water in the card, although it must be present to nourish the flowers. Likewise, the Emperor does have an emotional side, but he keeps it hidden and shows himself only as calm and confident.

The rams' heads on his throne invoke Mars/Ares, archetypes of war and aggression. We are left with no doubt that the Emperor earned his throne through political and/or military combat, and that he has no qualms about using his power to maintain his rulership. He has created order out of chaos, stability out of uncertainty; his role is to maintain that order and stability.

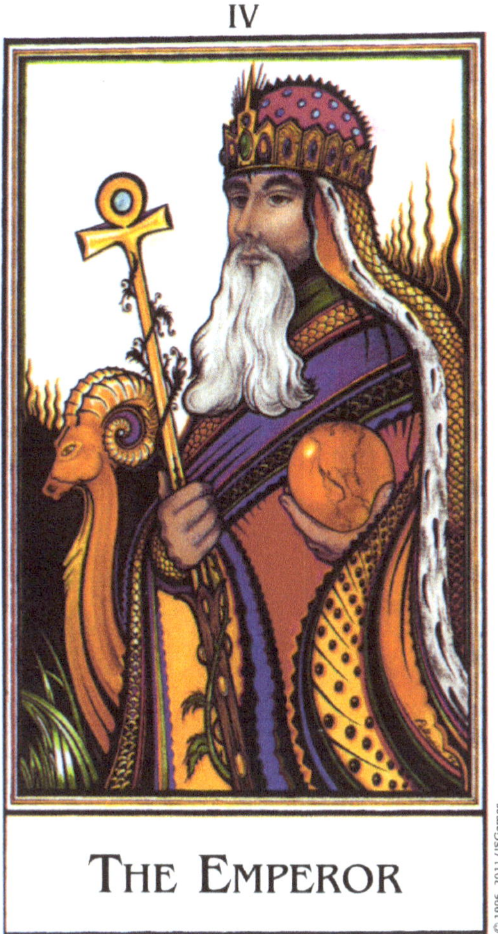

He is a leader. His grey beard signifies virility tempered by experience. His ankh scepter encircled by a flower, he wears the finest robes and jewels. His strength and intelligence have brought him riches. He is an enlightened monarch.

Despite his white beard, the smooth face of this Emperor indicates a younger man than we see in the *Aquarian* Emperor. He looks off into the middle distance, not regarding us.

The scales of his headdress echo those on the High Priestess; he derives his power in part from ancient lineage, and displays this proudly. The blue starlight stones from the Empress' gown adorn the Emperor's crown and decorate his ankh scepter, linking the pair. The dark stones on his robe are smaller versions of the sun, linked to the sun-colored orb he holds.

He seems to be standing next to a ship with a ram's head prow. As with the *Aquarian* Emperor, we do not see any water, but we know water must be present to support the ship and the plant life. Our Emperor controls his emotions very closely.

The green, natural vine becomes a stylized metal adornment on his scepter, showing that this is a man who tries to shape even Nature to his will. This is human creation, inspired by, but not identical to, organic forms.

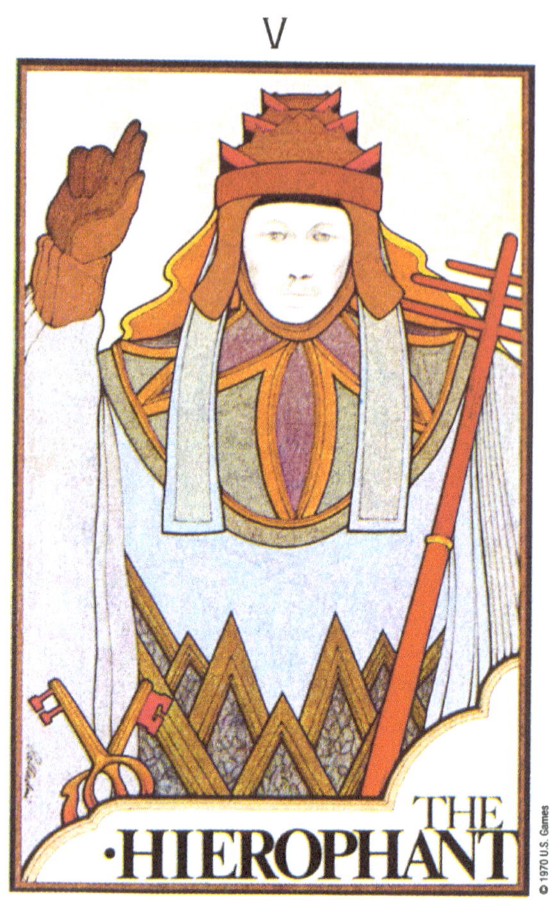

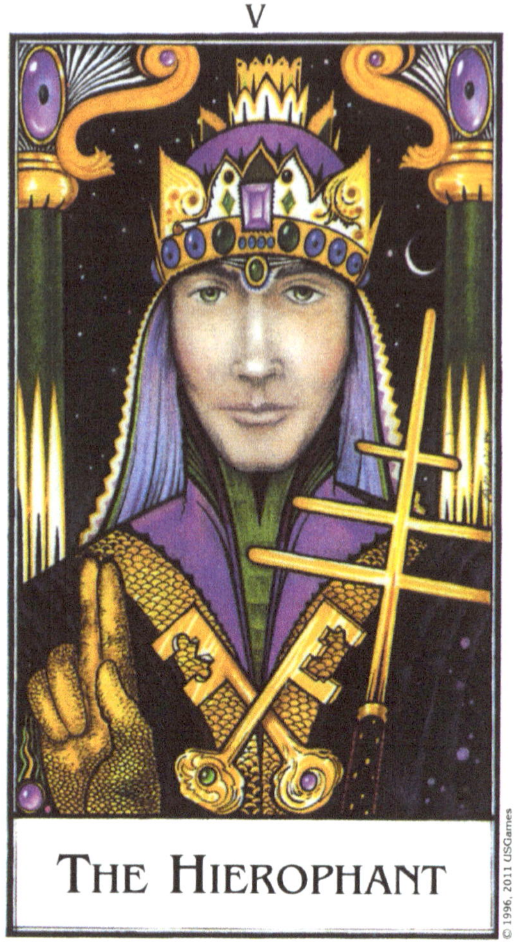

He came rapidly out of my pen and Magic Markers. He was stern, his hand raised in a secret sign. Then I met the The Hierophant of The New Palladini Tarot deck. I had learned much about life in the 25 years between the two decks. The new Hierophant wears a jeweled crown. His hand gives the sign of concealed truths (Christ is often pictured giving this sign). He represents the power of belief, the kinship of faith. His expression is the secret smile of serenity, of oneness with the universe.

He symbolizes all things righteous and sacred, and the salvation of the human race.

His hand raised in blessing, the crozier of his office at his side, the *Aquarian* Hierophant engages directly with the viewer. The yoke of his robe bears a flower petal design, and with his elaborate headpiece his face becomes the center of the flower. It seems almost like a costume that wears the person, designed to de-emphasize the wearer. The individual in the role is not the focus; the focus is the role itself.

His robes are ample, yet simple, and his staff and keys are unadorned. He does not need fancy trappings to indicate the status of his office—the office itself carries its dignity. The symbols of the office are present but not directly controlled by him; they are only symbols, not tools for his actual use.

He appears to rise out of the earth itself, having grown organically into the role of teacher and leader, rather than taking it as the Emperor takes his throne.

As spiritual leader of the community, his role is to create rituals that create ecstasy—taking us out of our ordinary consciousness and putting us in touch with the divinity in ourselves. He does this in proven ways according to rule and prescription. His headpiece reflects the order and symmetry of the continuity of his teachings; the text does not change, the actions are the same, and all must be done as it has always been done.

The *New Palladini* Hierophant appears younger, as though he is new to his role and still growing into it. He wears his robes and headpiece more closely, a second skin for him instead of a costume. He relies on his formal robes and symbols of office to lend gravitas and authority as he becomes accustomed to his responsibilities. He sits in his temple, observing forms and protocols of his office, emphasizing his status and reinforcing the roles and hierarchies of the community.

His round headpiece is more like a tower than the fortress-like symmetrical one worn by his *Aquarian* counterpart. It is still highly architectural in appearance, reinforcing the idea of the order and tradition he embodies. He does not hold his crozier or keys; again, they are symbols of his office, rather than tools he uses to perform his duties. The keys are crossed on his chest, over his heart chakra. Like the Emperor, the Hierophant keeps his emotions tightly controlled.

Like the High Priestess and the Emperor, he wears mailed armor, calling to mind a fish or snake and the wisdom associated with those creatures, as well as reinforcing the lineage of his authority.

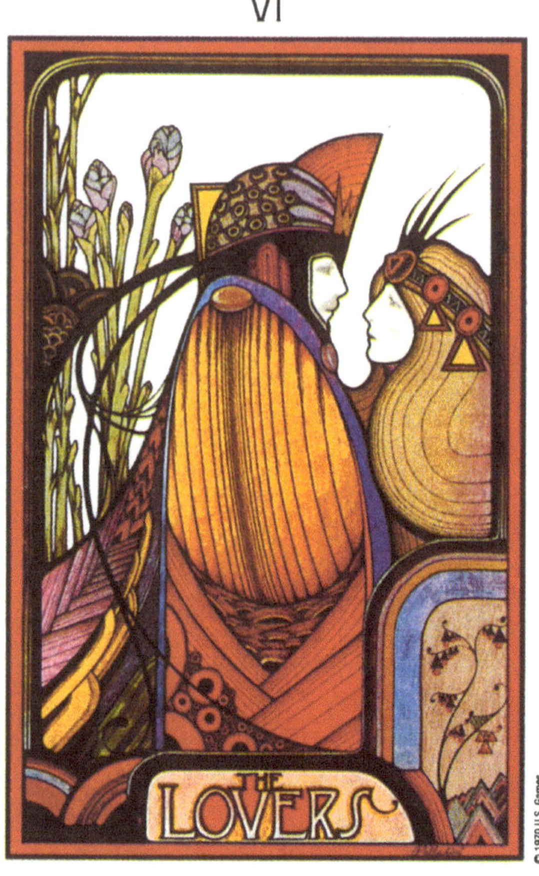

This one of my favorite Tarot images. I love the man's swooping helmet. I love the woman's resolute honest gaze. The colors are vibrant like stained glass.

I drew myself as the man. The woman was imagined, a soft beauty with long dark hair, perfumed and sensual.

All the intricate designs came flowing out of me. I barely had any knowledge of Art Nouveau or Art Deco, and yet the images came forth onto my canvas.

The Lovers are joined in strength and honesty. There is mutual respect. They are two halves of the same soul, two hearts beating as one.

Suddenly, we have a card that moves beyond the subdued medieval palette and sings with color and emotional passion. The first card to feature two figures instead of one lone person, the Lovers card leaps out of the deck with its vibrant jewel tones.

The couple, mature and confident, are physically close, although not directly touching. They are emotionally open and vulnerable to each other. The Lovers here are fully connected with each other, and yet remain intact as individuals. They see each other clearly, each with open eyes that reflect a true image of their lover.

In an attempt to feel better about our relationship, we may project upon the other person our ideal of the perfect partner, not seeing them for who they truly are. We refuse to see, and to accept, our partner's true self, and wonder why we feel disconnected from them.

We may, through fears about our own inadequacy and avoidance of rejection, wear a mask to appear to be our partner's ideal. We refuse to show our true self, and then wonder why we feel unloved.

A relationship based on projections and masks cannot thrive. Our projections fail. Our facades fall. We must face the truth: the relationship is not real, and cannot be sustained by illusions and self-delusion. We must see our partner clearly, and be seen clearly by our partner, for the relationship to be real. Not ideal - *real*.

These are innocents. Their love is new, vibrant, and true. They walk naked through a garden.

She wears flowers in her hair. Behind the man is the Tree of Life, bearing 12 fruits. The Tree of the Knowledge of Good and Evil is by the woman, around which twines the serpent. They are Adam and Eve, full of youth and love. This is the card of human love, as part of the way of truth and life. He is strong and watchful. She wears the expression of the sensitive life. Beauty and love will overcome.

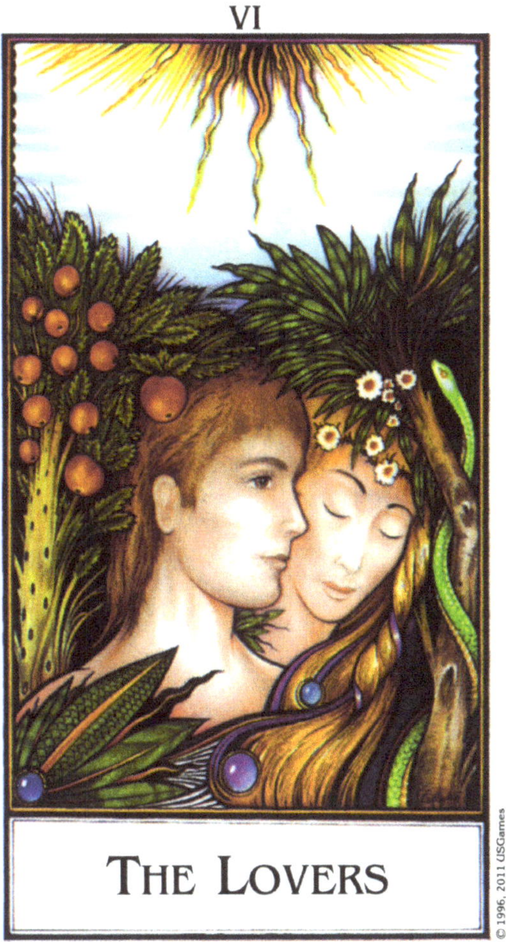

The couple here look much younger, newer in life and in relationship. The surroundings show Adam and Eve in the Garden of Eden, before the serpent has tempted Eve to eat the apple from the Tree of Knowledge.

Unlike the *Aquarian* couple, they are physically vulnerable to each other in their unclothed state, which paradoxically hides their emotional vulnerability.

The man looks away, and the woman looks down, eyes closed. They are not looking at each other, not ready for the kind of emotional and soul honesty that develops in a long-term relationship. They are still developing their individual identities, so their relationship identity is not yet formed.

We must be in true relationship with our own self before we can be in true relationship with another. We must be able to see our own Self—the glorious, divine Soul and the fallible, mortal human—must be able to see honestly, and love wholly, our own Self in order to love another Self.

They will learn, in time, to see themselves and each other clearly, as the *Aquarian* couple does, and experience the joy of deep connection. They have many experiences ahead, and much to learn, as the serpent in the tree waits patiently to start them on their journey.

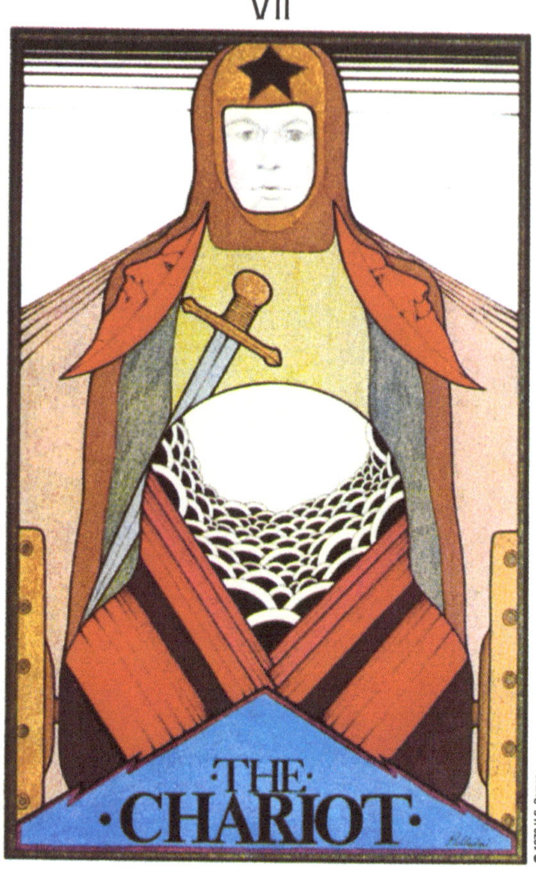

A resolute man, garbed for battle. He rides his swift chariot. His sword is close at hand. He controls the tension between opposites. He wears two crescent moons on his shoulders, mirror images of each other. His is a balanced life. He triumphs over all difficulties through perseverance. Never give up.

This card shows us a charioteer much larger than his vehicle. We wonder how this being could fit inside this chariot. The Chariot here is a symbol of the driver's will; no actual vehicle is required.

The driver's ambitions make him larger than life. He fills the frame, the flowing lines of his cloak extending past the frame of the card and offsetting any sense of heaviness we might otherwise feel. Here we have someone who knows his will, and knows how to direct it to achieve his desires. His plan may not be perfect, or even successful, but he is confident in his abilities and aims.

The charioteer's face floats as the full moon above the two crescent epaulets of his armor, and he wears a large star on the brow of his helmet. Channeling his emotional energy and intuitive wisdom, he moves forward confidently, if not always thoughtfully.

He does not hold his sword, or even touch it. Rather, the sword of the mind rests balanced on the edge of the chariot; the intellect is held by the will, rather than guiding the will.

We see a princely man wearing the hood of the Sphinx. His beard is the beard of the ancient pharaohs of Egypt, and a falcon protects him with its golden wings. He brandishes a jeweled sword, and wears two crescent moons on his shoulders. The wheel of the chariot below him is like the rays of the sun, with a jewel at its center. He conquers on all planes: the mind, the heart, the world. He speaks of science, progress toward equality, balance, and harmony. A strong man with noble goals.

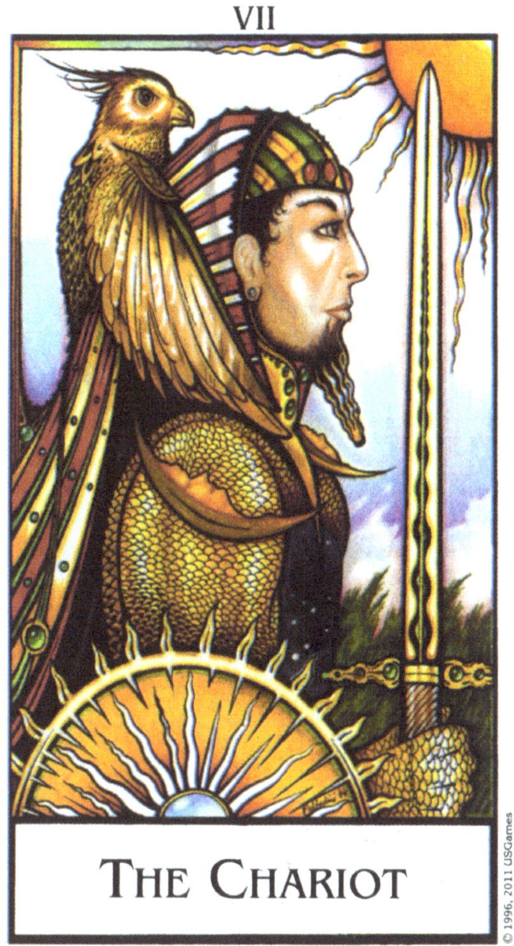

Moving even further from the idea of a physical vehicle, this card shows only a wheel of the chariot. The energetic meanings of the card are carried visually by the lines and colors indicative of movement.

The figure clasps his sword (Air) confidently, clear in his thinking, certain in his purpose, and focused in his pursuit of his goals.

The smaller sun on the wheel echoes the actual sun in the sky, bringing Apollonian reason and rationality to drive the chariot.

Perched on the charioteer's headpiece, the bird echoes the energy of the mind directing the will. As a living creature, the bird represents wild thoughts and untamed impulses, which provide the driving energy that is shaped by the rational mind of the sword and sun.

Before we take the reins, we must be sure we are ready and able to control the chariot, or we risk Phaeton's fiery fate, a sad end to grand plans and ambitions.

The charioteer himself occupies the space of the full moon between his two crescent moon epaulets, reminding us that our emotions and intuition are necessary to balance the intellect and will so that we make decisions and take action based on our whole selves, not based solely on one aspect of ourselves.

VIII

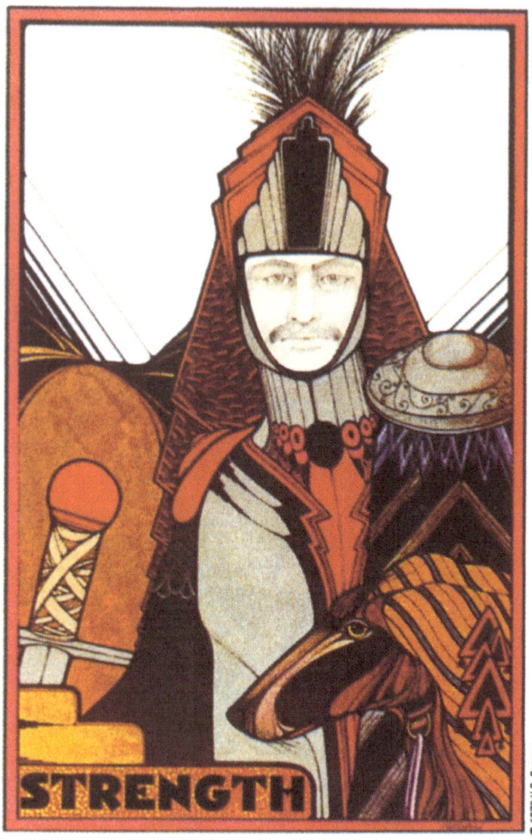

A Knight of power, action, energy, and courage. His faithful dog is strong and smart. They are brute Strength, warriors and friends. Through power, persistence, and spiritual energy comes triumph. Man and beast work together.

An intensely masculine version of a card that almost always depicts a female figure, the character in this card seems to be the Charioteer, matured, growing into the role of the Emperor. He has not yet conquered his empire, but he has made progress.

Armor, sword, and shield provide protection—if one has the strength to use them. Armor requires great physical core strength to wear, to move in, to fight in. The sword and shield likewise require strength and skill to use effectively; otherwise, they are only props for show, providing no advantage. Worse, if we do not have the strength to use them well, they can be taken from us and used against us.

The dog, drawn with flowing geometric patterns, almost blends into the figure's cloak, with little but its eye and muzzle to give it shape. The leash hangs slack, showing us that the animal is bound to the person by more than dull resignation or coerced obedience; loyalty has been earned, trust has grown over a period of time. The dog and person understand their bond and know that working together multiplies, not merely combines, their strengths. The whole is greater than the sum of its parts.

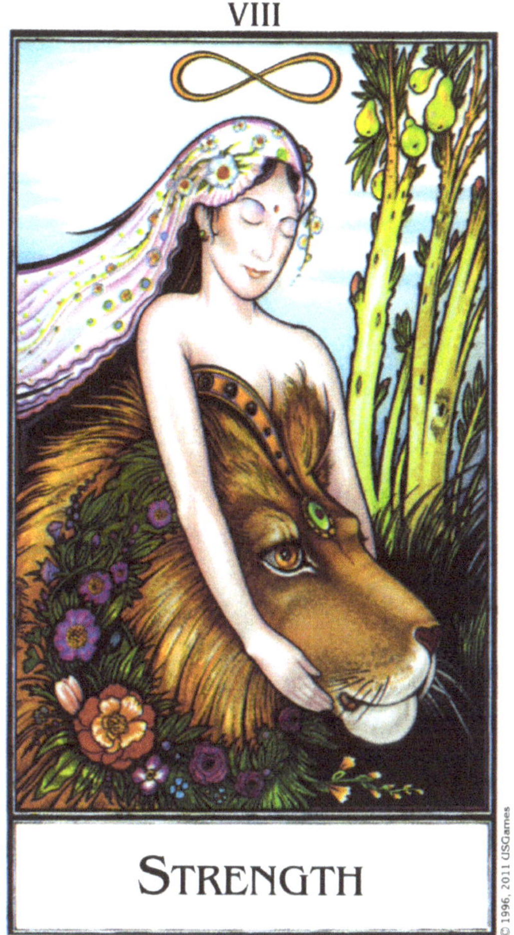

When creating my new deck, I wanted to balance ideas that were in my Aquarian Tarot. The brute strength of my Aquarian warrior needed tempering. Both man and woman are needed to balance life. We see a young woman who closes the jaws of a mighty lion. She holds firmly, but gently. The lion wears a chain of flowers. The woman wears a flowing veil which has a garland of flowers woven into it. Over her head, we see the sign of infinity, the same sign we see over the Magician. On her face, an expression of the inner contemplation. She is the victory of the power of the spirit over brute strength. With her help, peace will overcome war.

Here we return to the expected representation of a woman and a lion. Whereas the figure in the *Aquarian* card seems to be the evolution of the Chariot, the woman here is entirely her own story, *sui generis*.

Confident of her own strength and capabilities, she requires no symbols to show the world. She wears only a veil upon her head, and only the smallest of pearl earrings.

The manner in which she holds the lion, however, suggests more than simply restraint of the creature. She appears to wear the lion as a gown. She has become one with the lion, adorning it with jewels on its brow and a wreath of flowers woven into its mane. The lion seems utterly content, aware of its own strength and respecting the woman's strength. Again, the idea that working together multiplies rather than simply combines their strengths is apparent, as is the bond of loyalty and trust. She holds the lion lightly, and he does not resist.

The woman's strength guides the lion; the lion's strength protects the woman. The two are one, a partnership based on true understanding of respect for both self and other.

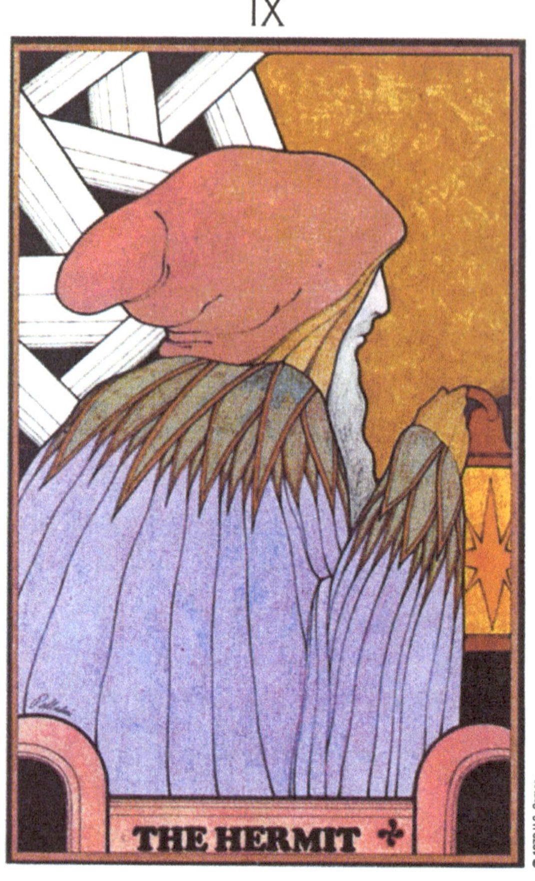

The Hermit has withdrawn from the world. He carries his lamp to illuminate the darkness. He meditates upon the deeper meaning of life. He seeks truth. He hides his face from us. He could be me . . . or you. He seeks knowledge in the dark, hidden places.

Aquarian: The Hermit leads, lighting the way with his lantern. He does not look back to see if we follow; that is not his responsibility. His role is to provide illumination on the path; it is our choice to follow to wisdom, or to remain in ignorance.

Even if we choose to stay, to resist change, we are changed by our awareness of our choice. Our ignorance is no longer comfortable and safe. We are not content to remain in darkness, despite what we tell ourselves, no matter how very justified we felt in refusing the call. Our unenlightened state now chafes and binds, a way of being that no longer fits our soul. Once we know something, we cannot un-know it.

We can choose to follow the path of wisdom at any point. We cannot make up lost time or distance on the path; our willingness to undergo the journey—however long we may have delayed its beginning—will move us forward at the speed of our soul, once we say "yes" to the path.

We cannot see the Hermit's face. We must trust that this is our teacher, the teacher our soul has sought. This Hermit teaches obliquely, not speaking for long stretches of the road; then asking questions for which we must find our own answers; then, at last, explaining things to us. We must develop our own understanding before we can understand another's perspective.

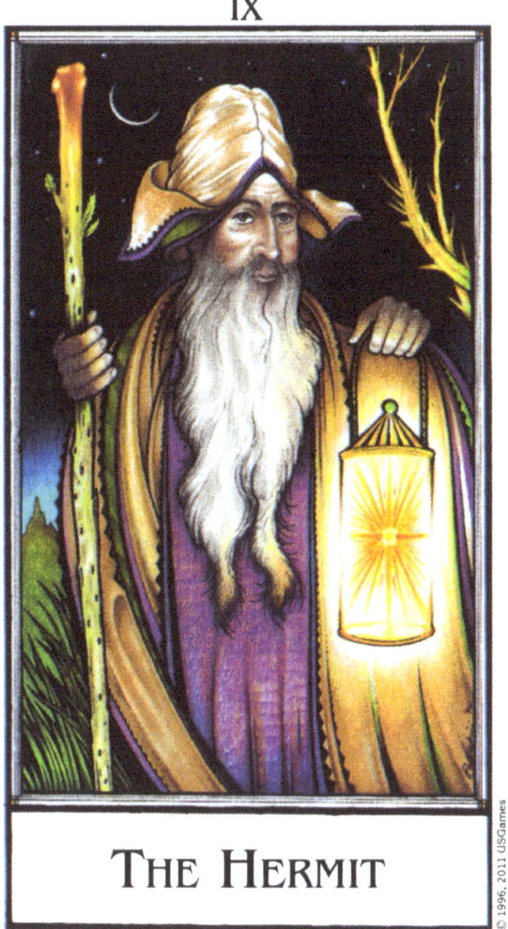

The old Hermit, dressed in rough, simple clothing, carries his lamp in the darkness. The lamp contains a star, and is the light of the world. His lamp throws light into the dark places. This is the card of attainment of a higher plane of existence.

In his solitude, the Hermit has gained knowledge and spirituality. He stares intently at us as the crescent moon rises.

This Hermit engages us directly, illuminating the current situation so we can make our own choice whether to stay, to follow, or to choose another path. This Hermit, too, is detached from our decision; he will continue on his path, regardless of our participation—or lack thereof—in the journey.

We cannot know where our choice will take us, or what will happen. We make the best choice possible, based on the information we have at the time. The choice is good if we choose honestly, regardless of the outcome. The choice is bad, regardless of the outcome, if we knowingly choose based on false information, false hopes, false motives. We know in our soul that we are making a bad decision, and fool ourselves into believing it will somehow turn out well. A good decision may not always have a good outcome, but a bad decision always leads to a bad end.

What matters is the now. Now is the time to decide—to choose movement, stasis, or regression. The Hermit tells us the time for thinking, pondering, and considering is over. No analysis paralysis permitted—you must decide, even if that decision is a to refuse to decide. That is as valid a decision as any, although perhaps not the most useful one.

If we choose movement, we are not guaranteed any specific outcome. We will experience the journey, we will have the opportunity to gain knowledge and develop wisdom—but the Hermit does not guarantee a safe, easy journey with a happy ending. He guarantees only that he will light the path. We have the responsibility to see the path clearly and to walk it bravely, wherever the path may go.

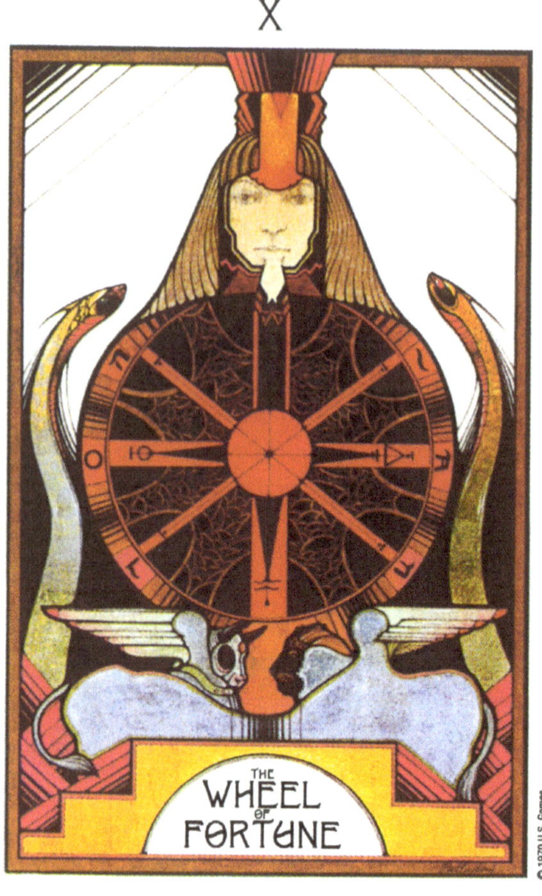

A strong pharaoh surmounts the Wheel, upon which Hebrew letters are inscribed, spelling the name of God. Sacred snakes stand guard. Winged figures of a bull and a lion support the wheel: the bull for strength, and the lion for courage. Strength and courage to face the ups and downs on the Wheel of Life. Destiny and fortune ride upon the wheel as it spins.

The Pharaoh's head rises directly from the Wheel itself; the Pharaoh is one with the Wheel, influencing and influenced by the Wheel's rotation.

Instead of the animals or human figures often seen clinging to the Wheel, we see two snakes on either side, detached from the Wheel, and two winged creatures at the base of the Wheel.

The four letters of the Tetragrammaton are clearly visible, but only two of the four Arabic letters we expect to see are visible—the A and the O, the Alpha and Omega. The usual place for the T, at the top of the Wheel, is covered by the Pharaoh's beard. The usual R at the bottom is simply a blank space. We ourselves must supply the missing letters to complete the word, just as in life we must participate in both the quotidian and cosmic processes to complete our journey.

We must act, and be acted upon. We make our plans, we take action, with no guaranteed outcome. The only constant is change, and the only thing we can control is our own self—our thoughts, feelings, and behaviors.

We act, we react—all we can control is our own actions and reactions.

The Universe always has the last spin of the Wheel.

The ancient wheel is inscribed ROTA. The sacred name of God is written in Hebrew upon the wheel. The Egyptian Sphinx is above. The eagle and bull are below. At the center are the four great elements of nature: Earth, Air, Fire, and Water. The Wheel of Fortune symbolizes the perpetual motion and change of a fluid universe, and the flux of human life.

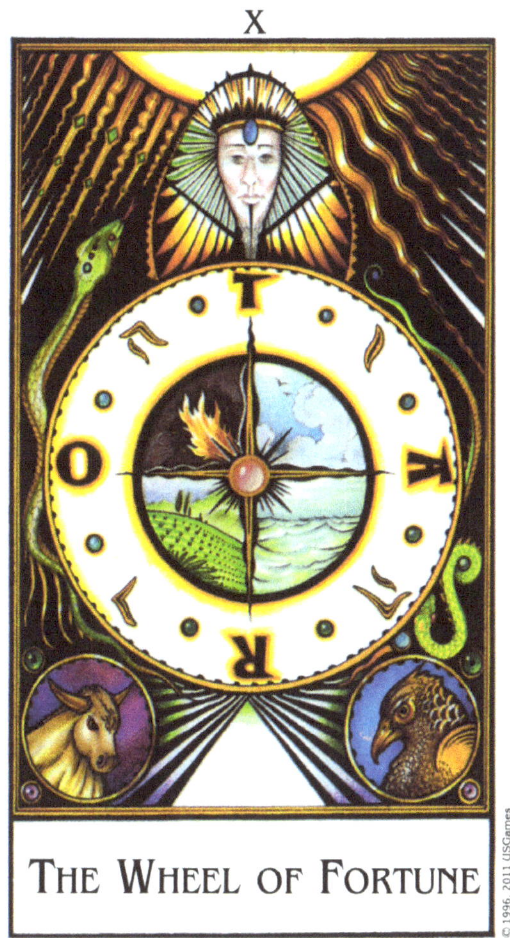

Here, the human figure seems to float above the Wheel, attached but separate.

We have the four letters of the Tetragrammaton, the four Arabic letters spelling TARO, and the four elements at the center of the Wheel. The card is more easily grasped on the visual level, requiring less intellectual effort to apprehend than the *Aquarian* card.

Instead of two snakes rising in parallel, we have one snake surrounding most of the Wheel. This suggests Kundalini energy rising, the snake looking past the human face and beyond to the sun—the natural power that governs and cannot be disregarded.

Human will is a considerable force and can create and cause many events; however, the Universe starts and stops the Wheel, regardless of our will.

The cameos in the bottom corners feature an ox and an eagle, two of the four symbols often seen in the Tarot, representing body and intellect. We do not see the lion and the angel, the usual other pair, representing will and soul. Their omission is another reminder that we do not have absolute control; we do what we can, and the Universe has the final spin of the Wheel.

XI

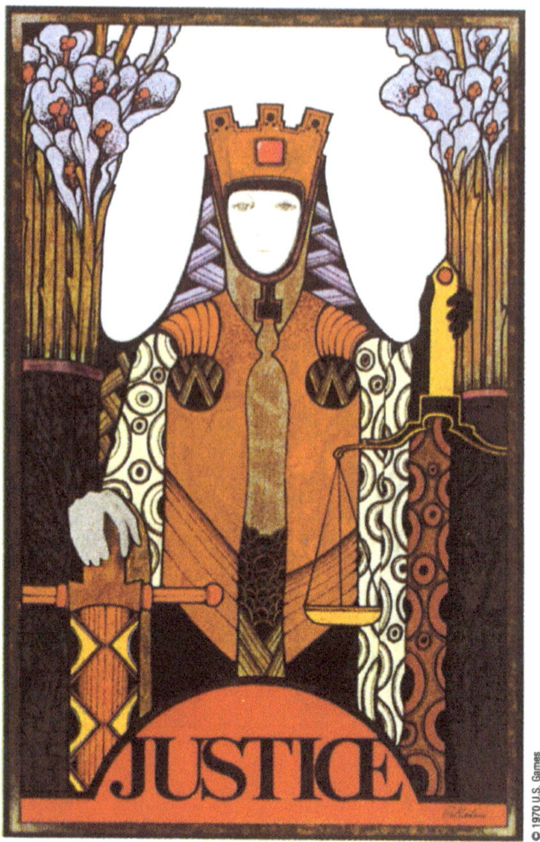

A strong warrior surrounded by flowering rods, she holds in her left hand the scales of justice and in her right hand the sword of justice. The sword is still sheathed within its scabbard. It is not yet time.

The scales are balanced: the essence of life; equality between mind, body, and spirit. In order for that balance to exist, one must have a sense of oneself and one's life. You are accountable for your actions.

Change results from prior events. Free will is everything. Choose wisely.

The figure in this card is placed between two stands of flowering rods which are anchored in planters, recalling the pillars in the High Priestess card. Justice carries the number 11, which reduces to 1 + 1 = 2, tying this card to the High Priestess numerologically as well as thematically.

Her sword and scales create a second, smaller visual reference to the pillars, giving us four pillars to contain and bind the card's energy. She also wears a four-sided jewel in her crown, furthering the visual emphasis on order, stability, and groundedness, a magnification of these qualities as represented in the number four of the Emperor.

Like the High Priestess, the woman herself is the Middle Pillar of the Tree of Life, the balance between Severity and Mercy. Real justice requires the balancing of these qualities. The innocent are freed, the guilty are punished as appropriate to their crimes—but no more.

The second pan of the scale is not visible to us, reminding us that we cannot know everything. We have our version of events, our facts, our truth, but we do not have The Truth. We need to let go of our preconceptions if we wish to see the complete picture and fully understand Justice.

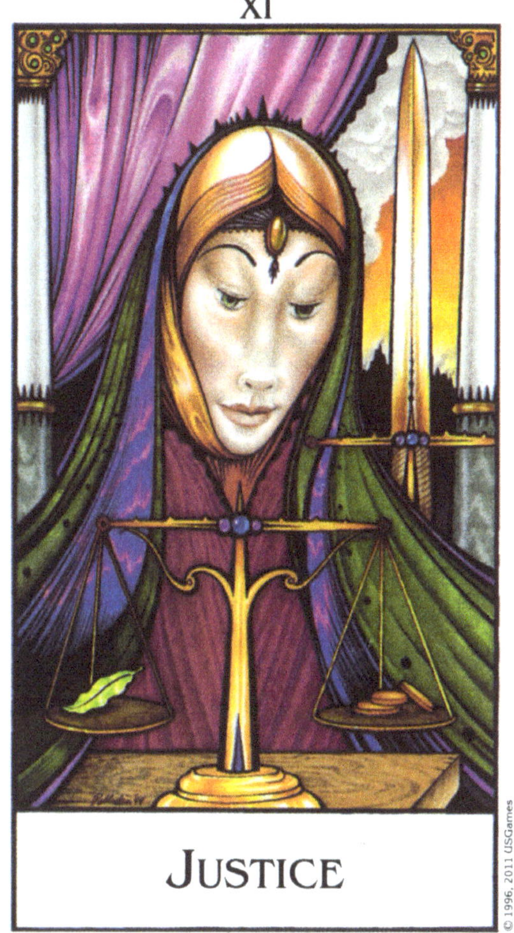

A woman, seated between pillars of marble and alabaster, contemplates the golden scales of justice.

The scales balance between a green leaf on the left and money on the right. Nature and greed are at war. Behind her awaits the sword of justice. Should the scales become unbalanced; the sword will right the situation. When man transgresses too far upon nature, the sword avenges. Justice will always triumph. Not laws. Not rules. Justice.

The woman does not challenge us or engage with us. Here, she is focused on the work before her of discerning Truth in order to achieve Justice. Like the High Priestess, her numerological partner, her temple is defined by pillars and a veil. Like the High Priestess, she is richly dressed in heavy robes to underscore her authority.

She sits between the Pillars of Mercy and Severity, embodying the Middle Way. The pillars also create a separate space, apart from the chaos of life, a sacred temple dedicated to the idea and the practice of Justice.

She does not hold the sword or scales. The sword appears to float next to her. The scales are small enough to fit on her table. She weighs three coins against a leaf, weighing the cost against the value, the tangible against the abstract. All things have worth, regardless of whether they have a monetary value. The use of a leaf, rather than the Feather of Ma'at seen in other decks, emphasizes the intangible and ephemeral in balance with the material.

This figure of Justice ties more closely with the Empress than the Emperor. The lush countryside in the background, and the vibrant green hues call to mind the authority of the Empress as a ruler based in natural law. The visual connection to the Empress creates a more balanced sense of the feminine and masculine energies than is found in the *Aquarian* Justice card, in its heavily masculine setting.

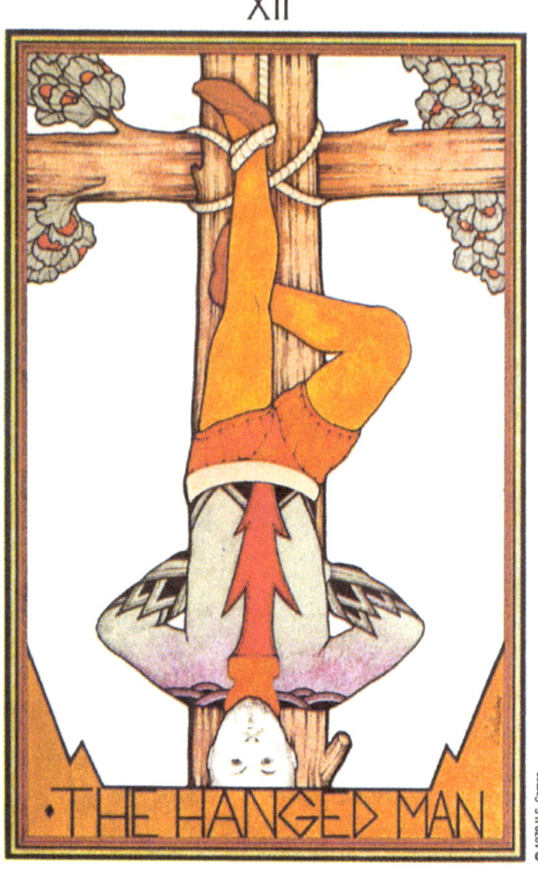

Looking back, I should have changed the name of this card. I think it is more properly "The Hanging Man." He is suspended upside-down from a fruitful tree. He is exploring the outer world and his inner self by changing his point of view. He is seeing and learning things he could not otherwise know.

The man is stripped down to his medieval underclothes; the trappings and appearances are removed to clearly see the foundation of the person.

We see the patterns of crystallization on the figure's sleeves, and a softened version around his neck. As he undergoes his transition, the limited viewpoint and preconceptions are fading, not yet replaced by fully formed new ideas. We must release the old way of being before the new can take hold.

The flowering branches on the tree indicate that this passage is indeed about growth, even if this is not clear to us as we go through the process.

He hangs by his left foot, indicating a subconscious process of choice in the matter. He did not plan to be here, yet here he is. He acknowledges and accepts the situation.

He knows that struggling against the bonds, the tree, the process, will only prolong matters and delay his release. He is accepting of the situation, even if he has not yet reached a state of grace in his acceptance. You do not have to like the situation, but you do have to accept it before you can move through it to a new situation.

A long-haired young man is suspended from a beautiful blooming tree laden with fruit. The tree is in the form of a cross, and his legs also form a cross. A golden aura radiates from his mind. His face expresses deep entrancement and meditation, not suffering. He is suspended between heaven and earth. Viewing the world this way, the young man sees deeply. He knows that there is no death. Death is a portal. Another life awaits.

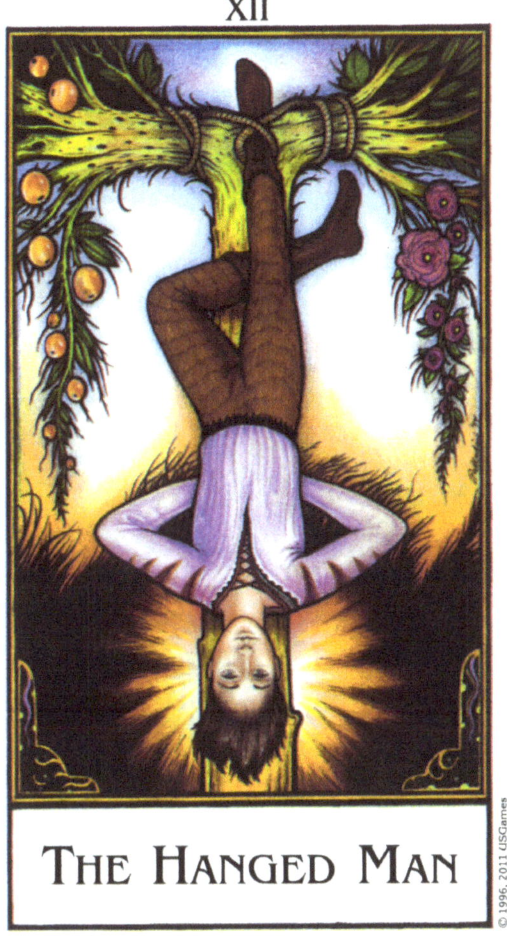

The figure here also undergoes a transformation, but in a very different manner from his *Aquarian* counterpart. The abundance of vibrant vegetation suggests a more vital and natural process, compared to the aridity of the *Aquarian*.

He hangs by his right foot, showing us that he stepped onto the tree knowingly, consciously, understanding that he will be changed, and with no expectations of what that change will be. He surrenders his will, his need for control, and waits to see what comes next. He understands that he must release the limiting illusion of control in order to tap into the true power within himself.

He is willingly suspended between the physical and mystical words, pausing the action of his life. In between the material and spiritual worlds, he realizes his true self as the place where the two worlds meet. This realization allows him to move forward from a place of peace and clarity, along a more authentic, soulful path.

The nimbus of light around his head emphasizes his state of conscious release. With grace of spirit and awareness of mind, he allows himself simply to be in the moment and undergo the transition, without expectation of when it will end or how it will turn out.

He trusts himself, he trusts the process, and he trusts the Universe.

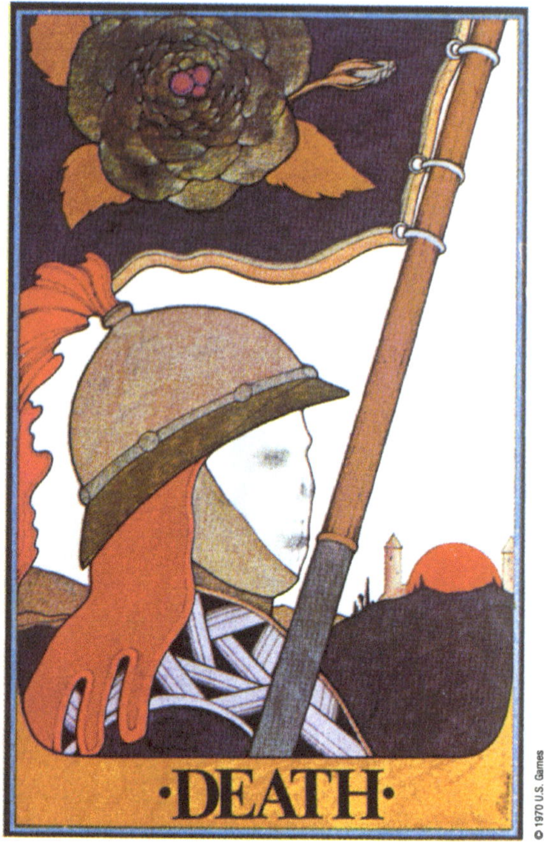

Do not fear this card. Death comes to us all, great and small. Death is part of life. It is the portal from this world into the next. The skull remains behind. The spirit moves on.

This card is about change. We all live, die, and move on. All things change. In fact, the Universe changes daily. The death of one thing leads to the birth of another.

Life makes us an offer we cannot refuse: In exchange for the privilege of being born and experiencing the fullness of life, we accept the inevitability of our death.

We fear Death. We deny Death. We defy, bargain, beg, argue, and plead with Death. We ignore it, or rush to embrace it. Perhaps we even learn to accept it. The one thing we cannot do is escape it. Death marches on, unstoppable.

Death here is seen as a soldier, resolutely performing its duty. A red sun sets between two towers in a barren landscape. The few trees, the symbols of life energy, are small and distant silhouettes as Death carries us away from Life.

As an organic process, Death cannot be stopped—delayed, perhaps, with interventions, but not prevented. At some point, the organism fails. Our heart ceases beating, our blood stops flowing, our brain ends its fabulously complex system of chemical signals, and our body dies.

What happens next? No one really knows. Religions have their stories: Pagans may speak of the Summer Lands; the Buddhists teach of the Nine Lands; the ancient Greeks told of the underworld of Hades; the Abrahamic religions have varying concepts of Heaven, Hell, and Purgatory.

No one actually knows, and the stories we tell of reward, punishment, and resurrection are attempts at consolation and reassurance that, while our bodies may cease to be, our unique selves will not be lost to Death and Time.

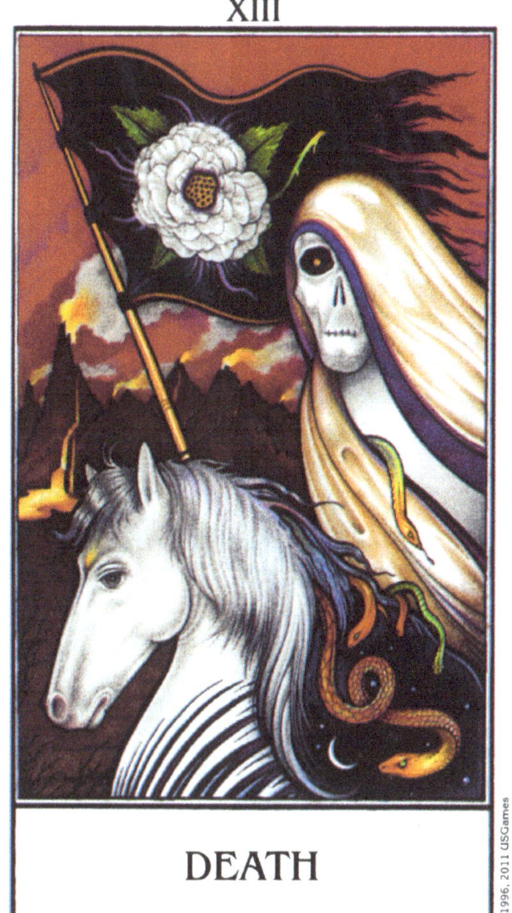

Death rides his striped steed through a fiery landscape. Snakes slither from beneath his robe as he carries the banner of the white rose: the rose of innocence and fertility. Rebirth from blood to seed to new bloom.

All living things must die. It is a natural process. Death is just a passage to new life.

Death in the *New Palladini* is seen as a messenger on a pale horse, itself unsubstantial—part horse, part energy, part night sky.

A snake crawls out of Death's robe. Snakes spring from the horse's mane. The red sky is filled with smoke and fire from the volcanoes. Lava flows in a river of fire down the mountains and across the plains towards us.

The only hope is found in the night sky. Our only way out is to become one with eternity, to let go, dissolve, become an impersonal star in the sky of the Universe.

The meaning of the Death card is simple and clear: The situation is dead. You are at the end of it. You must let go of your fear and let go of whatever it is you are clinging to, or is clinging to you. The situation is not going to change for the better. The end is here, and the time to repair, or mend, or heal, has passed. Acknowledge the death, mourn the loss, and move on.

This card rarely signifies an actual physical death of a person (or pet, for that matter). In over 30 years of reading for others, I have seen it come up indicating an actual death only once , and that was in a reading for a client who had been diagnosed with a terminal illness.

Unless there is a strong reason to do so, reading this card only as a physical death is too easy. Examine the other cards in the reading to determine what in the client's life is passing or ending, and how the client can navigate the transition with grace.

XIV

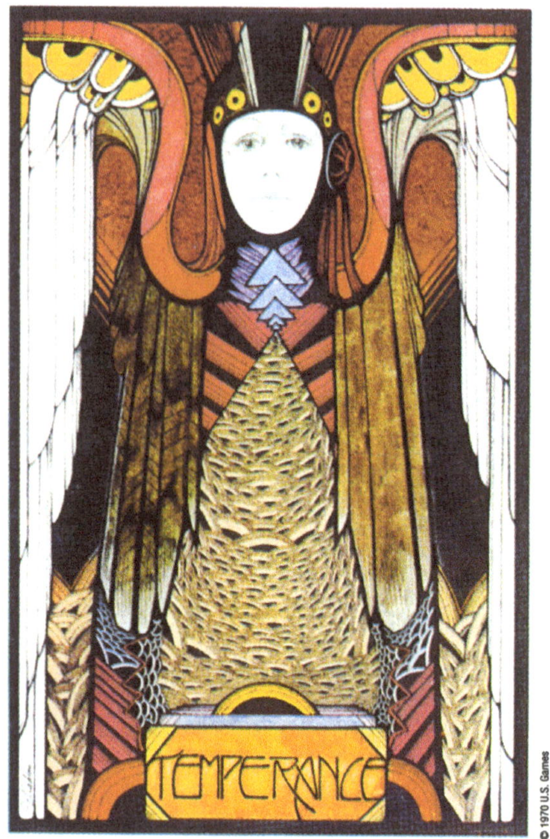

A winged angel, strong and confident. It has been tested by life, but only made the angel more powerful. This temperance means restraint, moderation, and justice.

To make steel stronger it is tempered. Heated until glowing red and then plunged into cold water, the steel comes out better, harder, and more resilient.

We must undergo the same process. Each day brings new tests, new mountains to climb. We are remade, re-formed, formed again. Tempered. From this process comes wisdom and strength.

The *Aquarian* Angel of Temperance is overwhelming. Her wings fill the picture, extending outside the frame. Colors and patterns, light and shadow, mix and weave, confusing our eyes and our mind about what we are really seeing.

Her expression is calm, neutral, giving us no clues as to how to act or what to expect in her presence.

The *New Palladini* angel is imposing, as angels are , but not overwhelming. The angel fits within the card—a cool, quiet nightscape. She radiates light, calm, and serenity. She focuses on her task, moving water between two cups. The flowing river of emotional calm and the tulips growing from the solid earth under the night sky give us a sense of reassurance and familiarity in the presence of this otherworldly being. The energy here is calm and contained, and we feel we can be part of this scene, even if we are unsure of our role in it.

Temperance can be seen as the watery companion to airy Justice, creating a balance between opposites. Discerning what is, Temperance adjusts our thoughts, words, and actions to bring them into alignment with our realizations and need for growth. Temperance tells us to remove what is not helpful or healthy so we can make room for that which heals.

An angel, neither male nor female, with jeweled wings, stands by the side of a river. The angel pours the essence of life from one golden chalice to another. The angel wears the rays of the sun on its head, an aura of deep understanding. This card harmonizes the spiritual, psychic, and material natures of mankind. It symbolizes the secrets of eternal life, and the perpetual flow of existence.

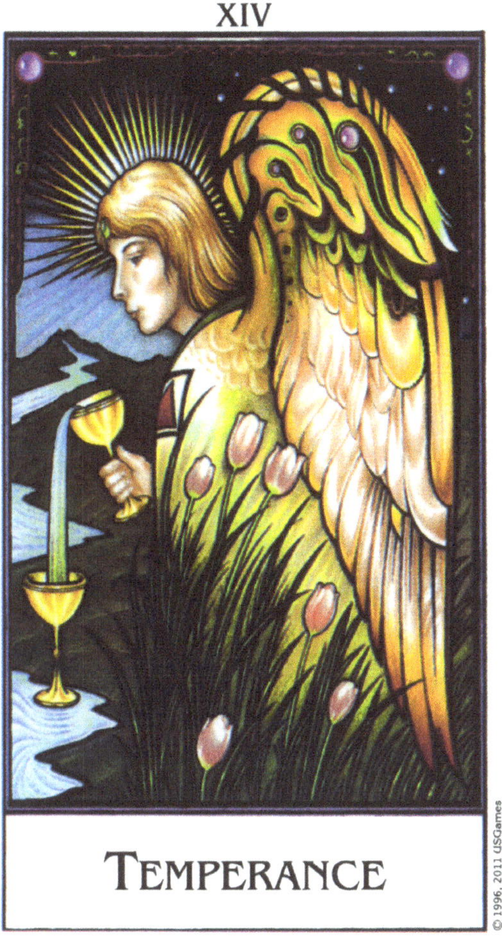

The fire triangle on each angel's chest speaks to us of the need to take action on the results of our contemplation. Knowing what needs to be done is a necessary start to the process, but it is not the process. Until we act on our knowledge, we are not making best use of it; without action, no one and no thing benefits from our knowledge, not even our own self. The water will not pour itself. We must lift the cup and tilt it to start the flow.

Temperance also refers to the process of tempering metal to remove impurities and make it stronger and more flexible. The metal is heated, sometimes it is beaten, and then cooled. This process of heating, beating, and cooling is repeated until the metal reaches the desired state of strength and flexibility. So, too, events and experiences in our lives temper our minds, our emotions, and our souls, imparting useful—if sometimes painful – lessons to help us evolve into greater awareness.

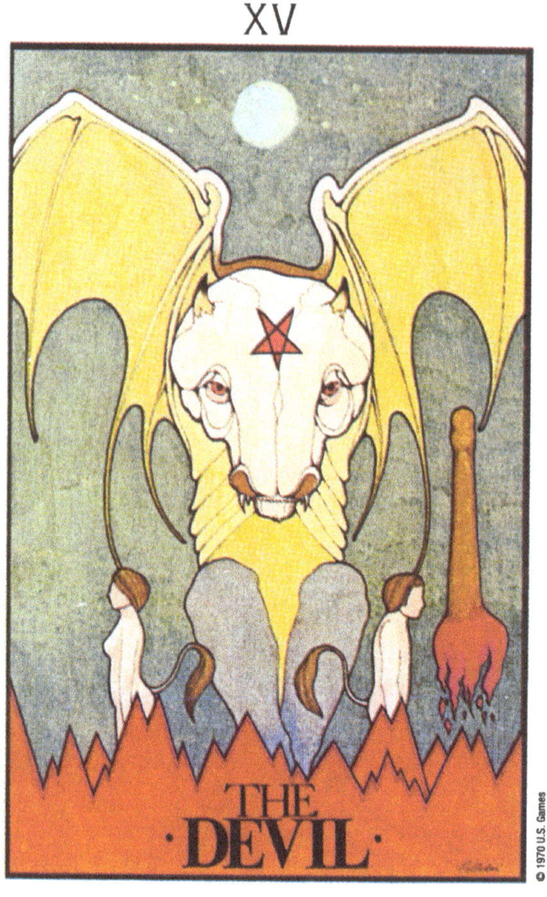

The Devil is a beast, inhuman, without heart, soul, or morals. A truly destructive force, it will do anything to destroy love and peace, for it can easily influence and control us. Material things are its lure to lead us away from our true divine nature. It perverts truth, and punishes good. The Devil is the agent of darkness seeking to extinguish the light.

Hello, Devil, our old friend! Along with Death and the Tower, this card is one of the least favorite in the deck. We see the Devil, and immediately go into Bartleby the Scrivener mode: "I would prefer not to." And yet, here the Devil is, and he must be given his due.

In Christian teachings, the Devil is Lucifer, the fallen Angel of Light, who disobeyed God and was cast out of Heaven to be the Angel of Darkness and to rule Hell. What a job! Banished from the light of Divine Grace, sent into eternal darkness and flame, and put in charge of countless miscreant souls.

After a few thousand years, it's all the same. There's nothing new under the sun, or in Hell. And yet, the Devil must do his job, finding new ways to trick humans back into our old, bad habits, or to develop new ones. The negative creativity which springs from the Devil's boredom is the same destructive energy which we use to justify to ourselves that we have to remain in the bad job, continue the unhealthy relationship, or persist in self-destructive behaviors.

The Devil here is much in the Rider-Waite-Smith (RWS) tradition: We see a bat-winged demon, inverted flaming torch, human figures with animal tails burning in flame. Here, however, they are not wearing chains. They remain in their captivity as a matter of habit, not knowing (or perhaps knowing, but not believing) that they can simply walk to freedom. They are ruled by their animal natures and their minds cannot understand their peril—or their possible escape.

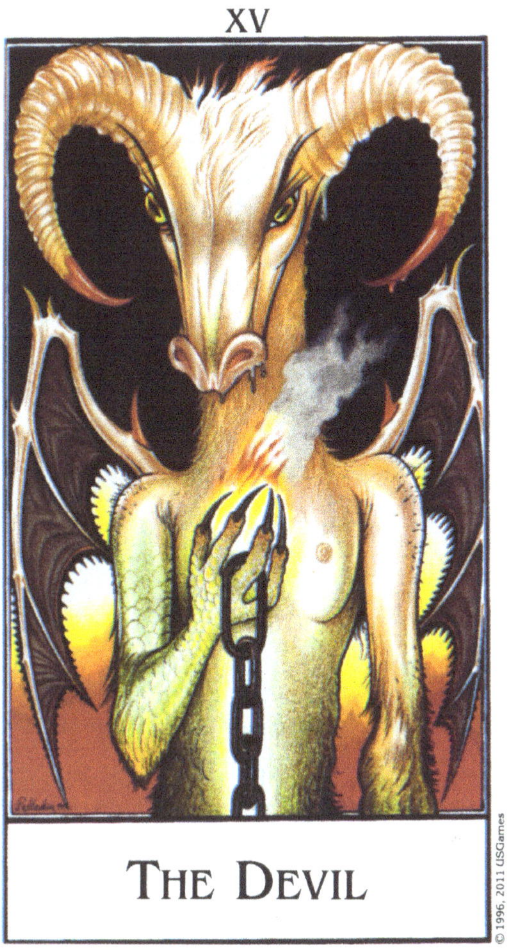

I see the beast more clearly now. His sharp horns are tipped with blood from piercing the hearts of lovers. He holds the chain of addiction in his claws. His green scales are the scales of the snake that tricked Adam and Eve into giving up the paradise of nature, the Garden of Eden. They traded everything beautiful and natural and good for knowledge. Then, everything changed, and they were cast out into the wilderness.

This Devil is more dangerous, both in appearance and in approach. His horns drip blood (not his, we can be certain), and his wings have sharp horns of their own, some likewise bloodied. Fire and smoke leap from the claws of his right hand, which holds a heavy black chain. We cannot see his left hand, but we can be certain of its potential danger to us. Perhaps it holds the lock to close the chain; perhaps it holds some other device to inflict pain.

The Devil challenges us, dares us to take him on. We can hear him: "You're smart, you're clever. I'm just a little old Devil sitting here. You can put on the chain, and break free, Houdini-like, any time. You know you can outsmart me." And so, telling ourselves we can beat the Devil at his own game, we take on the chains of addiction, compulsion, and self-destruction. It's all fun and games until you're trapped in Hell and can't get out.

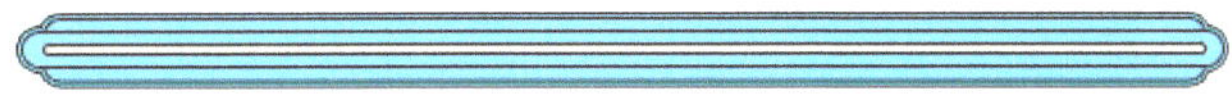

The Devil asks us to identify the Devil in our lives. How have we chained ourselves? To whom have we given our power, leaving us defenseless and vulnerable? What behaviors, thoughts, and feelings are keeping us trapped?

You cannot use the same thinking that created the problem to solve the problem. See the Devil for what it is. Name it, and so enable yourself to reclaim your power, break the chains, and walk away.

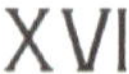

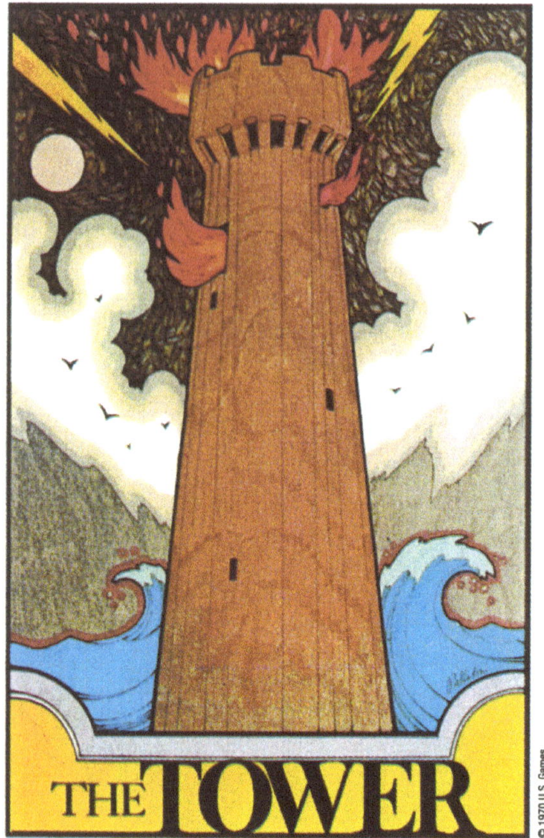

The Tower is under attack. Fire burns, while tsunamis blast its base. The storm rages. You are the Tower. Life tears at you, trying to destroy you. You are forced to change your thinking, your lifestyle, your goals. Out of chaos will come enlightenment.

Be strong.

Lighting! Fire! Chaos! Destruction! Most people are put off by their initial encounter with the Tower card, and are upset when it turns up in readings. And yet it is just another archetype—a dramatic and startling archetype with a powerful message that can tell us much if we can work through our feelings of dread to hear the message.

The *Aquarian* Tower is struck by lightning, engulfed in flames at the top, and beset by a rising flood at its base. Winds batter it. All we need is an earthquake to complete the elemental assault. Birds flee the Tower, battling the winds to escape. We see no humans in the picture.

The destruction of the Tower in the *New Palladini* is less dramatic visually, but just as thorough. Lightning strikes crack the structure, which burns at both its top and base, sending flames into the sky and surrounding land to spread the devastation. The mountain itself is cracking (there's our earthquake missing from the *Aquarian*), hastening the fall of the flaming structure.

Tower moments are often created by an external source—a natural disaster, such as a fire, flood, tornado, or earthquake. Sometimes it is a disaster of human origin—the loss of a job, a home, or a person close to us—that is as devastating as any act of nature.

Tower events can also be self-inflicted—a drug overdose, a sexually transmitted disease resulting from our carelessness, a loss from an investment we knew was unwise when we made it.

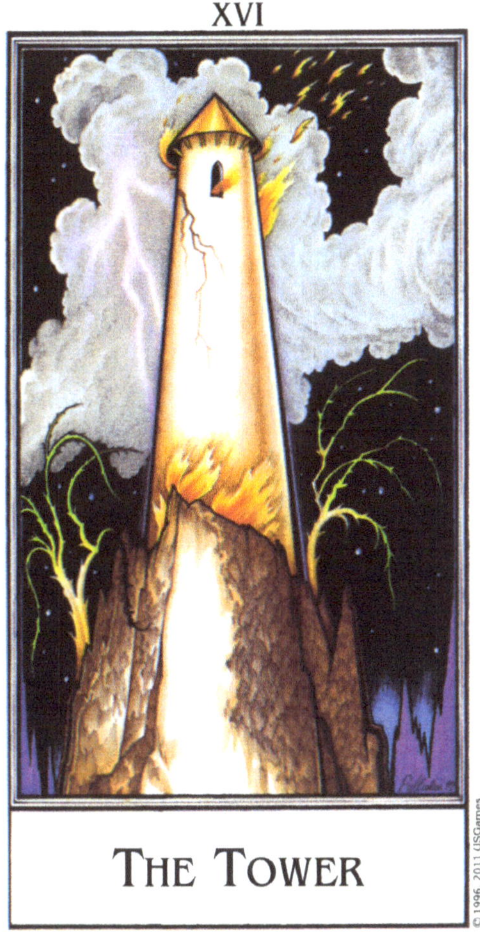

A great round Tower stands upon a rocky cliff. Twisted trees cling to the sheer sides of the mountain. A bolt of lightning leaps from the rolling storm clouds and strikes the side of the Tower, fracturing it. A fire rages within and licks at the Tower's foundation. This card represents the ruin of the life when evil prevails within it.

The common factors are the suddenness of the timing and the radical collapse of some part of our life that was previously intact. The Tower is broken, destroyed, gone. We cannot move back in, cannot continue to live life in the same way. We must move out and move on, or we perish in the burning rubble of our life.

When the Tower comes up as a warning, its message is unequivocally clear: Change is required—now. Not when he stops drinking. Not when she quits gambling. Not when the weather is better. Now. The situation is dangerous. The Tower is unsafe and cannot be repaired. We have one last chance to free ourselves from the limitations and negative environment in our Tower. If we do not move to free ourselves, the Universe will see to it in its own way and time. You can undergo change at your pace, or on the Universe's schedule. Leave now, or be prepared to dig yourself out of the rubble of your life when it all falls apart.

If the card represents an event (or events) that has already occurred, you can use it as a turning point in the reading by pulling additional cards showing the way forward, how to move away from the rubble and move on with life. Sometimes the ruins require a great deal of cleanup before complete freedom can be obtained. Sometimes the only thing to do is walk away from the ruins. Work with the cards to find the way forward.

XVII

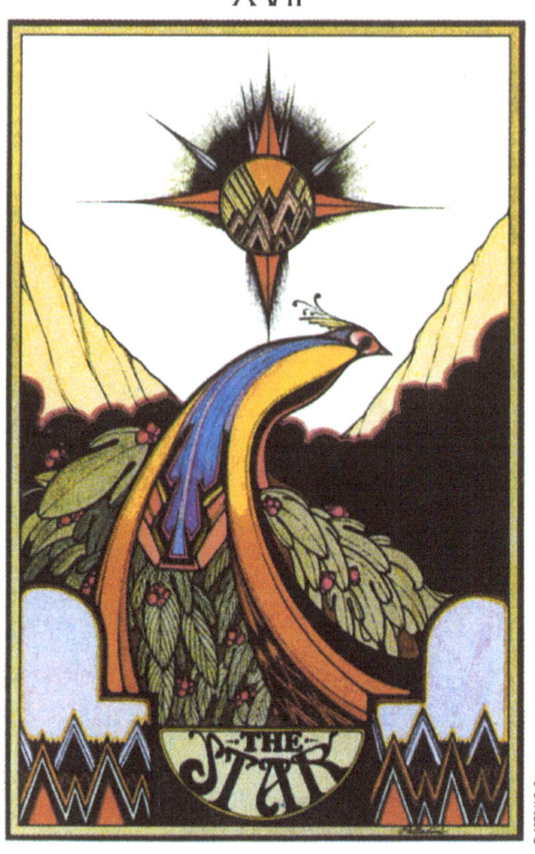

A mysterious dark star blazes in the daylight. It is the Star of Inspiration. It brings hope of transcending the trials of life to seek truth and beauty always. A magical bird spreads its feathers under starlight.

Leaving the chaos of the Tower behind, we find ourselves in the restorative card of the Star.

The *Aquarian* Star bursts forth out of darkness into a white sky. Its rays extend like the antennae of an artful satellite, surrounding a stylized sunrise over mountains. The eight-pointed star is Polaris, the North Star. Following its light, we navigate safely to a place of peace and grace, a harbor of safety for our souls after the harrowing passage we have just experienced.

The eight-pointed star also symbolizes the idea of squaring the circle. It occupies a place halfway between the two shapes, a meeting place between the square of matter and the circle of the ideal, bringing Earth and Heaven together.

The visual focus is, however, the magnificent bird in the center of the card. Filling much of the card with its sweeping wings, the bird seems a manifestation of the angelic energies of the Star. The vivid, celestial blue of the bird's plumage is found in the Lovers and Moon cards, and these three are the most intensely colored cards of the *Aquarian* deck.

Perched in a berry bush which speaks to us of sustenance and nurturance, the bird gives us a glimpse of beauty and hope after the dark passage which began in the Death card.

The sky is filled with stars: a great radiant Star of eight rays, surrounded by lesser stars, all of eight rays. A woman in the foreground fills her golden cups and pours the waters upon the land, irrigating it. On the right, a bird sings in a small fig tree. The woman is Truth and Beauty. She distributes the water of life freely. She is the process of rain and growth. She is the daughter of nature, inspired by the rays of The Star.

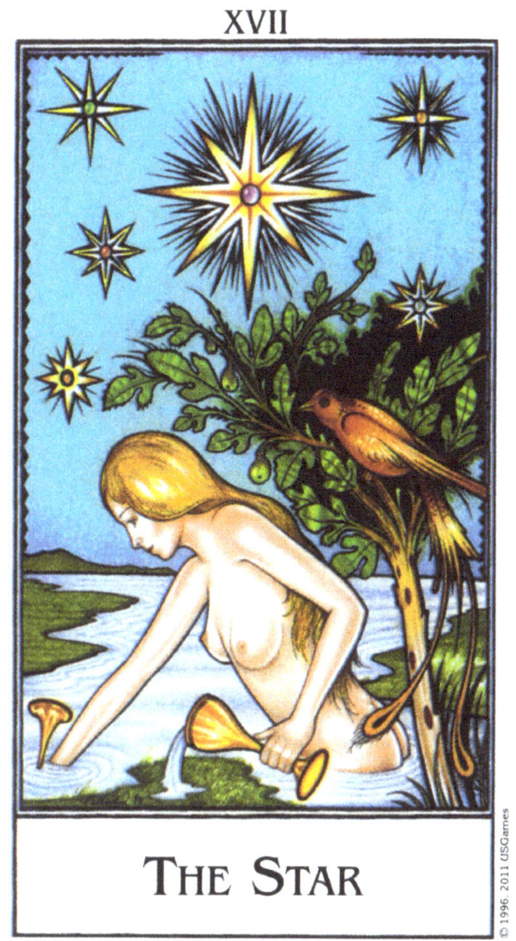

The *New Palladini* Star is closer to the Rider-Waite-Smith image. A bird in a tree watches a woman in the water, while several stars shine above. The bird's plumage, while elaborate, is not as colorful as that of the *Aquarian* bird. Its perch in the fruit tree here corresponds to the *Aquarian* berry bush.

Unlike the Rider-Waite-Smith, the woman here is standing in the water, rather than kneeling next to the water. She is immersed in her experience, retrieving the waters of healing and hope to pour on the ground, much like Kwan Yin blessing the earth. The woman is calm and intent in her purpose, working gracefully and peacefully in the starlit water.

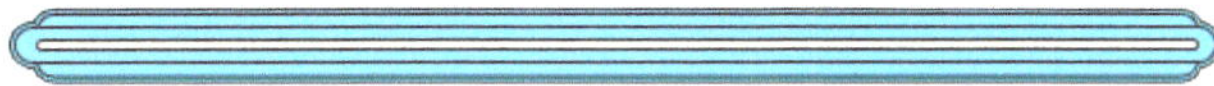

The Star reassures us with time and space for hope and healing. The Star reminds us to restore ourselves physically, mentally, emotionally, and spiritually through self-care. The Star restores our hope for our life, and our belief in our best self, leading us into a period of inspiration and re-creation, so that we re-find our way and rediscover the best in our soul and our heart.

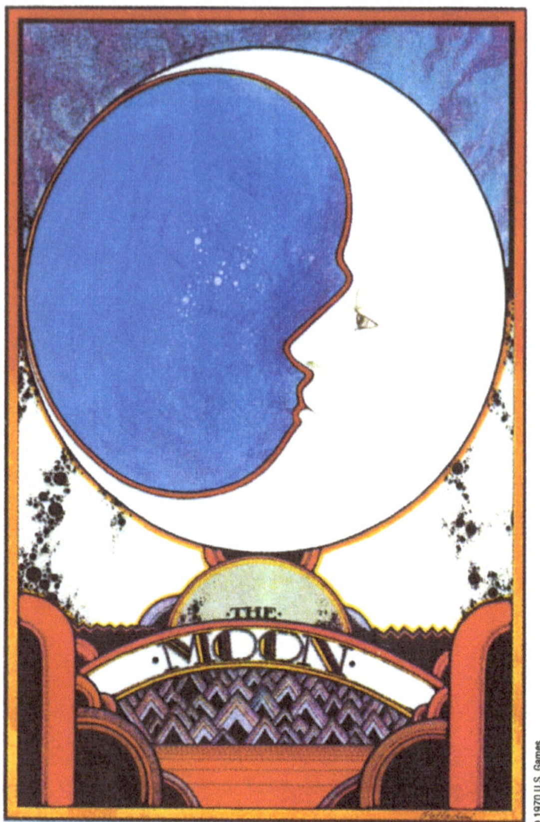

© 1970 U.S. Games

The Moon and I are old friends, you see. The Moon is sister to the Sun. She shines only because she reflects the majesty of the Sun, our star. Dreamily, millennium after millennium, the Moon has drifted by overhead, pulling up the waters of all the oceans. She influences women's fertility, and makes people fall in love.
I have been in love with the Moon for a long time. She has been my friend, my lover, my mother; my Lady Moon. I go to her when I need help.

My Moon card is resolute, staring deeply into the heart of the Creator.

Our celestial journey continues with the Moon card. Magic, mysteries, and secrets are the province of the Moon. From romantic poetry to lunatic ravings, the Moon moves us in seemingly inexplicable ways.

The *Aquarian* Moon shares its brilliant, celestial blue with the Star and the Lovers cards. The color is soothing and inspiring, a vivid contrast to the stark white crescent Moon. The Moon hangs against the backdrop of a dark sky above and lunar landscape below, an artistic symbol imposed over the actual lunar surface.

The Moon pulls us, draws us up and out of our rational daytime selves, invites us to revel in emotions, intuitions, and dreams, to explore and express our fluid, lunar self.

The eye is open, the mouth is closed. The Moon sees everything, and says nothing. The Moon is wiser than we are, who often see nothing and say everything.

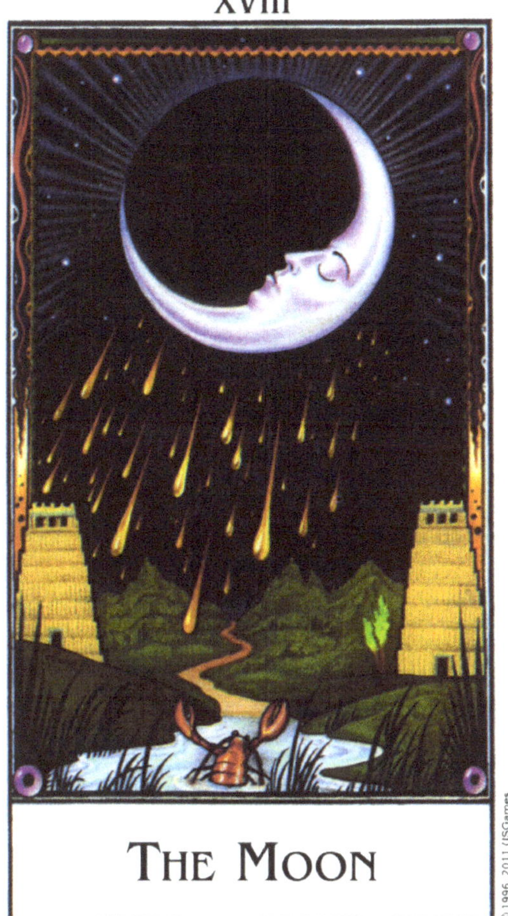

The Moon is meditating. From her fall golden drops of thought.

Twin ancient towers flank a road, which leads between mountains to the horizon. In the foreground is a pool of water, from which a sea creature emerges. The lobster raises its claws in reverence to the Moon.

The Moon brings inner peace, thought, contemplation in her silvery light.

The eye of this Moon is closed. It sleeps, along with most of the world. Having called us out of ourselves, it leaves us to our own devices and mischiefs.

The gold light falls to earth, infusing the land—and us—with lunar energy. The crayfish, too, hears the call, and, as the symbol of our wild nighttime self, responds and rises out of the depths to enjoy the night.

The dry path of rationality leads us to the waters of emotion, where we can immerse ourselves in the bliss of emotional freedom.

As a guide, the Moon encourages us to be honest about our emotions, both with ourselves and with others. By reconnecting with our intuitions and paying attention to our dreams, we can discover—or rediscover—important parts of ourselves to bring into our daylight lives for a more creative and emotionally rich way of being.

As a warning, the Moon cautions us to beware of illusions, especially the ones we create for ourselves. The darkness at the edges of the moonlight can make it difficult to see clearly, both ourselves and the people and things around us. The Moon reminds us to manage our emotions, rather than letting our emotions manage us.

XIX

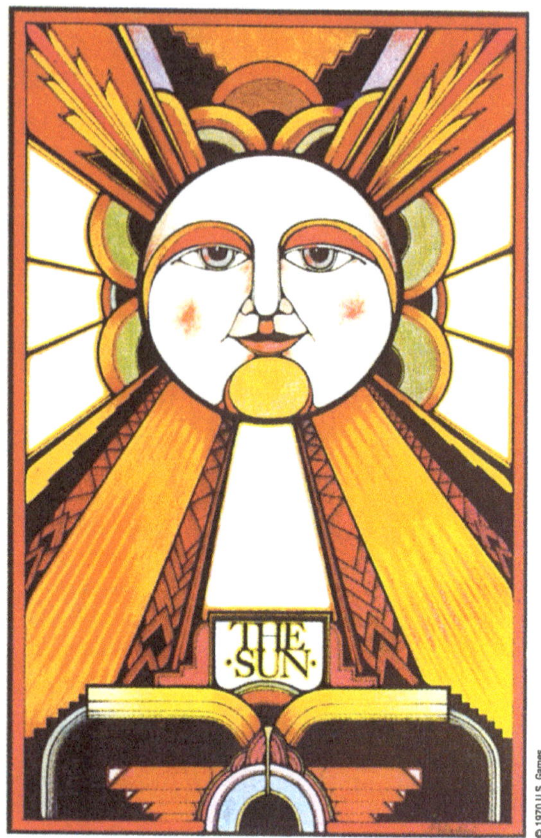

A radiant Sun bursts forth. In this card, Art Nouveau and Art Deco blend in the brilliant colors of the stained glass windows of my youth. The Sun looks young and happy. The Sun is content and free. It achieves goals easily because of its great energy and passion. Brother to the Moon, the Sun makes all things live.

The Sun card is the third expression of the number 1 in the Major Arcana. As the next step up from the Wheel (19 = 1 + 9 = 10), and two steps up from the Magician (19 = 1+9 = 10; 10 = 1 + 0 = 1), it is the intense top note to the energy of creation. The Sun is the source of manifestation energy for life on our planet. All living creatures depend on solar energy directly (plants) or indirectly (those creatures that eat plants) for sustenance.

Like the Wheel, which turns its course without regard for its effects, the Sun shines on everything—for good or ill. The bright sunlight required to grow roses and grapes is the same light that scorches the lilies. The Sun that warms our skin from the chill morning air is the same that causes blisters and sunburn if we stay in it too long. We are grateful for the light and the warmth after our passage through the underworld, but too much, too soon, can turn our gratitude to pain.

The *Aquarian* Sun is highly stylized, leaving us to create our own associations. The orderly arrangement of the sun's energy expressed in the geometrically balanced rays evoke Apollonian rationality and linear thinking, encouraging us to be joyful in clarity and creativity.

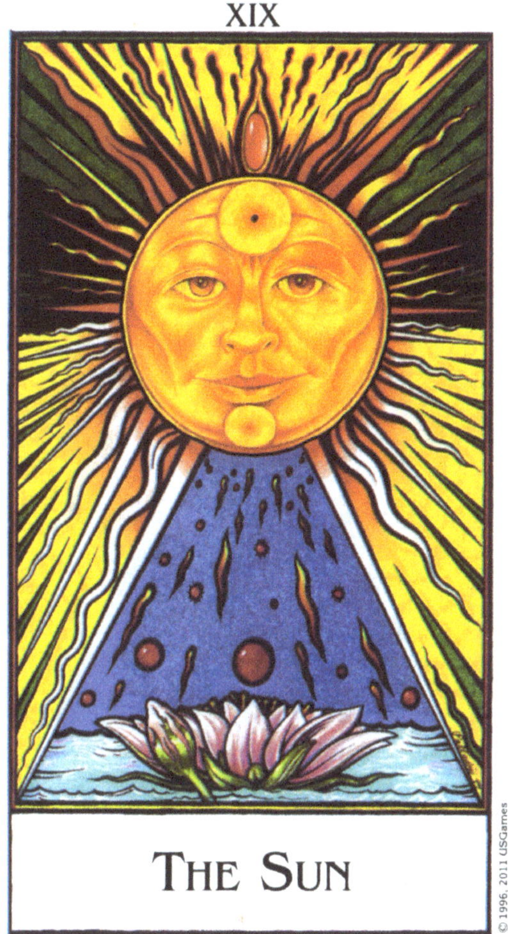

A wise Sun shines radiantly upon the waters below. Flames of inspiration flow down toward a blooming lotus. Things need light to live. The Sun is our star, amongst countless millions of stars in our own galaxy. Out here, on the edge of a spiral arm of the Milky Way, our Sun keeps us alive.

The *New Palladini* Sun also radiates energy, though in a mix of orderly geometric and gracefully curving lines, suggesting a creativity based on intellect and emotion, not just rational thought. The impulsive, random energy of Dionysus is tempered by the disciplined energy of Apollo, resulting in a creation that is both vital and precise. No excess, no misuse, no waste; all is precisely as it should be.

Energy falls in drops from this Sun to the ocean below, with a water lily and lotus growing in its light. The Sun also pulls up energy from the water, creating the cycle of rain and growth. This Sun takes and gives, generating a creative cycle rather than the unilateral, outwardly focused creative energy in the *Aquarian* Sun.

The Sun tells us to live, live large, live brightly, to burn and shine for all to see. Combining our emotional energy with intellectual power, we assume the role of Creator to bring forth new life, new ideas, new forms of living and being in the world.

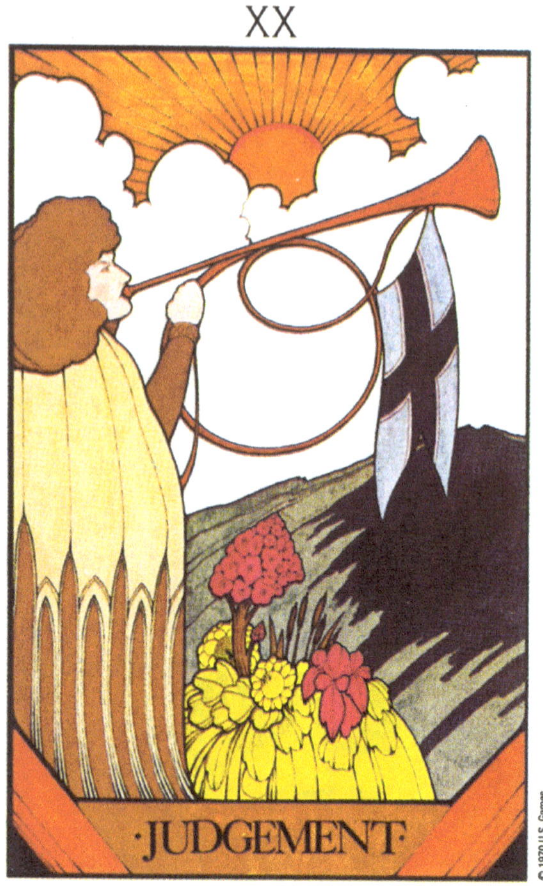

We all know it is coming. An accounting will be made. Did you do right? Did you try to help all mankind? Or maybe just your fellow man? Perhaps, now, you are led to deeper personal understanding, seeing your strong points and recognizing your weaknesses. The trumpet will soon blow.

Despite the similarity of the images on the two cards, the addition of one word—"last" —in the title of the *New Palladini* card gives it a very different quality from the *Aquarian* card.

Named simply "Judgement", the *Aquarian* card shows a figure with a trumpet, who almost seems to have summoned the sun itself with the power of his call. The clouds cast a shadow on the land, which diminishes as the sun rises. We, too, are called to awaken, to rise, to move out of the shadows of doubt and confusion into the light of life and reason.

Every day we make judgements - good/bad, right/wrong, healthy/unhealthy, nice/naughty, smart/stupid, on and on - all dualities, all sets of two, tying this card to the Priestess (2) and Justice (11 = 1 + 1 = 2). We judge ourselves, we judge others.

Judge not, lest ye be judged—where we judge others, we should look at our own actions, thoughts, and intentions. It is easier to advise others on how to remove the mote from their eyes than to take action to remove the board from our own. And yet, it is the board in our own eye that is our responsibility.

Changing the negative behavior—quitting smoking or drinking, changing our eating habits, leaving the situation or relationship—is a necessary condition, but not sufficient to create deep and lasting change. We have to address the emotional, psychological, and spiritual wounds underlying the behavior and heal them. Until we acknowledge and heal the emotions driving the compulsive behavior, we're just dry drunks, walking around with the same internal mess, and re-creating the external mess again and again until we make the choice to confront the real issues.

Our good judgement leads to awakening and renewal.

Our poor judgement also leads there - just on a harder path, and not as nice a place to wake up.

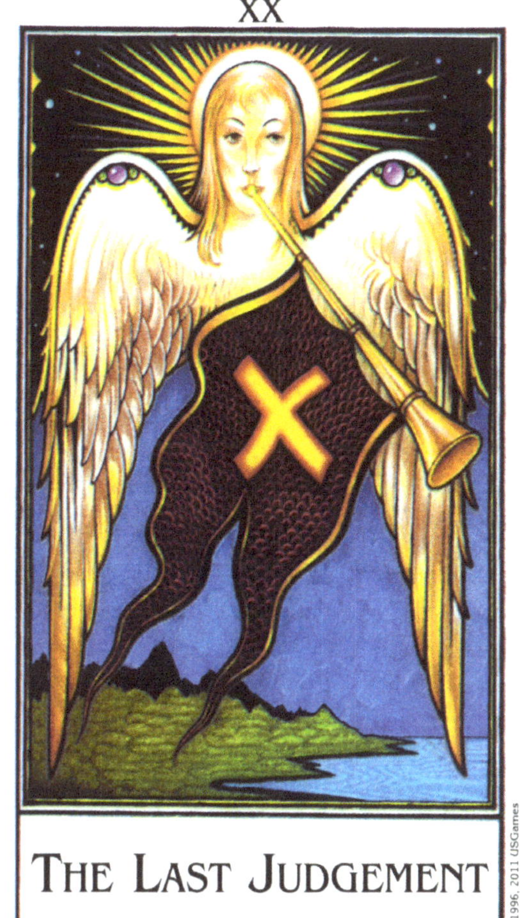

A great angel blows a bannered trumpet, with a cross emblazoned upon it. Her jeweled wings encompass the land and water. Her head is surrounded by a halo of light. When the golden trumpet sounds, we will move on in our life lessons—growing, stumbling, crawling, and trying to rise up, all at the same time. They call that Life. That is how we will be judged. You're born alone, you die alone, and in between, that's Life.

"The Last Judgement", as the *New Palladini* card is called, carries a specific connotation and denotation of the Christian biblical prophecy of the end of the world. Darkness covers the land. Inky night fills the sky, and, according to the story, human souls are filled with despair and dread. The angel Gabriel sounds his celestial trumpet to return light to the land and return hope to human souls.

The dead are wakened from their sleep, and their souls, along with the souls of the living, are sent before God for reward or punishment as the deity determines fitting to their lives—soaking in the bliss of Heaven for eternity, or roasting in the fires of Hell.

As the next degree of 2 in the Major Arcana (20 = 2 + 0 = 2), both Judgement and The Last Judgement raise the essence of Justice (11 = 1 + 1 = 2) and the High Priestess (2). Going back to the High Priestess, if we live in duly reflective awareness, we are just to ourselves and others, which means our judgements are sound and that we need not fear judgement by others, or the final judgement.

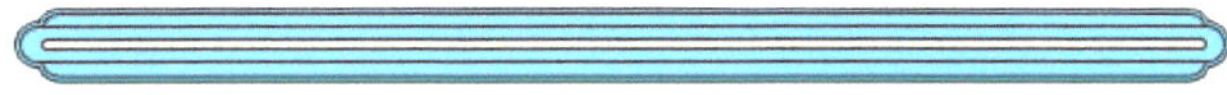

Whether Judgement or Last Judgement, the cards tell us that we must rouse ourselves from our current state of darkness (whether the mental darkness of confusion, emotional darkness of depression, or spiritual darkness of apathy), see the light, and make changes to bring ourselves back into alignment with our world, our community, and our souls.

XXI

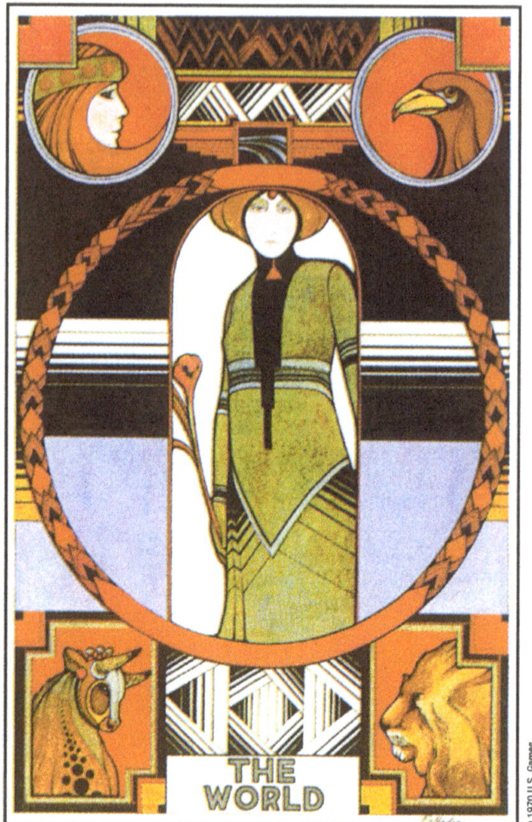

Move, change, see the World. Travel the Universe. Taste and feel and be all things.

Our World is complex. Many opposing forces wage daily battle. Inside of each of us, the same war goes on. One must know many truths in order to complete the journey.

Here at the World card, the decks flip alignment. The *Aquarian* World card echoes a standard Christian representation of Christ in glory, and the *New Palladini* gives us a secular image, which could also be interpreted as the symbols of any number of nature-based religions.

Like standard depictions of Christ enthroned, the *Aquarian* World features a central figure framed by a wreath, with the traditional symbols of the Four Evangelists in the corners of the image. The vertical and horizontal lines of energy can be construed as forming a cross shape behind the figure.

She is framed by a circle, echoing the Wheel of Fortune. Like the hub of a wheel, she is the center point around which all else revolves.

She hold a lily, emblem of orderly, progressive thought. She is the Mind of the World as well as the Heart of the World. A perfect balance of both humanity and divinity, the central figure, while not a typical depiction of Christ, she is presented as a strong, calm, self-contained being, much as Christ is presented.

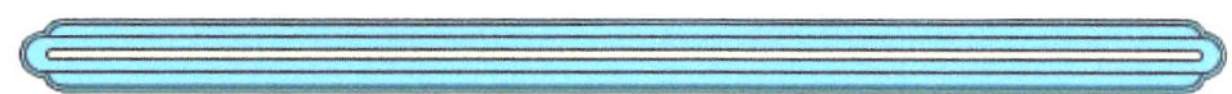

Despite the variances in the images, they carry a shared message: To live fully, we must choose to live in a state of grace, balancing among the elements, between humanity and divinity, between law and nature. We are dancing stardust, containing everything in potential and possessing the power to move from possibility to probability, and from probability to actuality, in the Dance of Life.

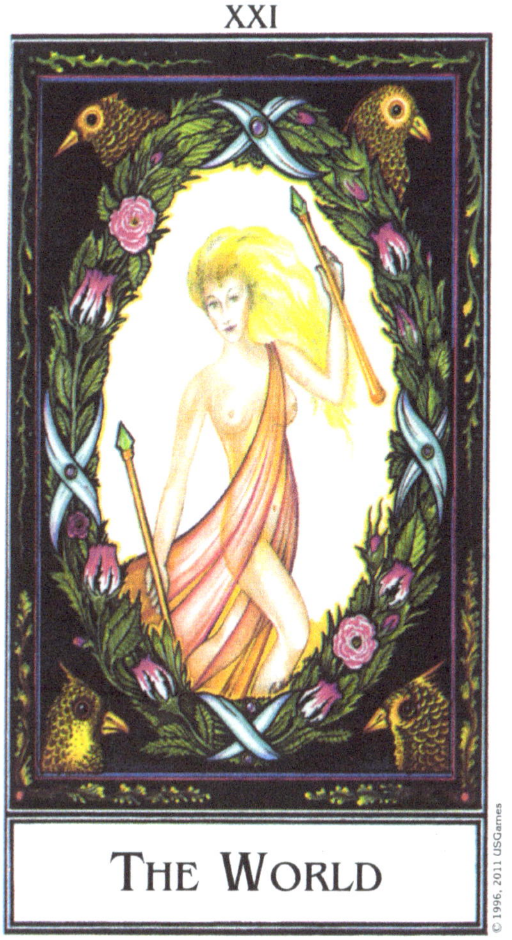

Then, 25 years later, came a revelation…I finally understood!

A great garland of pink roses surrounds the figure of Truth, who carries twin jeweled wands. She is a dancer, she is the swirl of the sensitive life, the human soul reveling in the earthly paradise.

This card represents the joy of life of the spirit, a life well-spent and fulfilling.

XXI

THE WORLD

This World image, while echoing the pattern of a central figure enwreathed and anchor images in the corners, does not go further in the same design direction. The central figure is a woman with wild hair, dancing joyfully—strong, but neither calm nor self-contained. The wreath is lavished with blossoms, reflecting the wild nature of the dancer, in contrast to the tightly woven geometric patterns in the *Aquarian* wreath.

The oval wreath can also be seen as a floral "0", mirroring the 0 of The Fool at the start of the deck, reinforcing the cyclical nature of the Major Arcana. Too often, we see the cards as a linear progression, when it is also easily read—and more interestingly read—as an endless cycle of spiritual growth.

The four birds in the corners are not specific species, and seem more like companions in her dance than stand-ins for religious historians.

The two wands she hold are the perfected forms of the wand of the Magician, and the Torah Scroll of the High Priestess. Combining the energies of the Magician (1) and the High Priestess (2) gives us the Empress (3), the feminine power of creation. The World card is also a 3 (21 = 2 + 1 = 3), thus emphasizing the card's connection with the Empress.

The Major Arcana threes can be taken together as:

Empress	+	Hanged Man	=	The World
Personal Growth	+	Spiritual Growth	=	Wholeness

Our development as a natural being under the tutelage of the Empress, combined with the spiritual development guided by the Hanged Man, creates in us the wholeness represented by The World.

The Minor Arcana
The Suit of Pentacles

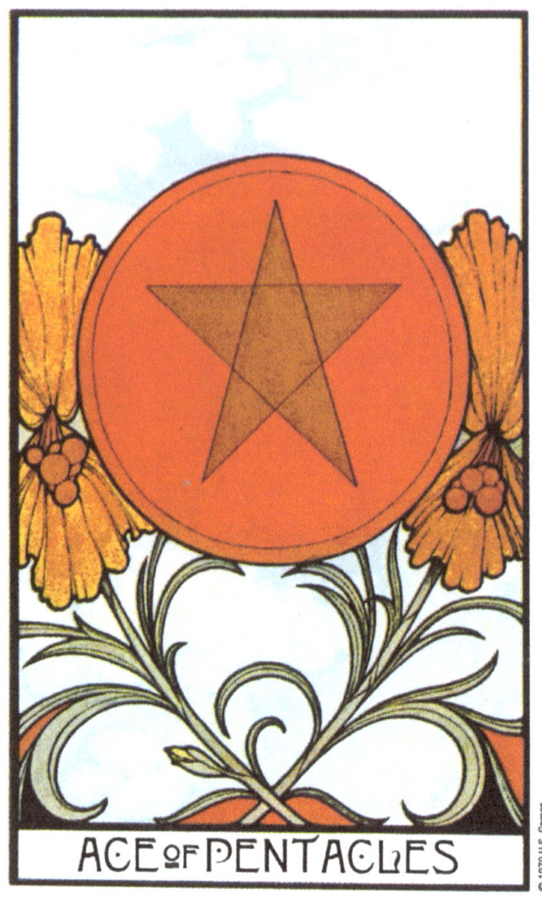

A red Pentacle is surrounded by flowers. A blue sky with soft clouds is behind. The Ace is happiness, growth, contentment, wealth, and the true riches of life. Man and Nature are unified..

The Ace is usually considered to hold the seed or potential of the suit. In the *Aquarian* deck, however, the symbol is depicted with the flowers in full bloom—a clear message of the power and potential, no guesswork required. Linking numerologically to the Magician, Wheel of Fortune, and Sun, the connection becomes even more apparent with the exercise of will, realization of opportunity, and manifestation.

The simplicity of the pentacle is framed by the elaborate flowers that support it. Nature can experiment endlessly; it has infinite time. Humans, bound by our physical and temporal limitations, must make choices each moment. Each possibility must be considered, and accepted or discarded.

The pentacle represents the potential and the manifestation of the potential. The final creation is the sum result of all our decisions and actions on how to shape the potential. Wise choices, timely action, and a dash of serendipity combine in our unique creation—a painting, a poem, a meal, a moment—something like no other, and that can never be exactly repeated or re-created.

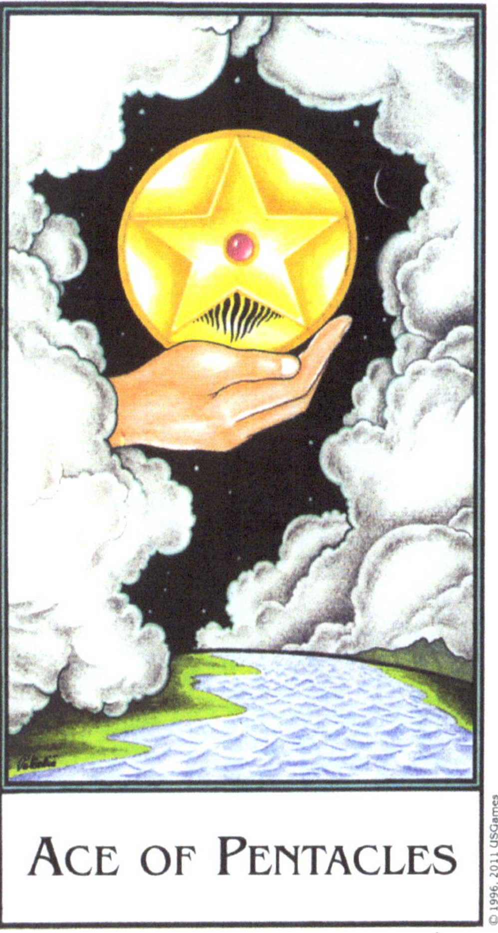

A hand emerges from clouds, holding a golden jeweled Pentacle. A great river flows through a verdant land under a midnight sky. Wealth, happiness, and a good, true life are offered to us all.

This version offers a more visionary concept of the Ace. Clouds clear and form a frame for the pentacle being offered, suggesting the inspiration of creation. The flowing waters provide the emotional energy of creation. The pentacle itself glows and shimmers with creative energy. Still a symbol of the physical and material world, this pentacle also speaks to us of the process and components of creation, encouraging us to experience the process of material creation as an intellectual and emotional journey as well.

The pentacle represents the potential and the manifestation of the potential. The final creation is the sum result of all our decisions and actions on how to shape the potential. Wise choices, timely action, and a dash of serendipity combine in our unique creation—a painting, a poem, a meal, a moment—something like no other, and that can never be exactly repeated or re-created.

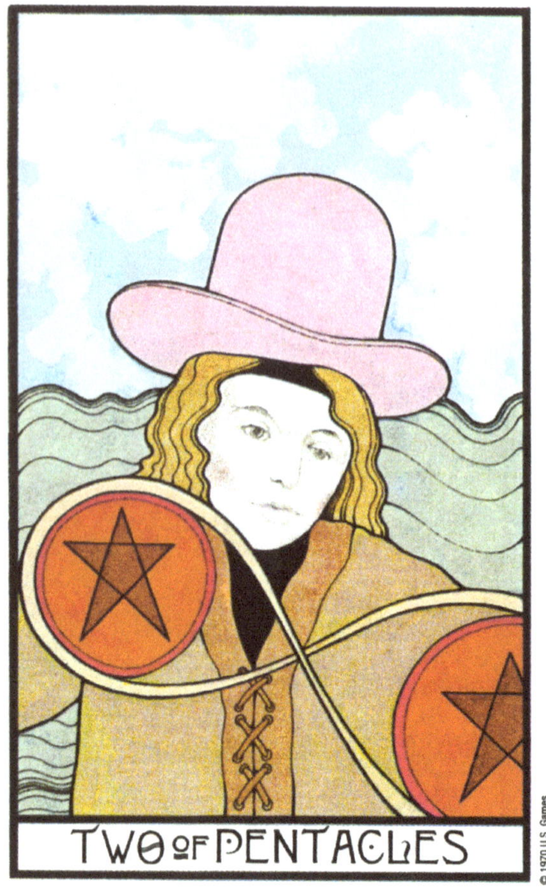

A woman with a strange hat holds the sign of infinity, which contains two Pentacles. Life goes on in happiness and joy, in a never ending dance. With skill, perseverance, and hard work, all things can be achieved..

The figure focuses on her pentacles, which float in the air and are bound by a lemniscate. She brings her emotional (water) and intellectual (sky) energies to the work.

The pentacles are separate from her, and she influences rather than controls them. She reflects on the possibilities, but has not committed to one or the other; she is still reflecting (like the High Priestess), considering her choices.

She must use her judgement (card 20) to decide what is right (Justice, card 11) before she can make a choice and take action to complete the work that we will see in the Three of Pentacles.

A curious young woman in fantastical clothes gazes upon two floating Pentacles connected by a lemniscate. The symbol of infinity reminds us that nature and life are never ending.

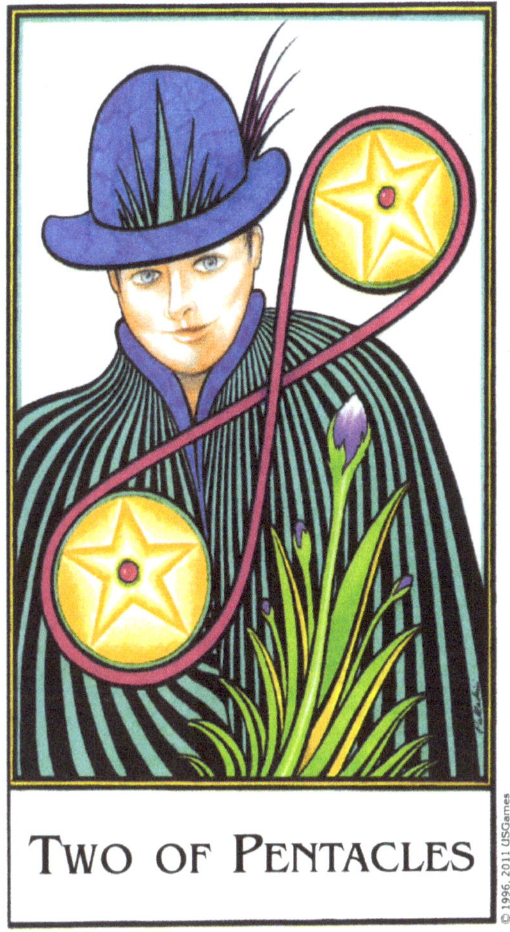

Here, too, the figure considers the pentacles floating in front of her, the possibilities and options. Unlike the *Aquarian*, however, she engages with her pentacles, looking at us to say, "See what I can do? And I'm not even finished!"

The striped cloak, the growing flowers, and the grass in her hat suggest the first level of completion. Progress has been made, initial results are in, and it's time to make decisions about how—or even whether—to continue the work.

With her direct gaze and her showy display of skill, she reminds us more of the Magician than the High Priestess. Like her *Aquarian* counterpart, she is aware of the need to make a good decision, but seems more concerned with impressing us by her cleverness and putting on a good appearance. She may not have mastered the form, but for her, the form is equal to, or perhaps more important than, the substance.

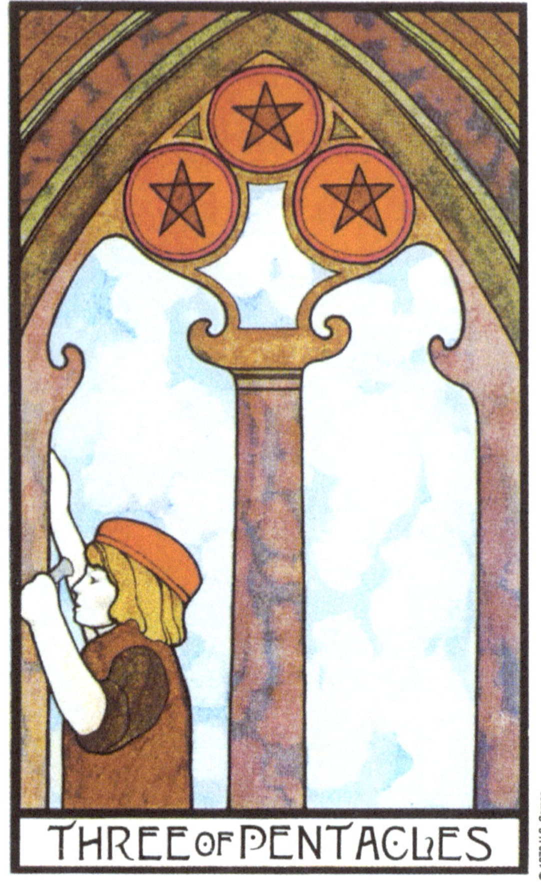

This is the card of mastery: skill, performance, achievement. A mason has built a mighty arch of the finest marble. He is proud of his accomplishment. His hard work has brought him happiness and the satisfactions of a life well lived.

As an echo of the Empress, the three is the card of creation. The agent (1) acts upon the object (2) resulting in the new creation (3).

The three complete pentacles crown the scene. The sculptor is focused intently on the third pillar, focusing his will on the work. Like the Hanged Man, the sculptor goes outside of himself, beyond his own limited scope, to find inspiration to create his art and his world.

The open sky suggests the mental effort needed to create. Creation is not simply a physical act; it requires an idea, a plan, and then action. We cannot do something without first having the idea to do it.

The rewards of creative achievement are great; personal satisfaction, perhaps material compensation, and acknowledgement of our achievements by others.

The card offers encouragement to keep focused, keep working, and also reminds us to keep the goal in mind—see how far we have come, and remember what we are working toward.

A sculptor pauses during his work to gaze out over a beautiful river valley. A flock of birds flies though the sky. He is carving an elaborate and richly detailed church window containing three Pentacles. With his simple tools and his great talent and skill, he has created a rich and magnificent life.

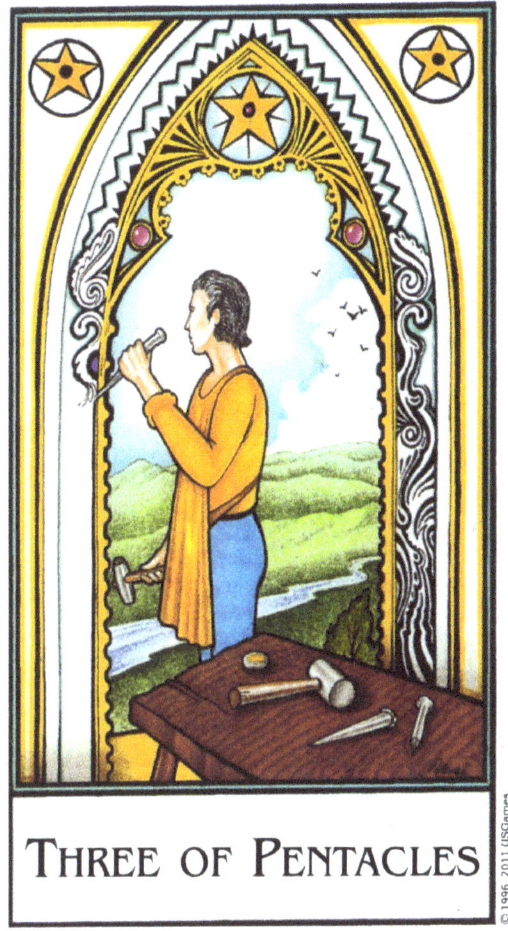

Although connected numerologically to the Empress, this card also feels like an echo of the Magician. The figure has his tools on the table; all he needs to create is at the ready for active use.

The sculptor looks away from us and away from his work. His chisel rests on the stone, ready for the next cut, but his attention is not on his work. He views the sky, the birds, the rolling hills, the flowing water—aware of what lies beyond the scope of his task, and perhaps finding inspiration in the elements.

The card asks us to consider our focus: Are we taken from our work by non-essential and unproductive distraction, or are we focused on work to the exclusion of other important parts of our lives? Where do we find our ideas and inspirations?

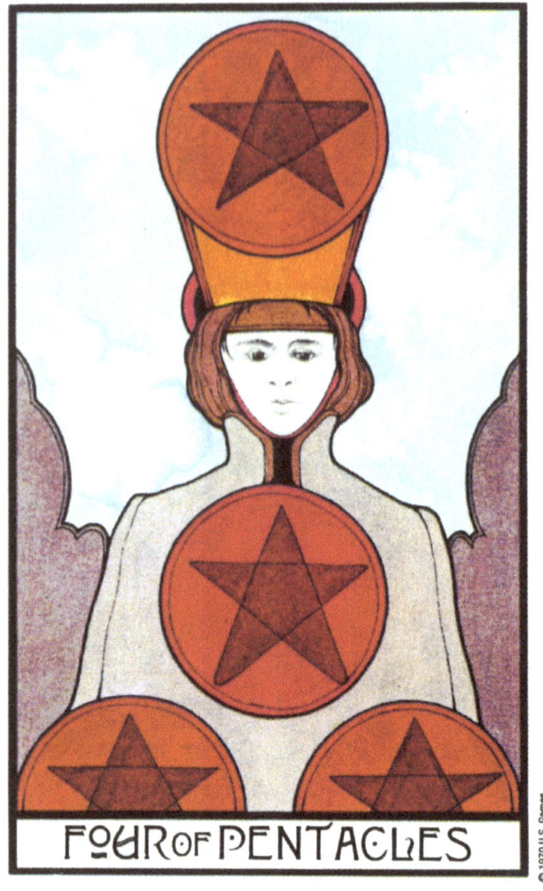

A young man crowned by a Pentacle denotes inheritance, legacy, the wealth of forbears and family. He is what his progenitors gave him; his lineage made him who he is today.

As in the Two of Pentacles, the figure's attention is focused on the pentacles. Three float before him; the fourth is resting on his headdress.

He considers his accomplishment, as though uncertain what to think about it. Caught in the current state, he is unable to see beyond, and so prevents himself from moving forward. This is not so much about resting on one's laurels as being stuck in the current pattern, perhaps unaware even of being stuck, and so being trapped by our own inability to see beyond what we have already done.

While it is important to acknowledge our accomplishments and give ourselves credit for our achievements, it is equally important to understand the need for continued growth. The aridity of rock and sky further indicate his lack of emotional resources, despite his material success.

A seated King holds a Pentacle, and another floats above him. His feet are firmly grounded in two more jeweled Pentacles. He is surrounded by flowering fruit trees. He has inherited the gifts of those who came before him, and to whom he owes everything.

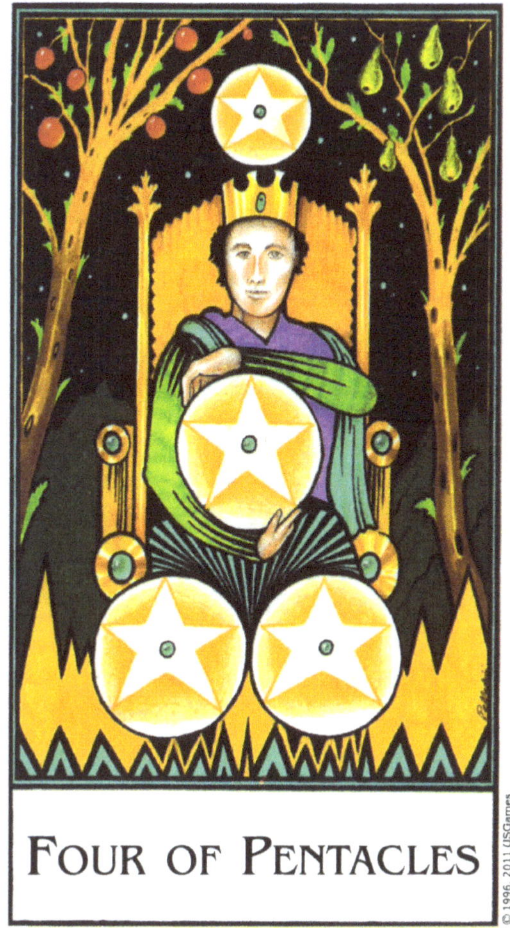

The figure here, unlike the *Aquarian*, is at ease with his wealth. The two pentacles in front are there for everyone to see and admire. He is able to enjoy them as well, and does so. He sits comfortably on his throne, holding a pentacle as though ready to spin it.

The pentacle at the top of the card does not rest on his crown, as is seen in many other depictions. It floats above him, a self-made sun in his personal firmament, a visible sign of his wealth and achievement.

He is framed by two fruit-bearing trees. Nature herself lauds his accomplishments and adds her abundance to his wealth.

He is free to enjoy his wealth. It does not bind or block him. Life is good, and he makes the most of all he has. The Emperor enjoys his life.

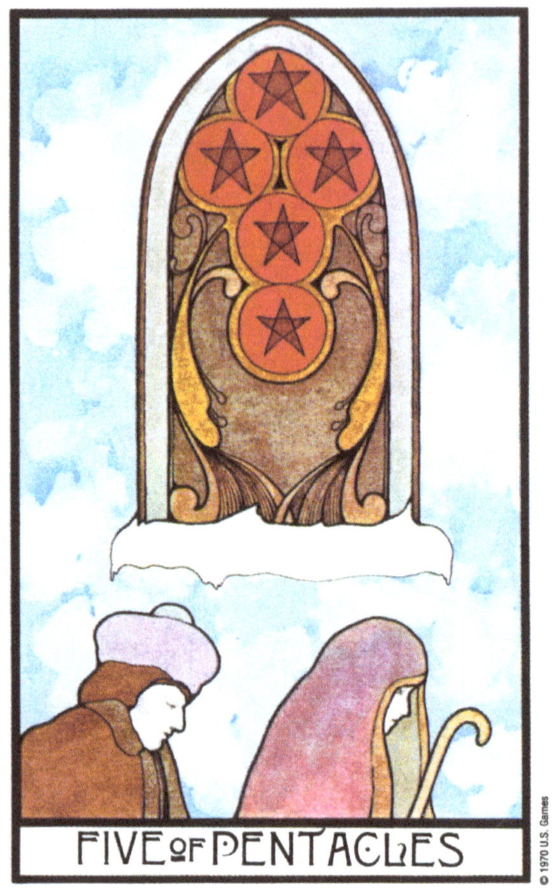

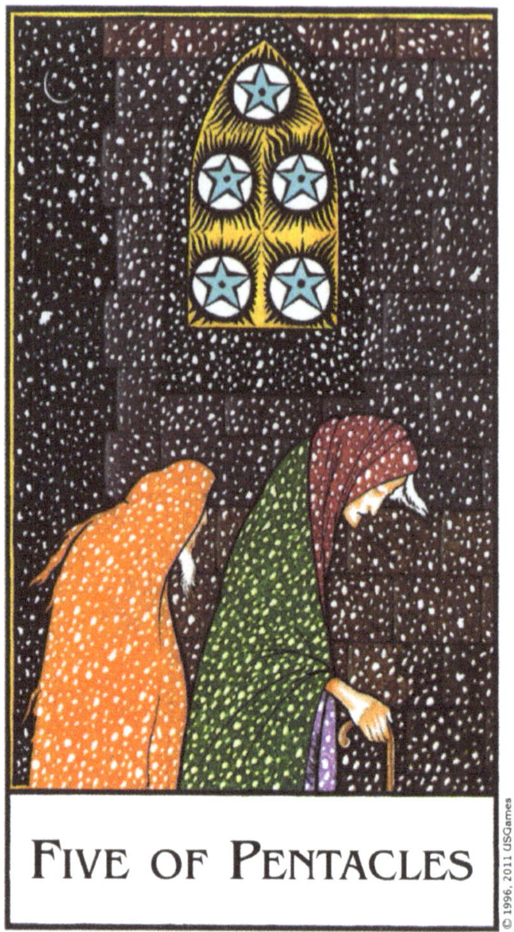

Two impoverished and lonely people wander through an uncaring world. They are homeless and hungry. We see them every day in our streets. Do we notice them, or even care?

They walk past church windows containing Pentacles of hope and money. They have only to enter within to change their lives.

This is probably the least-favorite card in most RWS-based decks. The 10 of Swords? Scary, but manageable. Death? Frightening, but inevitable. Poverty and affliction as depicted here? *Terrifying*.

Unlike most depictions, the pair in the *Aquarian* card are not elderly, not clothed in rags—yet the image conveys the sense of absolute deprivation, outside in the cold and snow. The window may represent the warm, comfortable home they have left—or perhaps a place of refuge to which they are heading.

We cannot see the door; we do not know whether they walk towards or away from it, or even whether they know there is a door leading to a place where they can find shelter, warmth, and support.

They are down, but not destroyed. The card tells us there are as yet untapped resources, however meager. We need to be aware of our wisest uses of the resources we have to move back into a place of material security.

The situation in the *New Palladini* card is more dire than in the *Aquarian*. The pair are obviously older, more frail, more beaten down by time and circumstance. Like the *Aquarian*, they do not look at the window. Is it the unbearable pain of loss of the place they are leaving? Or are they so conditioned to hopelessness that they are unable to even look for possible shelter? Again, we cannot see the door to the place, and perhaps they cannot, either.

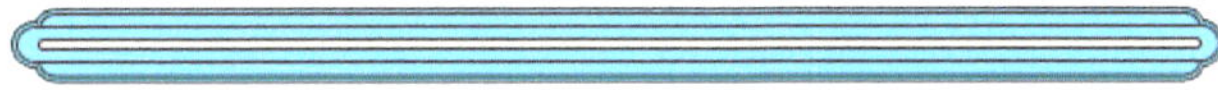

Sometimes you are not going to win. Sometimes the best approach is to acknowledge defeat, cut your losses, and move on. Take what you can, and go on to the next situation.

Do not let your losses blind you to what remains, or to new possibilities. The cards suggest that you do have resources you are unaware of, that there are possibilities you have not yet realized exist. Raise your eyes and see what can be seen; you may find just what you need, beckoning like a lighted window in the night.

Find your shelter from the storm, and prepare for the sunrise after the storm has passed.

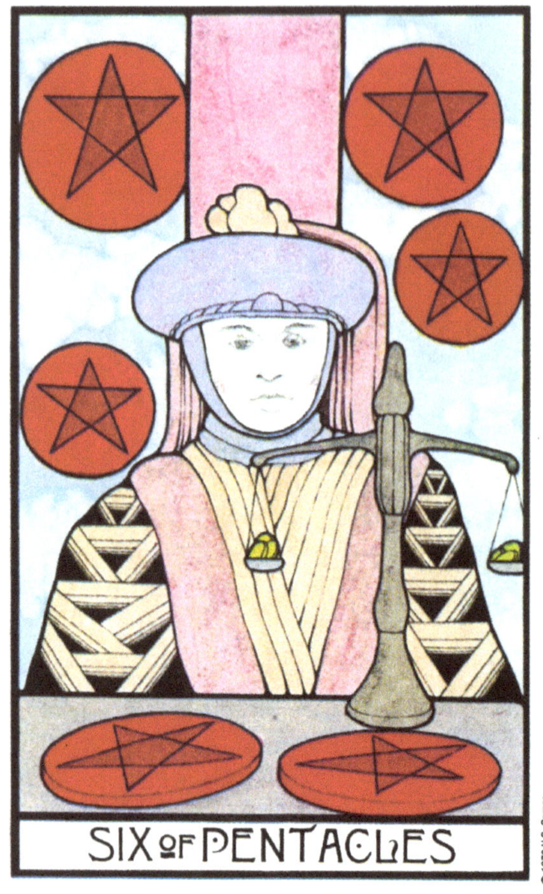

A resolute and serious person contemplates the scales of equality. The scales are balanced, with each side holding the same amount of money. This card symbolizes fairness in all things, particularly business and the proper sharing of resources.

The RWS and most of its clones depict a person dispensing coins to two of the figures. Here, we see a sole figure with his six pentacles, and six coins in his scales. The message of distribution of resources is still present, if less obvious.

The scales are evenly balanced, three coins in each pan. If we remove a coin to spend or share, the scale tips. If we remove all the coins on the outflow side, the scale is completely out of balance. We must then replenish the empty pan with new coins to restore balance. If we have no new coins, we begin to pull from our reserves. If we spend the reserves, the scale again balances—but both pans are empty.

Whatever resources the coins represent (actual money, time, talent, objects), the card reminds us to use them wisely and well.

The figure sits in front of a pillar, and his body forms a center pillar between the latticework sleeves of his robe. The figure is the balance, choosing between excess thrift and prodigal spending, between prudent investments and unwise ventures.

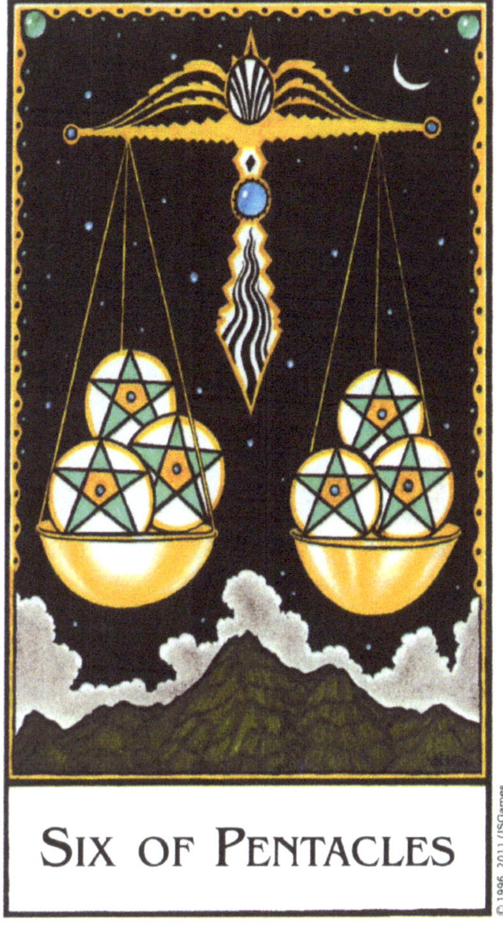

The golden scales of equality hover in a starry midnight sky. They are perfectly balanced, as all of life should be. Each cup of scales contains three Pentacles, creating equality and perfect sharing.

This card removes the human figure and goes to an abstract level with its imagery. The scales float in the air. The fulcrum has no solid base, yet the balance holds true. The principles also hold: Wise use of resources and an honest approach in all matters are absolutely required.

As a numerological reflection of the Lovers and the Devil, the Six emphasizes right relationship to the material world. Enjoy abundance, but refrain from overindulgence. Manage your resources wisely so that you can meet your obligations, save for the future, and share as you are able with those who have less. No waste, no excess, no deprivation, no exploitation. Find the balance of "enough", and live in that space.

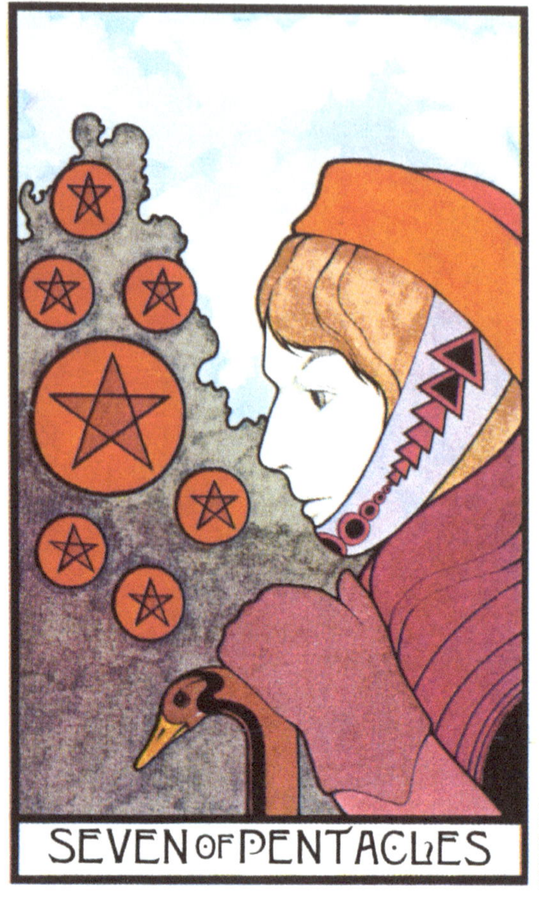

A serious young man gazes upon a tree upon which are seven Pentacles. He has raised the tree himself, with hard work and much care. He awaits the ripening of the fruits of his labor.

Hard work has brought forth the pentacles blooming on the bush. Varying in size, they may represent multiple projects in different stages, or accomplishments both large and small.

However, the figure does not see the results. He stares disconsolately at the base of the bush, unable to acknowledge the fruit growing at the top. Even the duck head on the walking stick looks down in disappointment.

The card suggest we step back, look around, look up, and see things as they really are. Disappointment and frustration may be part of our current reality, but they are not the only reality. Only by acknowledging what we have accomplished and what is available to us will we be able to move forward.

A richly dressed young man holding a jeweled staff contemplates a flowering bush. The blossoms are golden Pentacles representing money, business, and success. Through intelligence and a life of hard work, the man has earned his rich rewards.

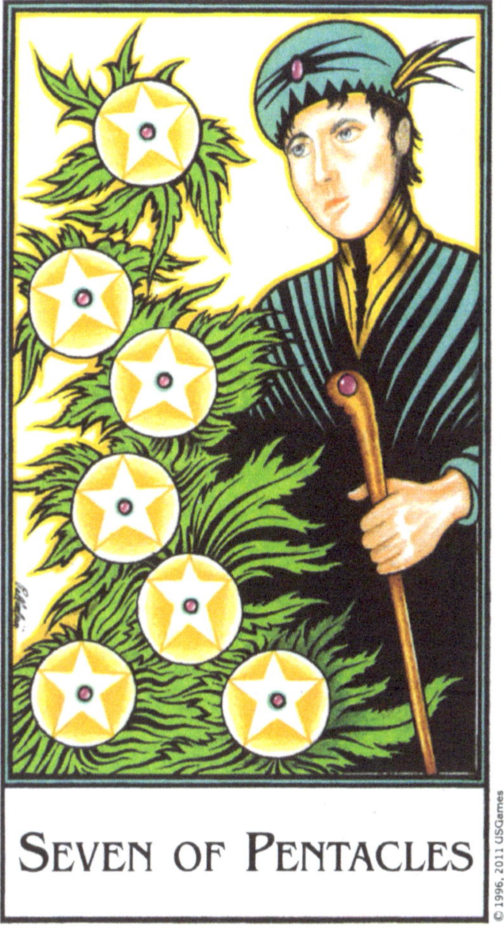

The figure here does look up, but still does not see the blooming tree. Rather, he gazes, unfocused, past what is, in an attempt to see what is yet to come.

Planning for the future is important. Setting goals and creating plans is required if we are to progress with what is important to us.

However, focusing solely on the next situation prevents us from being in the moment, which results in lost opportunities. Being aware of where we are, what we have, what we can do, right now, enables us to make plans grounded in reality while honoring our aspirations. If you can dream it, you can do it—you have to create the circumstance for it to manifest.

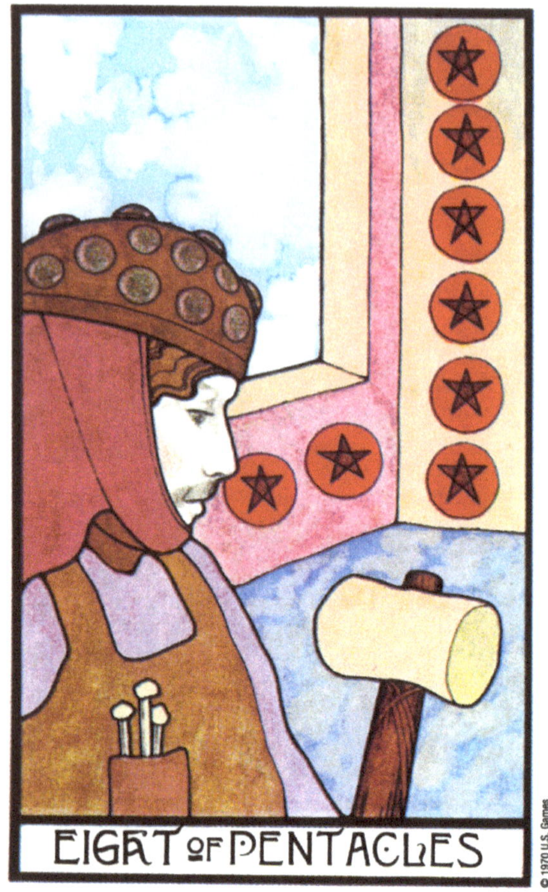

A hard-working craftsman holds his mallet, and wears a leather apron and helmet. He is concentrating on his work. With skill and perseverance, he has created eight Pentacles, which hang on the walls of his workshop. With unceasing labor and concentration, he has made his future; he is secure and successful in business.

The artisan contemplates his tools. The eight finished pentacles hang on the wall for all to see and admire. Rather than focus on the results, the artisan considers his tools, evaluating their fitness for continued use.

Step back and take a look at the whole scene. Acknowledge your accomplishments and revise your plans. Do you need to adjust your methods or timing? Sharpen your tools? Switch to another tool or medium?

Decide on the next action necessary to move forward.

Having decided, do it.

Move forward.

An artist at work, making Pentacles from precious metals and gems. He is concentrating hard, for his work is difficult. But he has succeeded. Each Pentacle is different, a labor of skill and love.

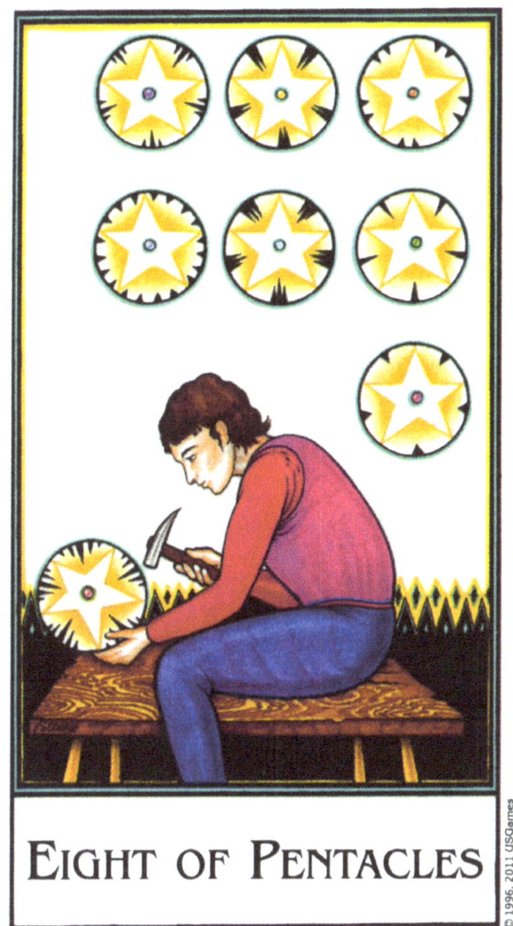

Practice makes perfect. The artisan has produced seven pentacles, and is finishing the eighth. The designs vary—but the quality of the work does not. Focus, practice, persevere. Feel the energy of the Strength card in this card. Feel the inspiration and hope of the Star in this card. The Star guides you as you do your work. Strength sustains you as you do your work.

Achievement requires work. Talent requires practice to develop. The only way for something to be done is to do it. Stop planning, stop discussing, stop imagining—take action and do the work.

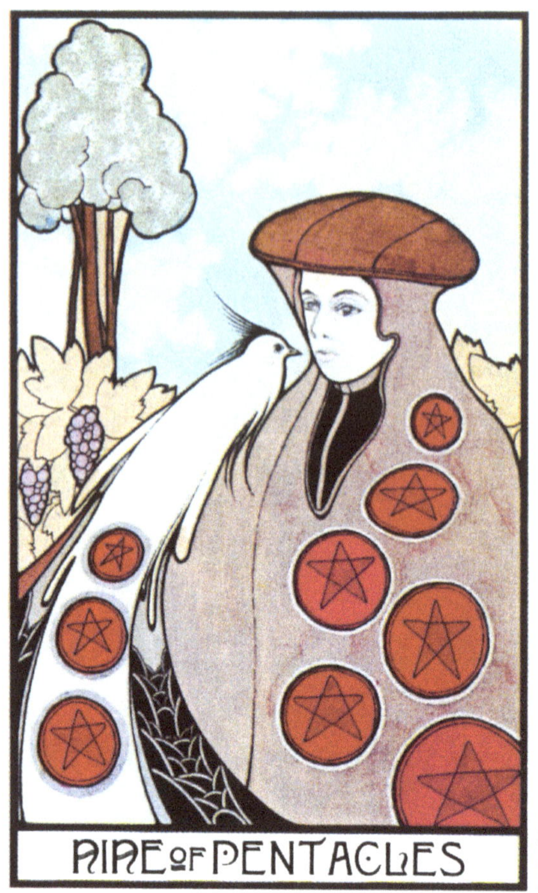

A young woman stands in a fruiting vineyard, gazing into the eyes of a magical white bird. She is sure and accomplished, and dreams of her bright and wealthy future. The grapes will be pressed into the wine of life. The bird and the woman's cloak are covered in the Pentacles of prosperity and happiness.

Surrounded by material comforts and physical abundance, our lady walks her garden with the company of her exotic bird. She seems to speak to the bird—perhaps of her contentment, or her loneliness, or both.

Material security is necessary for us to experience security on other levels. At the same time, if all our material needs are met while our emotional, psychological, or spiritual needs are unfilled, we are unable to appreciate our material abundance.

The card asks us to consider whether we are using our material advantages to soothe or supplant our other needs, or conversely, if concern about our material security is affecting other aspects of ourselves and our lives.

A beautiful maiden is listening to the song of a little white bird perched upon her shoulder. Jewels in the form of bunches of grapes contain nine Pentacles, promising a rich harvest of life's riches and joys: accomplishment, success, and knowledge of true wealth.

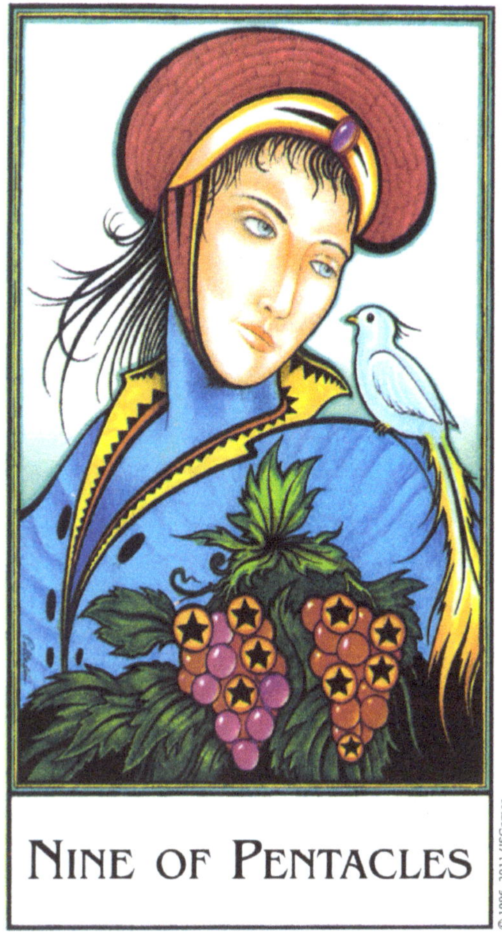

The scene here is similar to, and simpler than, the *Aquarian* scene. The wealth and abundance are more implied than illustrated, but we have no doubt that this woman has all she needs and wants for her material comfort.

Both women are isolated by their wealth, alone in their gardens, shielded from direct contact with the world by their walls. Likewise, their clothing shields them from direct contact with the immediate environment. This physical isolation renders them symbols rather than persons, preventing them from active experience and direct connection. They have become passive recipients of their prosperity instead of active participants, precluding the possibility of sharing their good fortune with others.

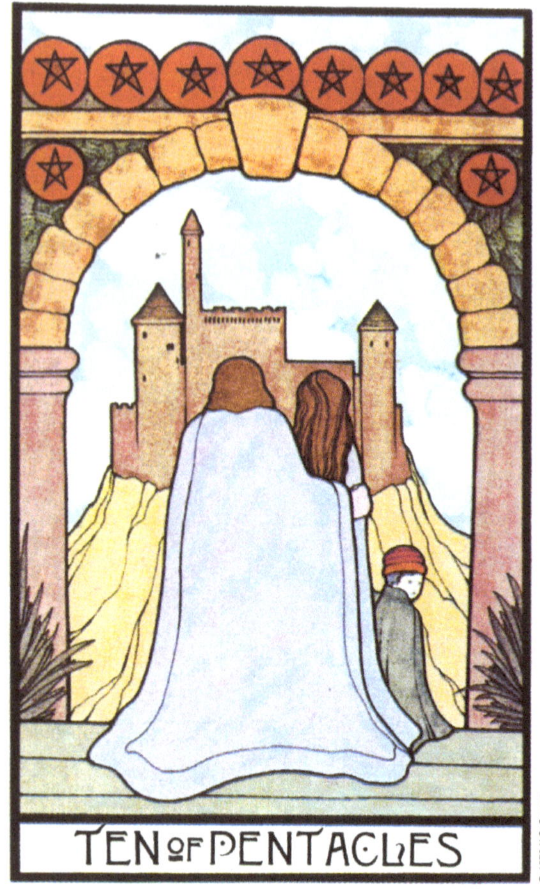

A man and his wife approach their beautiful castle. They are standing beneath the gateway arch of their home. Atop the arch, ten Pentacles bring wealth and happiness. Their little son turns to look at us, somewhat shyly. This is the card of family, fortune, and fecundity.

The card in each deck shows a couple facing a distance castle. Perhaps they are observing their own home from afar, or sharing a dream of their future. How we see it can tell us a great about our own present situation. Is it a card of a goal achieved, or a desire not yet fulfilled?

Hard work pays off, but not always with the expected result. Sometimes it is more, or less, than we expected; sometimes it is completely different from what we planned, and "more" and "less" are not applicable terms.

Something outside the scene has drawn the child's attention. He is secure in the home created for him by his parents, and this gives him the confidence and curiosity to explore his world, starting close to home.

In this card, the scene is quite arid, mostly stone and sky. The pair of shrubs seem almost as though they are made of the stone of the wall, rather than being vital plants. This continues the theme of the 9 of Pentacles—that material success does not automatically create emotional satisfaction. For us to enjoy our achievements, we must invest them with meaning, and we must find that meaning in ourselves and in our connections with those we love.

Whether those connections are with our family of origin, our family of choice, or with the universal family is for each of us to decide. The important thing is that we have those connections, and allow us to be nurtured, and to nurture others, through those connections.

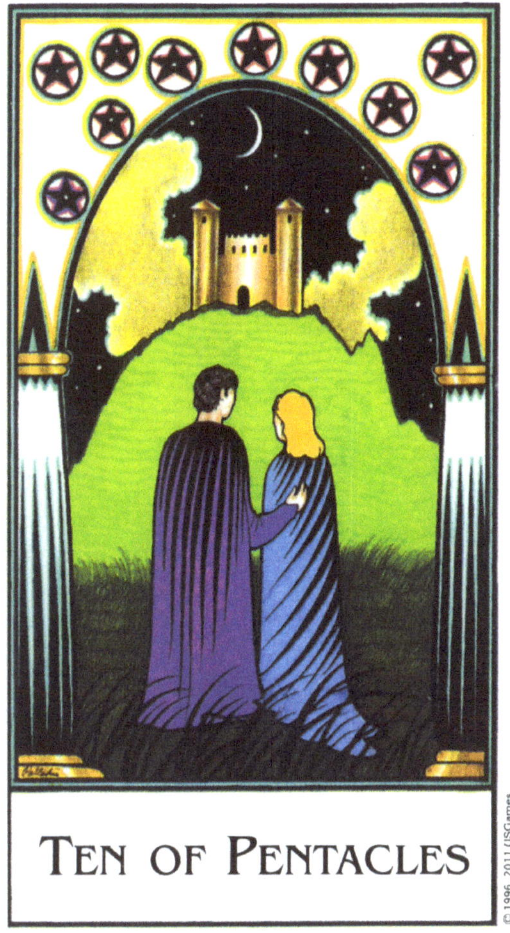

Under a great columned arch, a man gently touches his love. Before then, atop a green hill, stands their beautiful golden castle under a crescent moon. Ten Pentacles top the arch, signaling prosperity and plenty. A card of love, marriage and fulfillment.

This card shows us a lush, moonlit landscape, far from the harsh daylight and dry stone of the *Aquarian* landscape. This feels more hopeful, more likely that the pair are looking at what they have accomplished, rather than wishing for what is not. The waxing moon (a sign of increase) reinforces this feeling.

Echoing the manifestation energy of the Magician, this couple knows that they can accomplish what they set their minds to do. They have come this far, and are pleased with what they have done. They have created a secure base on which to build their next accomplishment, and this gives them the confidence for undertaking their next goal. They are prepared for the vagaries of chance held in the Wheel of Fortune, and ready to receive the blessings of the Sun.

While this pair does not have a child with them, the fecundity of the land provides encouragement for their own creative works. Whether that results in a child, a work of art, a business, or some other creation, the scene is set for manifestation and growth.

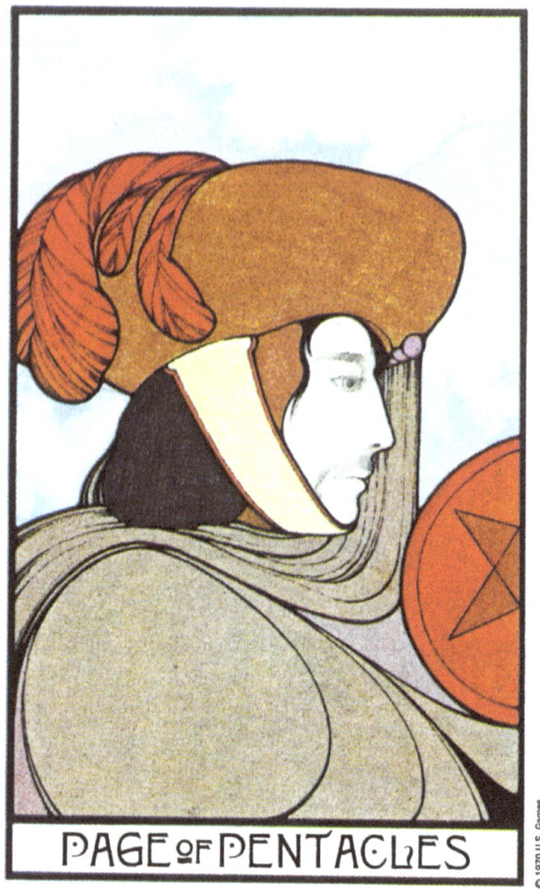

A dark, handsome man of serious demeanor who serves his Knight well, taking care that his master's needs are met. He is intelligent and hard-working, and hopes to someday become a Knight. He is watchful, patient, and wise.

The Pentacles, as the suit of Earth, are considered the slowest suit in the Tarot. The *Aquarian* Page bears this out. We see a man who seems far too old to be a page, and we wonder why he remains in this position. He contemplates his pentacle, perhaps wondering the same thing. He seems weighted down by his robes, his hat, the burden of his pentacle. As the Earth element in the Earth suit, he embodies heaviness. He does not even fit inside the card frame; he has outgrown his circumstance, but has not moved on for whatever reason.

We need to assess our abilities and our situation honestly and with care to give ourselves appropriate credit for what we have learned and what we are capable of doing. Perhaps we are so accustomed to being a Page that we have not realized we have actually grown into a Knight. Perhaps we are so focused on serving others that we have neglected our own growth, and we find that our circumstances no longer fit.

If we feel unprepared for change, the Page tells us that we have more abilities than we realize. If we feel unwilling to change, the Page reminds us that change is required, and we can either take the initiative to make the change we wish to happen, or deny the need for change and have it imposed upon us by the will of others.

Our souls have grown, our minds have expanded, our abilities have increased, and it is time for us to move on to a more suitable situation.

A youthful figure meditates upon a Pentacle, which hovers above his hand. He is gaily dressed and of happy disposition. Verdant mountains and a flowing river are behind him. His hard work and loyalty have brought him riches and joy. He will someday be a great and powerful Knight.

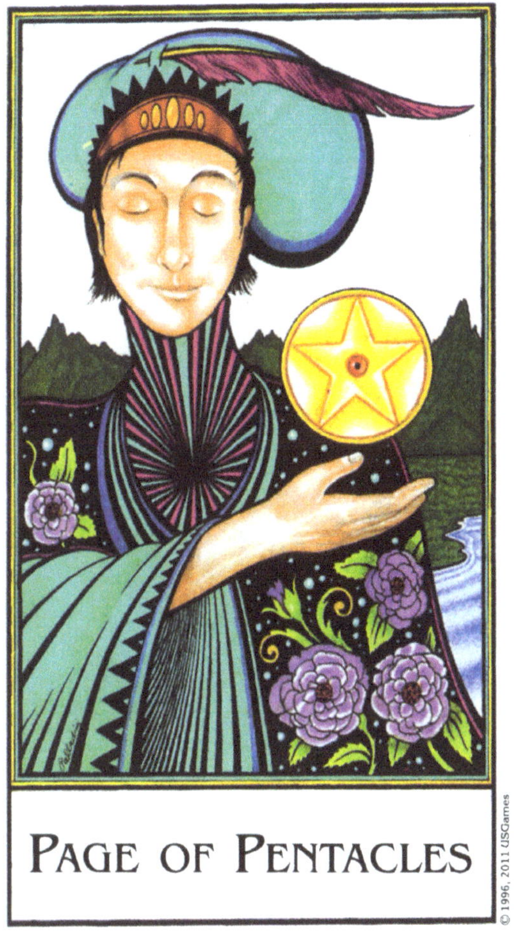

This Page, however, feels lighter. The green background, running water, and rich robes suggest a supportive material abundance, rather than material restriction. His eyes closed and a contented smile on his face, he gestures to his pentacle, which appears to float. He has learned to appreciate and enjoy his material advantages, although he has not yet learned to put them to full, wise use.

He seems content to stay in his present state, a comfortable childhood with adult privileges, and sees no reason why he should desire change. Life will require him to learn to manage his advantages as a responsible adult in order to retain them.

The ability to provide for one's self on the material plane is crucial to psychological health. Remaining in a materially dependent state renders us emotionally dependent, and limits our growth. We are not free to fully explore our selves and our true emotions for fear of losing the approval of the person who provides for us materially. We keep ourselves in a half-aware state, focusing our being on fulfilling the other's expectations and denying our own nature. Having our own resources, including material wealth, provides us a security that cannot be given by another person. We have created it, it is our own, and we can do with it as we choose.

This Page shows us that being able to enjoy the fruits of one's own labors is as sweet as the fruits shared with us by others, an that being able to share our abundance with others is even more sweet. Providing for ourselves, and for those we love, is a noble and admirable achievement.

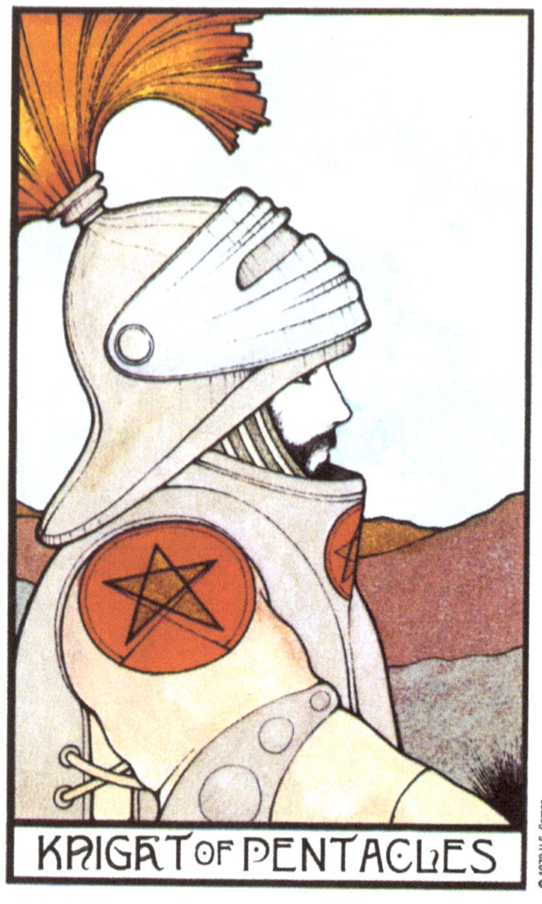

A bearded Knight in full armor bears the sign of Pentacles on his right arm. He rides through a rough, barren land, but he does not fear. He is stout, resolute, and brave. He gladly offers his strength and service to his King and Queen. He is responsible and hard-working, and gives his all.

The Knight continues the heaviness and inertia of the Page. As he is a Knight, we assume he is mounted, although the only indication of a horse is a small tuft of a mane in the lower right corner of the picture. For all we know, it might be desert brush.

The Knight wears his symbol for others to see, but does not see it himself.

He looks ahead, but gives no response to indicate what he sees. Perhaps more of the same—miles of desert and mountains. Or an oasis, or a village. We do not know, and he is not saying. His message to us seems to be, "Find out for yourself." As the fire element of the earth suit, this is not unexpected.

A Knight in bronze armor rides a strong, black stallion. He rides through lush green countryside, holding a jeweled golden Pentacle in his chain-mailed hand. He embodies righteousness and valor, and is a true and brave Knight.

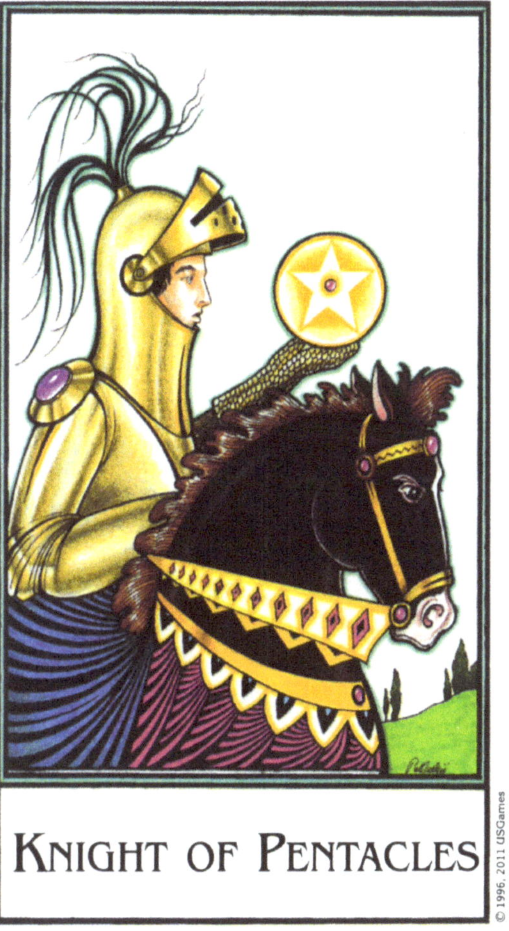

This Knight is mounted on a fine steed, bedecked and armored for the journey. He carries his symbol before him, perhaps as a reminder of the purpose of his journey. His armor is brightly polished and smooth, emphasizing his material advantages. The bit of background we can see is green and thriving, a more pleasant environment for an adventure than the arid desert.

Again, we do not know what the Knight sees. He, too, encourages us to mount our own horses and make our own discoveries..

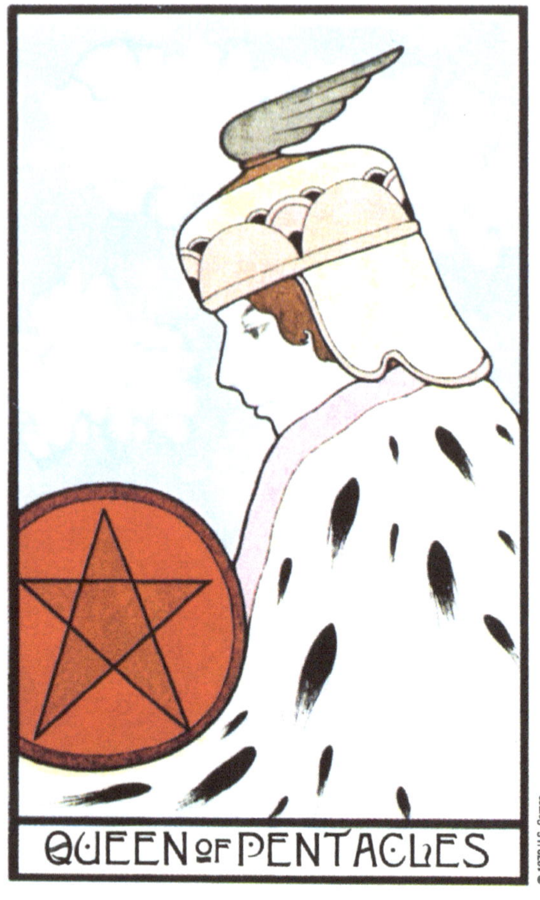

A dark-haired Queen in an ermine robe contemplates a Pentacle. She is wise and kind. She is a devoted wife, and offers love and security.

As with the other court Pentacles, she is weighed down by the trappings of her position. The pentacle seems to hold itself in place, and to hold her in her place.

She looks down, not seeing the pentacle, but seeing behind it. She understands the workings of the world, the machinery and machinations. This knowledge brings her power and advantage, but not always happiness. She is confined by her circumstances and her role. The cage may be gilded, but it is nonetheless a cage. As long as she must remain in it, she will do her utmost to ensure her comfort and advantage, and to keep the gears turning to continue to provide them.

Her position also allows her to secure comfort and advantage for her loved ones. She is wise, and skilled at negotiating the demands of life on all levels. She is devoted to those who are devoted to her, and fiercely protective against any who would try to harm her favorites.

She creates an abundant environment for herself, and welcomes into it those who have earned her respect and her trust.

The silhouette of a crowned Queen. She is the mate of the King of Pentacles, and is filled with the cosmic consciousness of universal love. In her mind glows the golden Pentacle of wealth, strength, and prosperity. She is a loving, supportive, and kind woman, a true Queen.

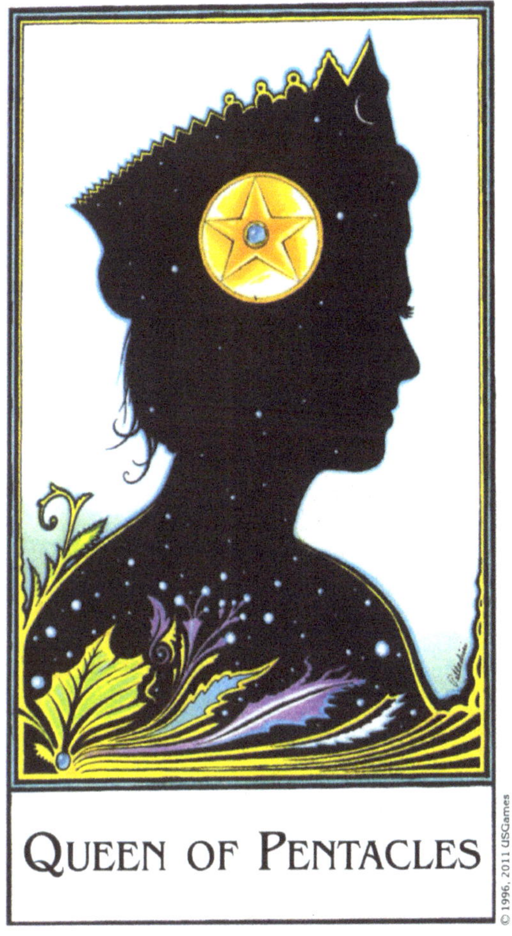

A star-filled silhouette renders this earthy Queen more abstract, as befits the water element in the earth suit. The pentacle is prominent in her mind, providing a practical grounding to her watery musings. Its placement emphasizes its importance, while leaving space for the sky and stars to inspire her thoughts as well.

Connected with the Empress through the power of physical creation, this Queen urges us to create with thought and care. She reminds us that resources are finite and precious, and to use them wisely to create the best possible life for ourselves, our loved ones, our community, and our world.

She is not trapped by her earth element. Her mind is illuminated by starlight, allowing her to see the subtleties of the material plane, and to shape them into beautiful, useful forms for herself and others to enjoy.

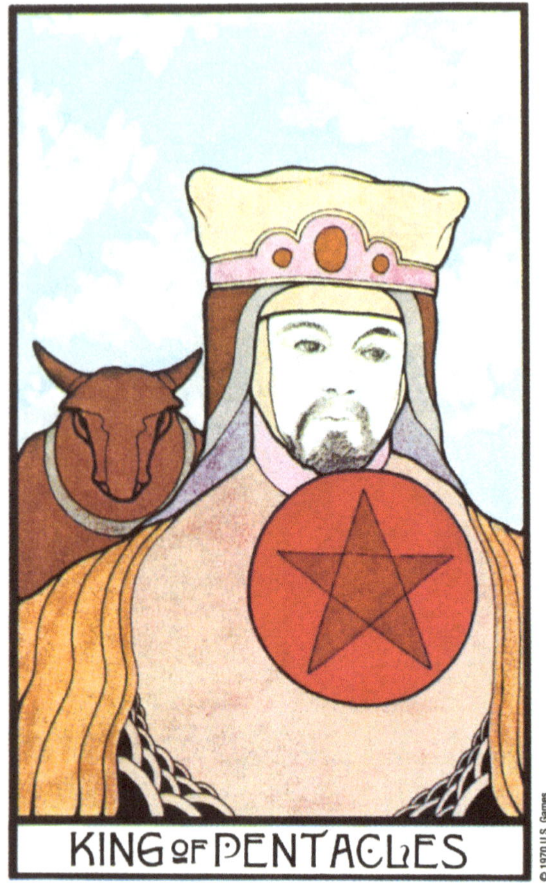

The King is a dark man of good intelligence and strong convictions. His face is kind, but resolute. He wears a Pentacle over his heart. He is a considerate and affectionate partner, and a wise ruler. Behind him, a strong, brave bull awaits. Through courage and hard work, riches will be achieved in a righteous manner.

The King, too, is weighed down by his robes, his roles, his responsibilities. The pentacle sits directly on his chest, covering his heart and throat. He must feel, say, and do only things that are suitable to a King; he is not a person, he is the King.

The bull behind him gives him the strength to fulfill his role, even though the person may wish to rebel and resign. Like the other court cards in his suit, his hands are unseen; he wields his power through giving direction, rather than taking direct action.

As the Air element in the Earth suit, the King may also remind us to be clear in our thinking before taking action. Say "yes" or say "no"—just be clear what you are agreeing to or rejecting before you agree to or reject it.

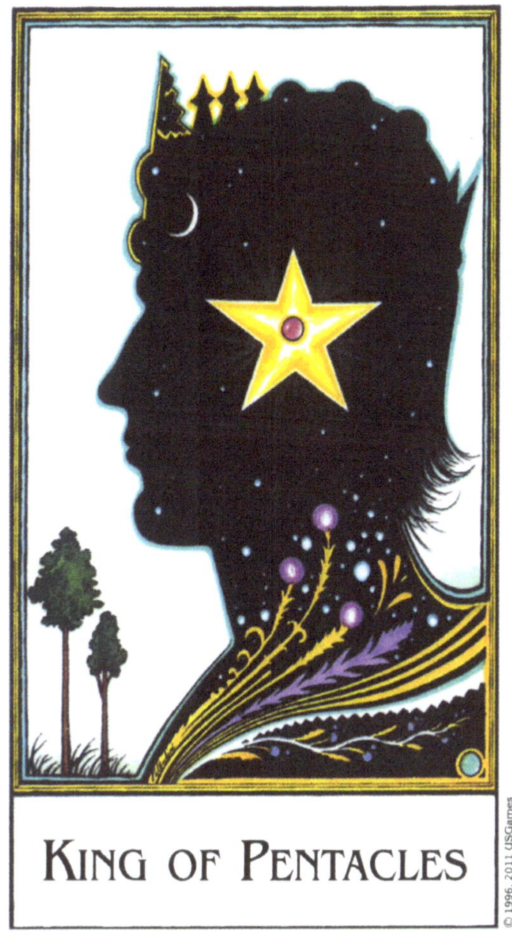

We see the silhouette of a strong young ruler wearing his crown. He is filled with a night sky and flowers, and a golden jeweled Pentacle. His wisdom and courage flow from Nature, and this knowledge will assure all the riches life has to offer. He is the wise King, in contemplation of all that exists.

A crowned silhouette faces his Queen, his mind likewise directed by the earth energy of his suit; he is still somewhat abstract. He fulfills his roles and responsibilities, but we do not even see the King—we see the outline of the King, a representation of the ideal of the King.

This abstraction of the Air element of the Earth suit tells us to disregard form and examine the content. We can be so blinded by our expectations, so dazzled or confused by appearances, that we fail to see what truly is the substance behind the form. Are we dealing with someone who is solidly grounded, who has the will and ability to keep commitments? Or are we dealing with someone who dresses well, speaks sweetly, and has no firmness of purpose?

Like the Queen, he is generous to himself, and to those close to him. He enjoys the privileges and comforts of his position, and feels he has earned them through his wise management of his kingdom and his people.

He encourages us to wisely manage ourselves and our lives, so that we can create our own position of advantage and comfort to enjoy and to share with our loved ones.

The Minor Arcana

The Suit of Rods

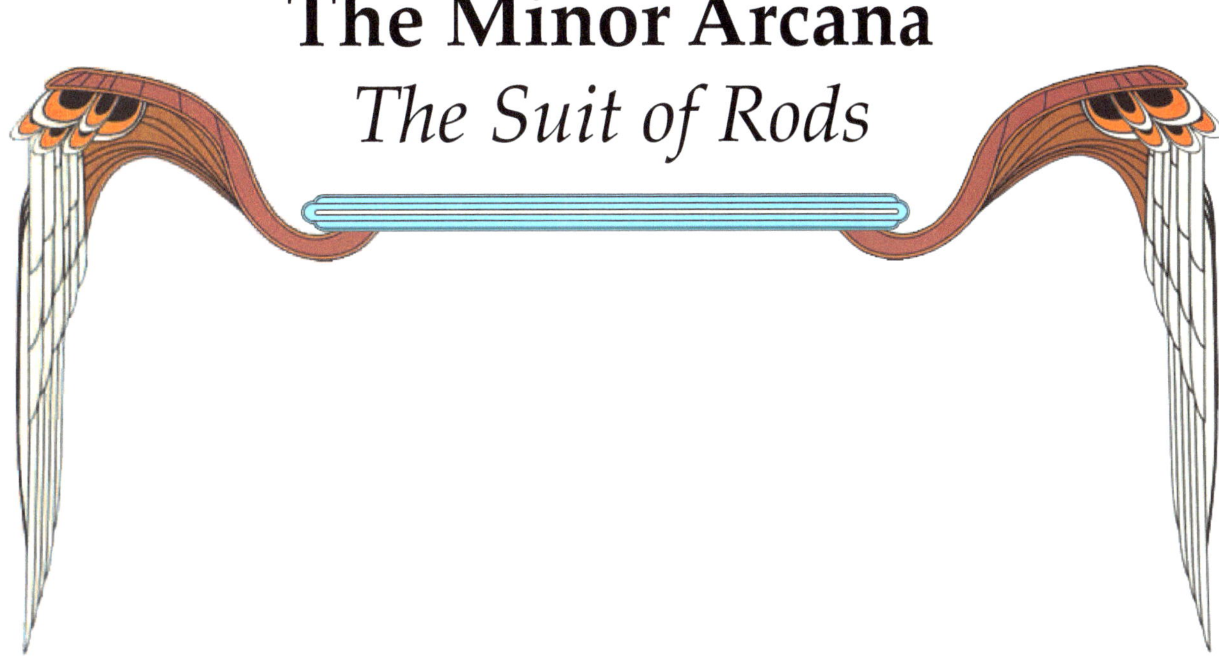

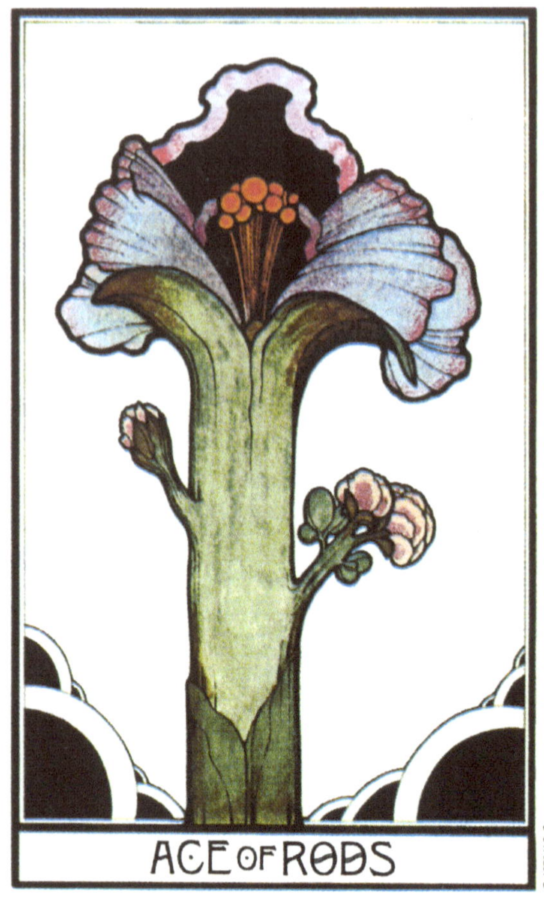

A flowering rod bursts forth. Full of energy, it signifies new life, love, birth, marriage, fulfillment, and creation. This card is the beginning of many things, ideas, actions, and new roads of life.

A flowering rod seems to grow out of sea of black waves of energy. With leaf, bud, and blossom, its stamen heavy with pollen, the rod's embodiment of creative energy is readily apparent.

The waves of energy that feed the rod remind us that creative energy is a combination of the emotions, the intellect, and the spirit, echoing the message of the Magician. The Ace reminds us that we can achieve great things through the focus of will and taking prompt, positive action to move things forward. Despite the vagaries of the Wheel of Fortune, the harmonious manifestation of the Sun is within our reach.

The Ace tells us that we have what we need to start, and now is the time to begin.

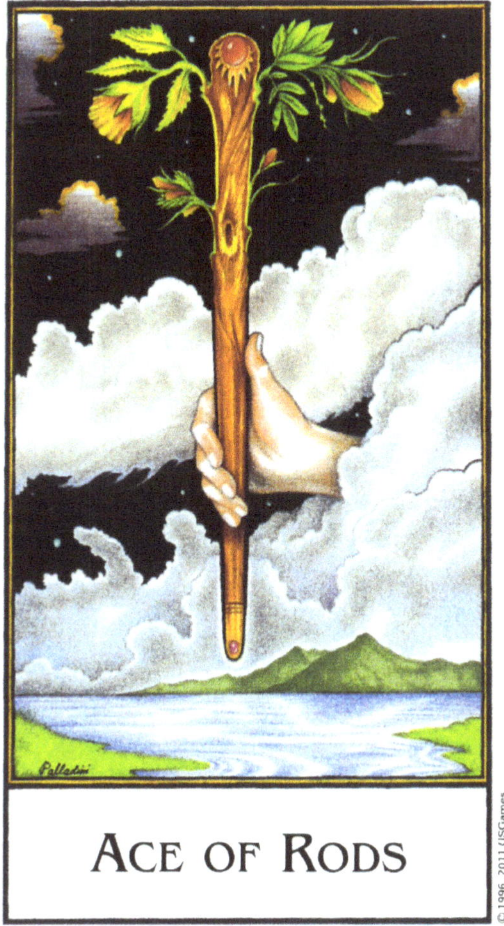

A hand emerges from the clouds at night, holding a flowering rod. It is like a magician's wand, and its energy flows from its top into blossoms of gold. Buds and flowers promise fertility and life. A ruby crowns the tip of the rod. This is the wand of a royal magician, signifying creation, invention, the source, family, origin, money, fortune, and inheritance.

The creative energy of the wand limns the edges of the clouds with its golden light. The rod itself is in full bloom, a vibrant expression of creativity, the buds a promise of continued vitality and fertility.

The sun-shaped jewel at the top of the rod encapsulates and stores the energy for future use. The components of creativity—intellect (clouds), emotions (water), and physical vitality (grass and mountains) —are more explicit here. The rod illuminates the world, its vibrance contrasting with the deep black of the night sky.

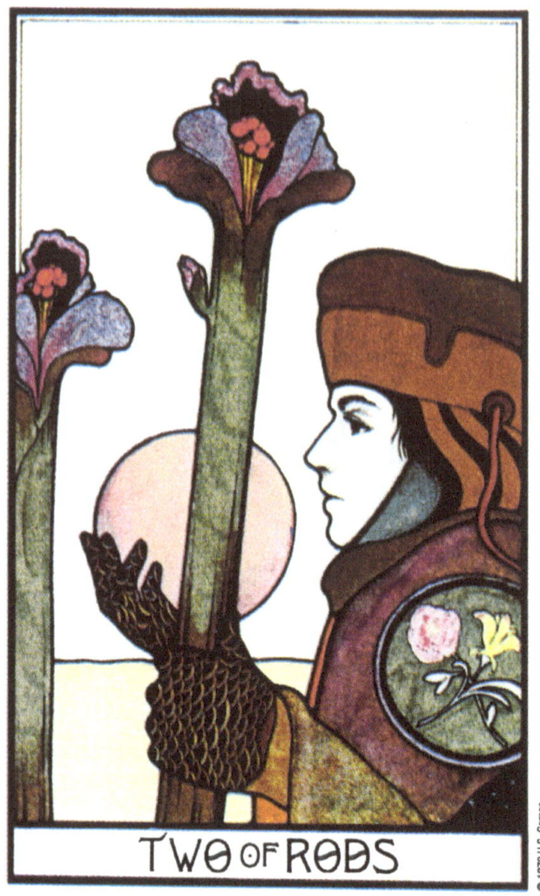

He holds the globe in his right hand. In his left, he carries the Staff of Dominion. All things are possible.

On his shoulder are the Rose of Desire and the Lily of Thought. He is resolute, but in his eye we see longing, sadness, hope for another life.

Holding a flowering rod and a sphere, the figure echoes the Emperor holding his scepter and orb. Whereas the Emperor has conquered his lands and earned his accoutrements, the person here has given himself more modest versions to symbolize his desires and goals. Holding the rod symbolizing his focused will, the sphere his concrete goals, the figure is calm and confident of his plans and his ability to carry them out.

The Rose of Desire crossing the Lily of Thought on the figure's badge tell us on yet another level of his will and his plan. He looks forward, towards the future, his power and plans in place. His mail gloves give him a firm grip and protect his hands as he reaches for more.

The second rod shows us he has resources at his disposal, and his confidence cannot be doubted.

A man of learning looks out from the ramparts of a castle. He carries two golden flowering Rods. His sensitive face reflects the sadness of wisdom amidst the chaos of the world.

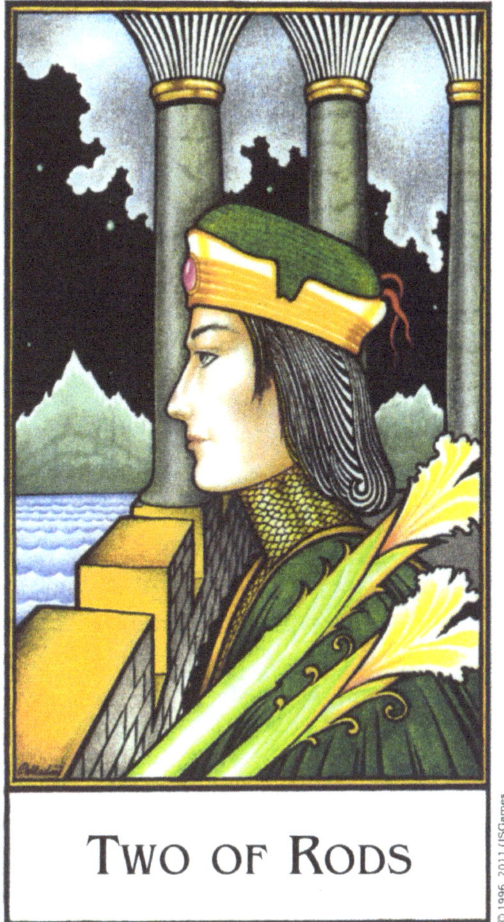

More like the High Priestess—his numerological match—than the Emperor, this figure likewise contemplates his plans, but does not seem to burn in the same way as his *Aquarian* counterpart. The lands, the night sky, and the flowing water convey a quieter, less showy confidence. The rods rest lightly on his shoulder, present and noticeable, but not obtrusive.

The orderly lines of the wall show the mental discipline required to create and carry out his plan.

Everywhere else, though, the lines of energy run amok in this card. Even the man's hair is made of contrasting lines moving in different directions. Despite his calm face, we sense the will, the activity, the effort expended to reach this point. He reflects, he plans, he plots—and he enjoys what he already has as he continues his quest for more.

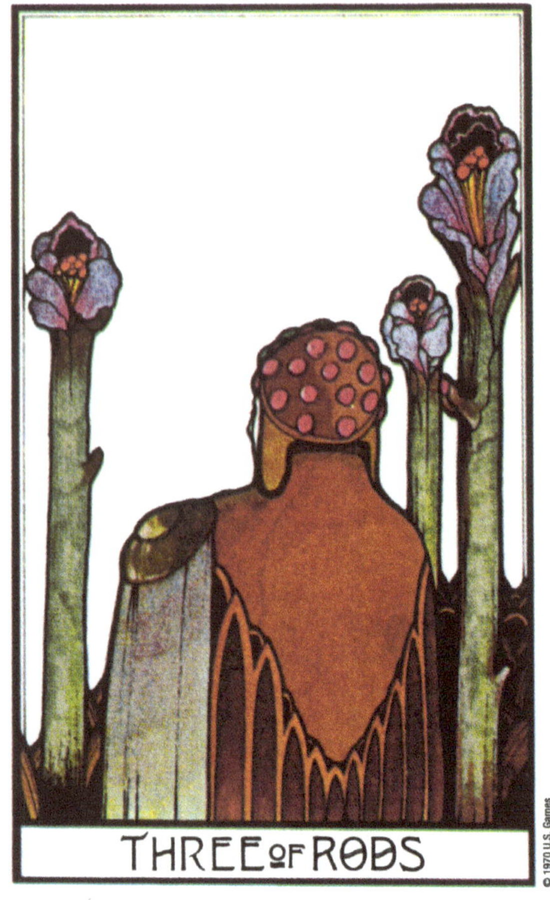

A man stands watch. Three Rods stand with him. They are guarding the route of trade and commerce. With their help and courage, the Kingdom will prosper. All things depend upon cooperation between humans and Nature, between nations, between individual people.

Love lives here.

Continued effort yields continued results—three wands now stand where there were only two before. The jeweled hat and richly trimmed robes attest to success achieved. The decorative badge has been replaced by an epaulet—a declaration of rank, and also protection from blows as one encounters obstacles and opposition.

The figure turns completely away from our view. We do not know if time has worn our seeker, or if he wears his wisdom well. He continues to look ahead, assessing opportunities and threats, adjusting his strategy to further his plans.

The King's guard stands on the shore, holding his royal staff. Two others stand with him. He watches a passing ship laden with the necessities of life. Upon his watchfulness rests the wealth of his country, his family, and his King.

He stands fast. He will not fail.

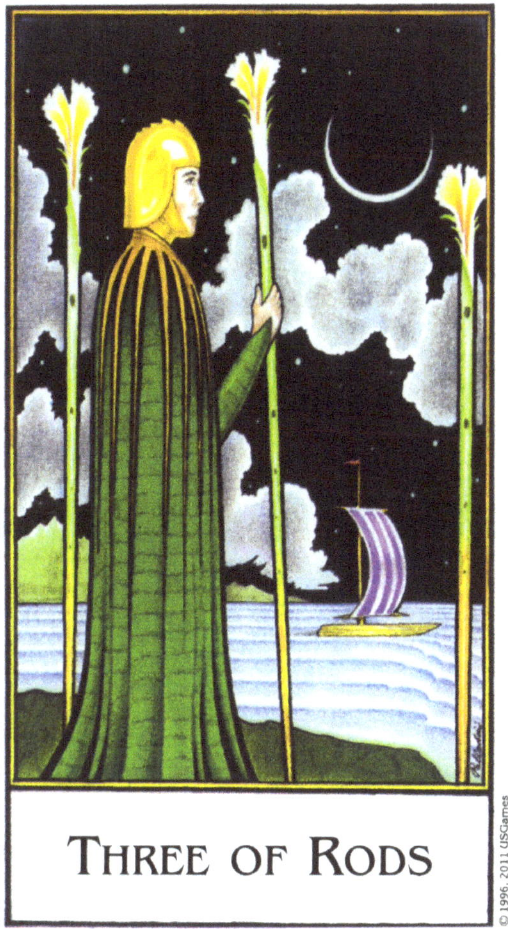

The energy lines calm down in this card after the high energy of the Two. The horizontal lines agree, the vertical lines run in parallel curves. Our figure is older, wiser, and still looks ahead. A ship sails to sea; perhaps the journey will be favorable and bring a fortune. If not, however, he has his three rods—his resources—carefully managed to prevent loss, and to recover from a loss, should one occur. His careful planning and nimble strategies keep him on a successful path, achieving his goals and increasing his resources.

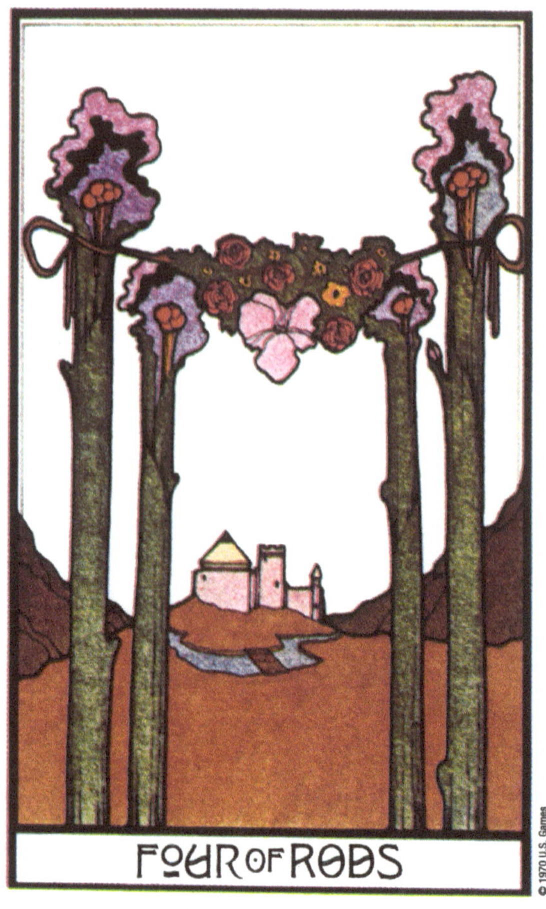

A stout, solid castle surrounded by a moat is framed between four flowering Rods. The Rods are joined by a garland of roses. Inside the castle, peace and prosperity reign. Harmony, repose, and emotional blessings reside here. Walk between garlanded Rods and enter this happy place.

Flower garlands are strung between four rods, indicating a festival or celebration. For the first time in the suit, we see actual water—emotional expression, perhaps even tears of joy.

Four is the number of manifestation, of completed creation. Your planning, efforts, and perseverance have paid off. Acknowledge what you have accomplished, express your joy, and share it with those who shared the journey with you. Enjoy the pleasure and pride of a job well done, a goal achieved, a creation brought forth. Let the celebratory energy renew and inspire you for the next phase.

Four glowing living Rods welcome you. They are festooned with flowers. A golden path leads to a castle made of the purest gold upon a mountain overlooking a land of happiness and rest.

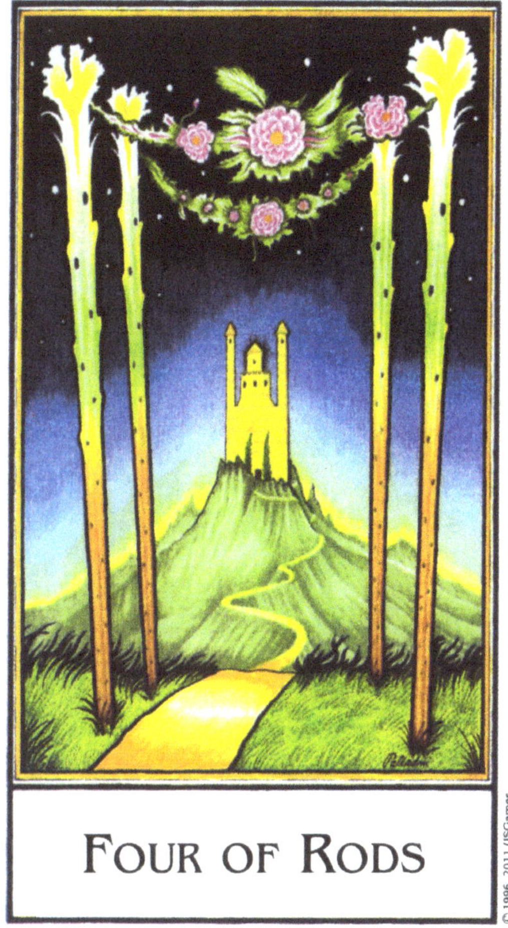

Similarly, we see a scene set for festivity, the green grass expressing the vitality of feelings in place of the water.

After our time of celebration, we need to move forward. The path here is clear and smooth. We cannot see it all the way to the castle; it runs behind the mountain before reappearing. We cannot know every twist and turn on the way to our destination, but we see the path continues on even after the castle. Our dreams call to us to keep moving on the path, going confidently and joyfully in the direction of our bliss.

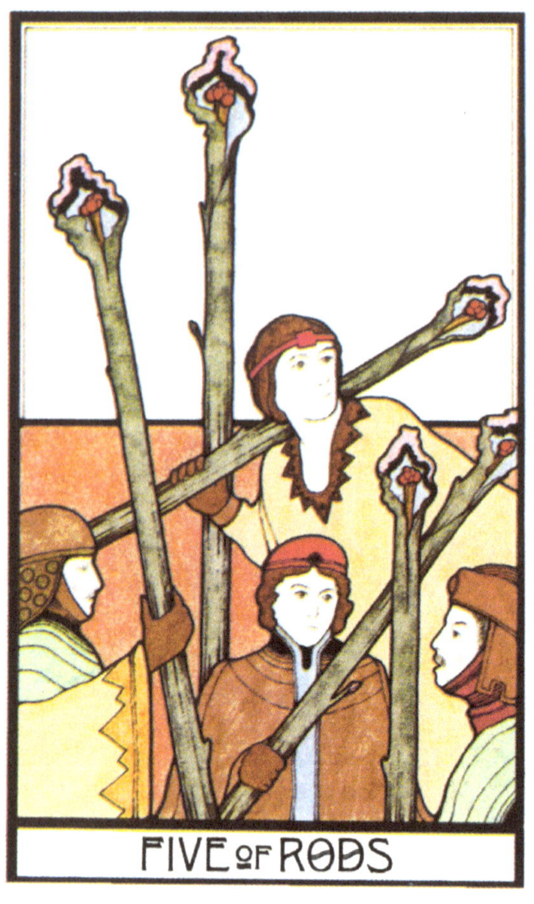

Four young men are confronting each other. They are armed with stout Rods. A fifth Rod awaits a new competitor. A strenuous battle is coming. They are still young and strong. Wealth and recognition await the victor.

The officer issues orders. One soldier stands at the ready. Another seems confused. The third soldier clearly has not heard the orders; he holds his rod casually over his shoulder and stares off into the distance. The fourth solder is absent.

When this card turns up, it is telling us to look at communication as the source of trouble in the situation. Are instructions and expectations unclear? Are we trying to involve people who are uninterested, or unable or unwilling to participate? Taking time to clearly define goals and roles will reduce chaos and foster cooperative action.

Five youths brandishing staves—not as in battle, but as a sport. They are competing, training for the real battles of life yet to come. Courage and wisdom will be required for victory.

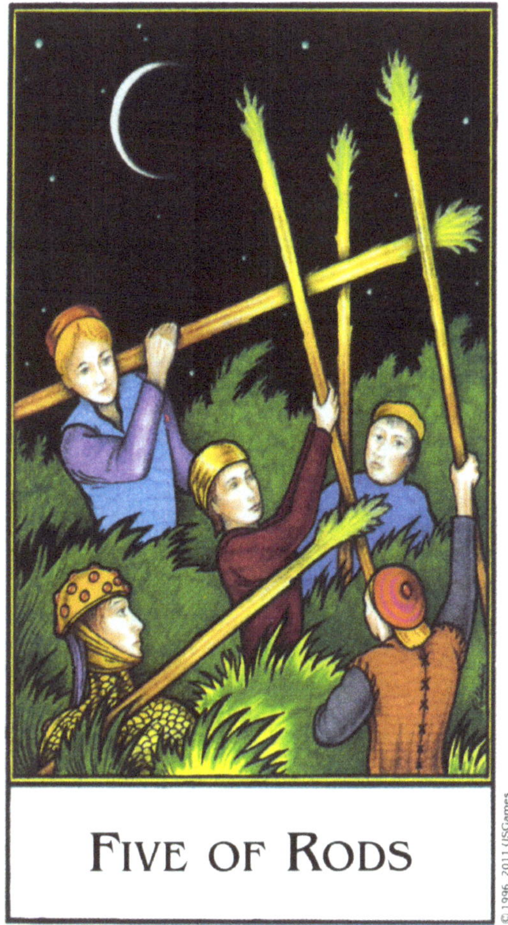

Having issued his orders, the officer stands back to watch his staff carry them out. Unlike the *Aquarian* card, the staff here are clearly trainees, new to the military life.

One youngster takes the lead, and his confidence inspires the second to follow him and to attempt to imitate his action. The other two seem rather baffled by the proceedings. One stands motionless, waiting for further instructions, while the fourth clearly has his own ideas of how things should be done.

Again, making the effort to adjust communication and refine plans is the way forward from the current chaos.

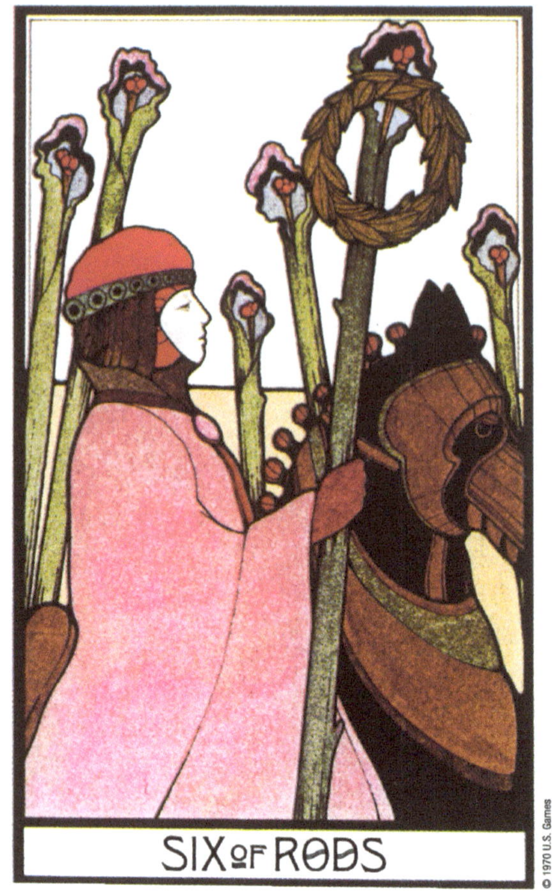

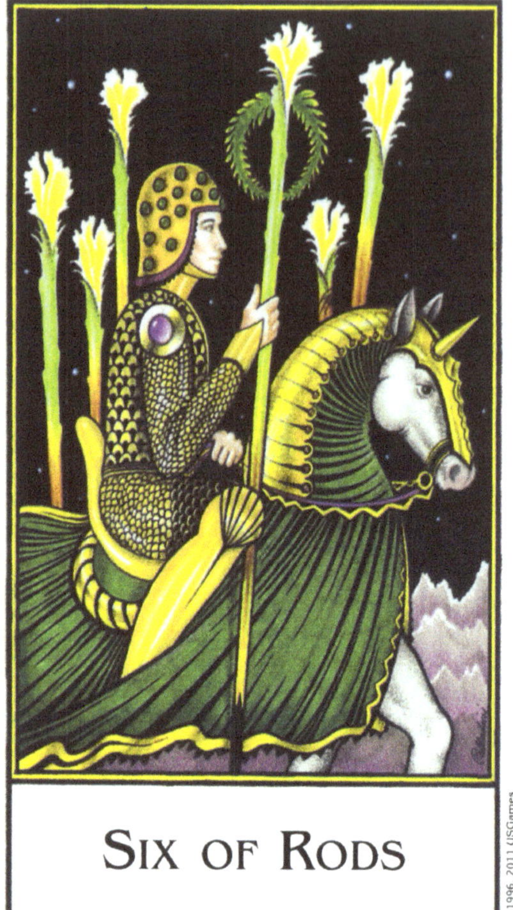

Both Knights are returning from battle. They bear flowering Rods topped by a laurel wreath.

It is the symbol of triumph and learning. Hope and knowledge are victorious over all enemies.

With the laurel wreath of victory hanging from his wand, the figure in the Aquarian card rides proudly and impassively in a triumphal procession. It is a strange parade, however—while the other rods are seen, their carriers are not. The rider is alone at the moment of triumph, elevated and separated from everyone around him. Unlike the Lovers, which shares the numerical value of six with this card, the figure here is disconnected from himself, and so is disconnected from those around him.

Like the Four of Rods, this card represents acknowledgement of accomplishment, but differs from the earlier card in its sense of isolation amidst the celebration. Seeking acknowledgement and approval from others removes us from our own sense of joy in our achievement. If we cannot celebrate ourselves, the plaudits of others cannot fill that need in us.

The victor in the *New Palladini* card also is alone amidst the celebration. He, too, contradicts the numerological correspondence to the Lovers by his isolation. His achievement has not brought him the satisfaction he expected, for he has no one close to him to share it. The approval of the crowd is pleasing, but not satisfying. He misses the one voice whose utterance of “Well done!” would make the achievement truly great in his mind.

He seems tired and anxious, as though stoically enduring the fulfillment of societal obligations so that he can retire to someplace private and quiet to shed the weight of his armor and the weight of societal expectations.

After great labor, celebration and rest are both appropriate; give yourself time for both.

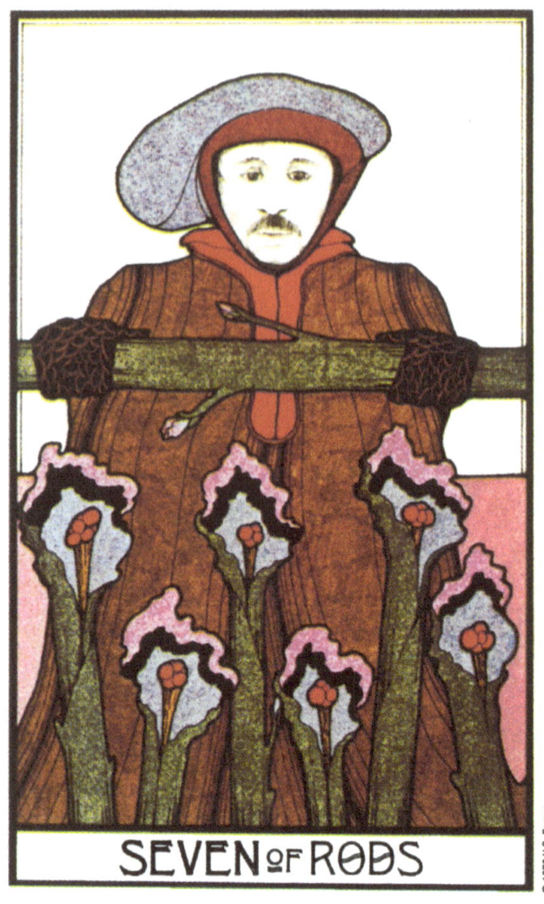

A man is outnumbered by adversaries. Through courage and persistence, he will be the victor. He is well armed. His flowering Rods are his weapons. His strength creates advantages in business, trade, or verbal war.

Unarmored, the figure has only his staff for both offense and defense. He faces the six opposing staves, his staff perpendicular to them.

He looks tired, worn from the battle, and uncertain whether to hold his defense or go on the offense. The position of his staff and his body language seem to call a halt to the battle, perhaps to regain his footing in order to renew the fight, or perhaps to parlay with his foes.

He holds his rod in front of him, across his chest, in a defensive posture, as if to say, "No further. No more." We are reminded to protect ourselves by establishing healthy boundaries in our relationships, and to remove ourselves from a situation which is unhealthy or dangerous.

If someone refuses to respect our boundaries, we can withdraw and refuse to engage further with that person. We do not have to prove to anyone that we are tough, or show how much abuse we can take; we do have to take care of ourselves, and to defend ourselves against abuse and misuse. We do not have to wait for a Tower (16 = 1 + 6 = 7) event to free us from the situation; we can free ourselves through our own choice and our own power.

The card asks us to consider our options and choose what is right, rather than what is convenient, easy, or expedient.

A strong young man brandishes his staff. He stands upon a rocky crag, surrounded by his enemies. He is not afraid. He has valor. Many times he has faced great odds, and many times he has won.

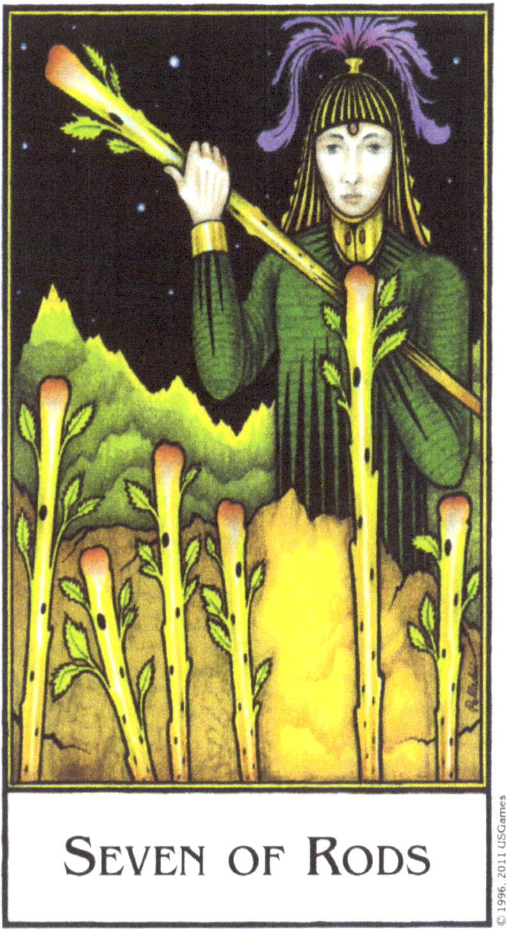

The figure here is similar, except that his battle occurs at night. The card questions whether we have enough light to see clearly who and what we are fighting. Are we battling something Other, outside our own self? Or are we battling our own demons, the discarded and disowned aspects of our souls? If we are fighting an external foe, we need to be clear about that person's (or thing's) strengths and weaknesses, and clear about our own if we are to find a way to victory, or a way to withdraw to safety if the battle is unwinnable.

With the Chariot energy of the 7, we are reminded that we must act from a place of balance and awareness. Sometimes a pause to consider is appropriate before taking action. Be sure of what you are facing before you decide whether to fight, to defend, to surrender, or to withdraw. Connected also to the Tower (16 = 1+ 6 = 7), the cards also tell us to be aware of things beyond our control when deciding how to proceed in our situation.

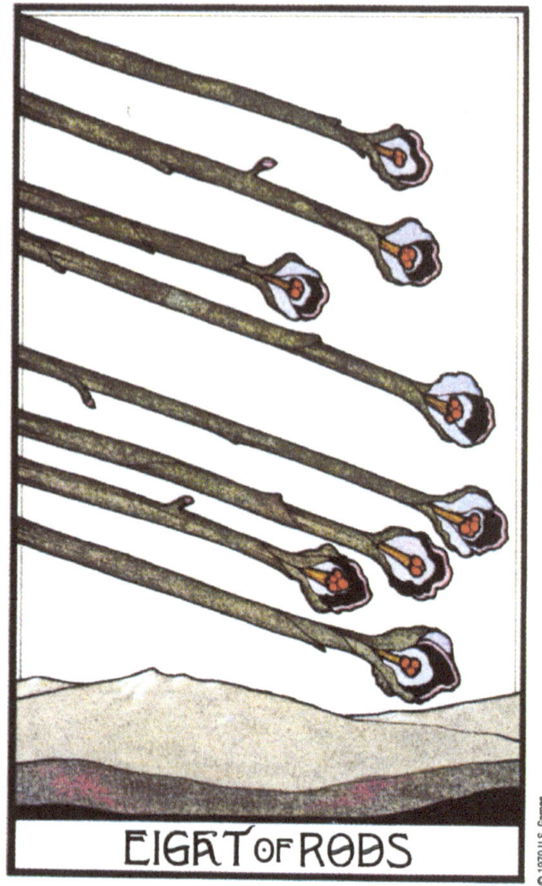

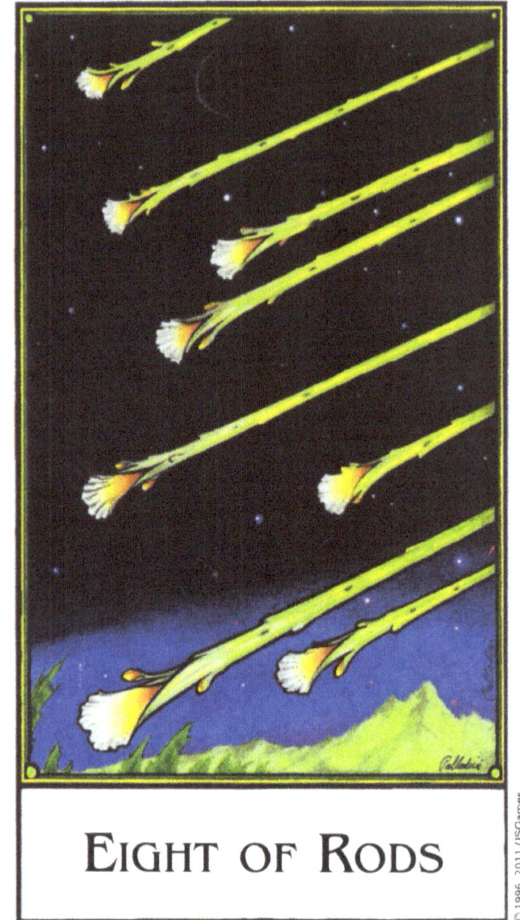

Eight magical wands fly through the sky. They are like arrows carrying news, messengers under the night sky.

The first light of dawn is just breaking.

They become Arrows of Love.

Eight flowering staves are completing their flight and are almost returned to earth. We, too, are near to completing our quest, our task. We are not yet finished, however; the card reminds us that part of the course remains, and we must complete it.

The rods in the *Aquarian* image are almost spent, painted as dry and sere, matching the arid landscape. To complete our work, we need to balance our energies of thinking and doing with the energies of feeling and being.

The wands in the *New Palladini* card are still green and vital, and head towards a green landscape. The energies here are more balanced, indicating a more even approach to completion.

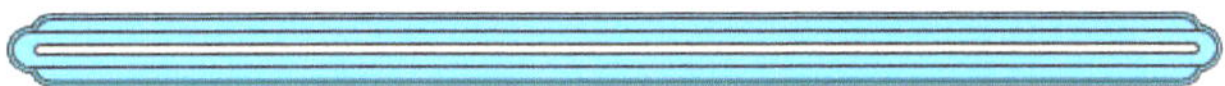

As echoes of the Strength card, both of these images remind us that strength comes in many forms. The rods represent not only our personal strengths, but the advantages and resources in our environment that can help us reach our goal. We are called to re-examine ourselves and our circumstances for new resources, or reinforcement of our existing sources, to speed us on our path.

The cards' connection to the Star card encourages us to remain hopeful about our plans, and to seek new inspiration, keeping us energized and engaged as we move towards completion of our journey.

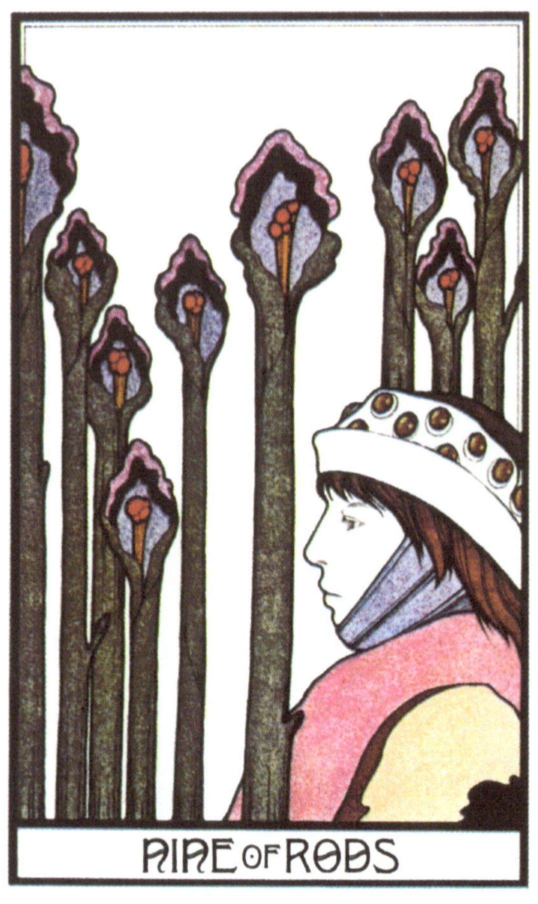

A stern-faced youth surrounded by nine flowering Rods. They give him strength. He would be a formidable opponent. His Rods stand ready to serve.

The rods from the previous card have reached ground, and have been arranged as a fence or a screen, establishing a secure boundary of protection. The ninth rod, held by the figure in each card, indicates the exercise of will necessary to complete that task, and, by extension, the larger task of which this is a part.

This figure seems exhausted by his efforts, reflected in the arid landscape as he contemplates the rod he holds. Perhaps he seeks reassurance that he has done the right thing, or that he has the ability to see the task through to completion.

Like the Hermit (9), the figure here withdraws to a quiet place for contemplation. He needs to rest, to assess the situation, and to devise a plan for completion. Shadowed by the Moon card (18 = 1 + 8 = 9), he is aware of the need to guard his thinking from illusions or false appearances, to focus on what truly is, and not be swayed by half-lit appearances or shadowy suggestions of the unreal. His job is to achieve clarity of thought based on accurate information, and to decide on the best course of action.

A man holding a golden flowering Rod seems to be waiting. He earned his red feathers by his courage in battle. His nine Rods glow under a starry sky.

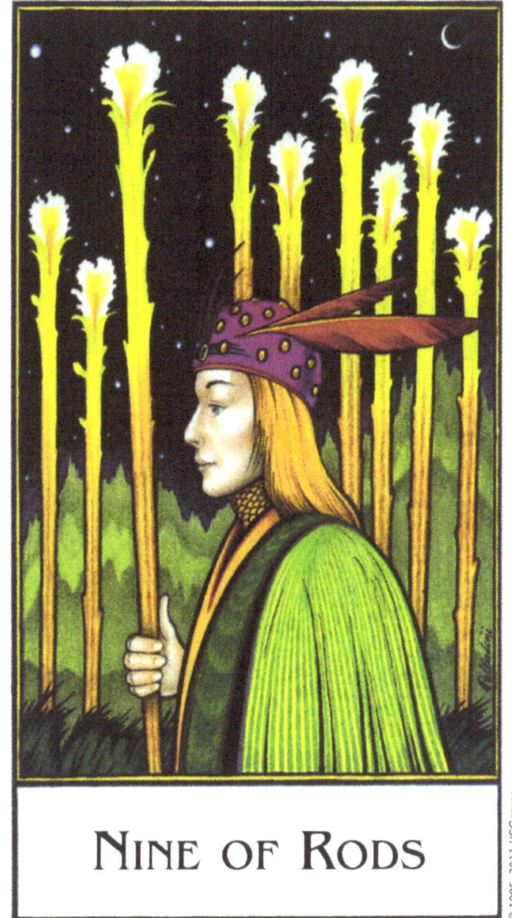

The figure here seems calmer and more confident, balanced by the vitality of his environment and energized by the matching green of his garments. Unlike his *Aquarian* counterpart, he is sure of his path; he contemplates his next action and does not question his choices or abilities.

Echoing the Hermit (9), the cards tell us that we have learned much in the process of reaching this point, and we must learn from our experience to make good choices to move forward.

We must take the time to step back, to re-assess and reevaluate our situation, our selves, and our path, in order to make the best decision for moving forward. Again, we cannot let ourselves by fooled by the half-light of the Moon into thinking that what is unreal is real, or that what is real is not so. Clarity of thought and clarity of purpose lead us to the right path.

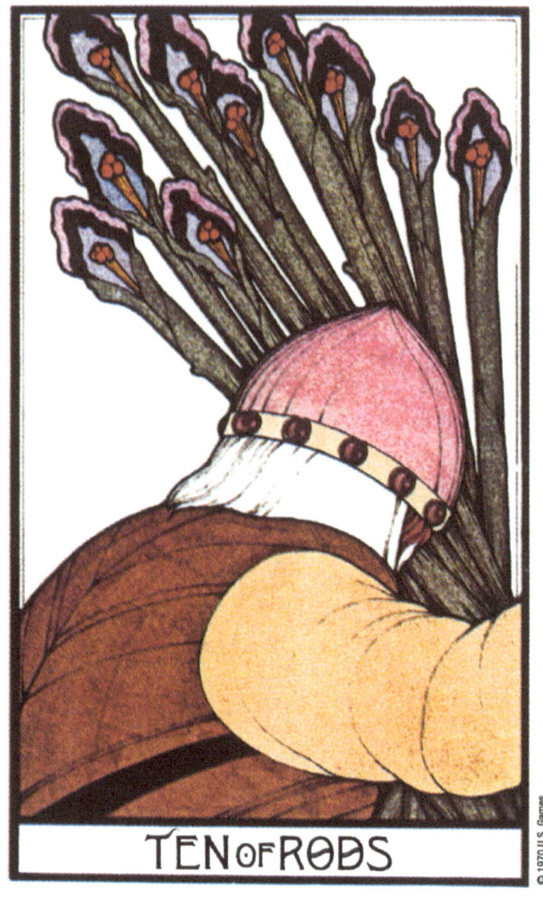

The load is heavy. Many Rods full of many emotions, many lives. The weight of life is tiring, yet we have no choice. We must struggle, continue, persevere. Rich and poor alike must carry their burdens.

The rods have been gathered, but are not yet bundled. We are so close to completion, but not quite there. We must remain focused on our goal and continue to do the work to reach it. Success is near, but not assured. The energy of the Magician encourages us to use our tools and move forward confidently.

We may also find that the energy of the Wheel of Fortune sends unexpected events our way, which may hinder our progress - or finish the job for us! The rewards promised in the Sun card (19 = 1 + 9 = 10) also encourage us to keep at our task and keep moving towards our goal.

Alternately, if we are trying too hard to control something that is already slipping from our grasp, consider letting it go and moving forward unburdened by the unmanageable and undoable. The Universe has other ideas about what we need to be doing, and unexpected opportunities presented by the Wheel of Fortune can lead to similarly unexpected - and often more pleasing - rewards.

A sad man carries ten long flowering Rods. They are ungainly, and are weighing him down. He is surrounded by thorny brambles. The mountains lie ahead. The road of life is long and rough. The burden is great. One must continue. Carry on.

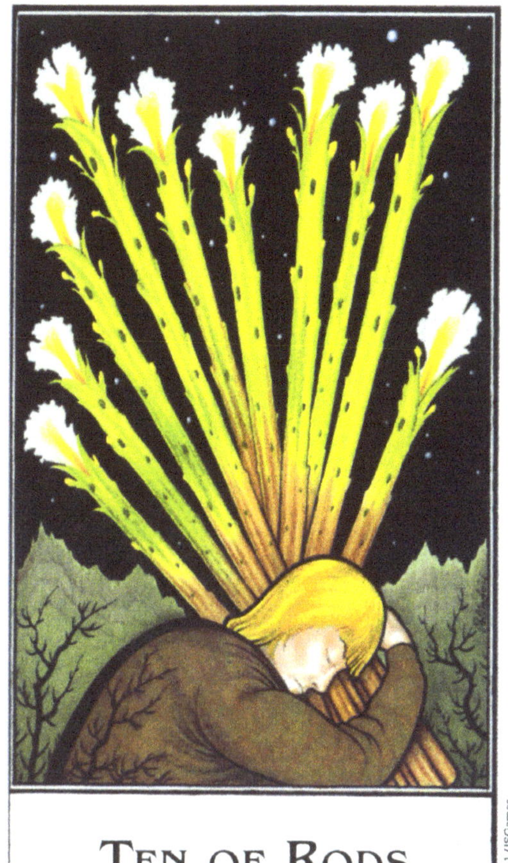

The figure here seems to have a lighter grip on the rods, although he also seems to have an easier time of managing them. He is accustomed to their weight, even if the burden is not easy or light. Perhaps it is ours to continue to carry, or perhaps it is time to release the burden and proceed on our path, unencumbered.

His head is down, his eyes barely open. He needs a touch from the Magician here, a whisper in the ear to look up, look around, and see where he is. He may be further along the road than he realizes, closer to the goal. There may be others to help him carry the rods. There may even be a cart to carry both him and the rods. There may be other possibilities, other advantages, but he will not know until he takes the time to open his eyes and see.

Related to the Wheel of Fortune (10), this card reminds us that we cannot predict the outcome of our efforts. We do our work, we carry our part, and yet the ultimate success or failure depends on so much we cannot control.

Our job is to do our part to the best of our ability, to make the most of the advantages we have, and to give ourselves to the work without reserve until the work is complete, or no longer needed.

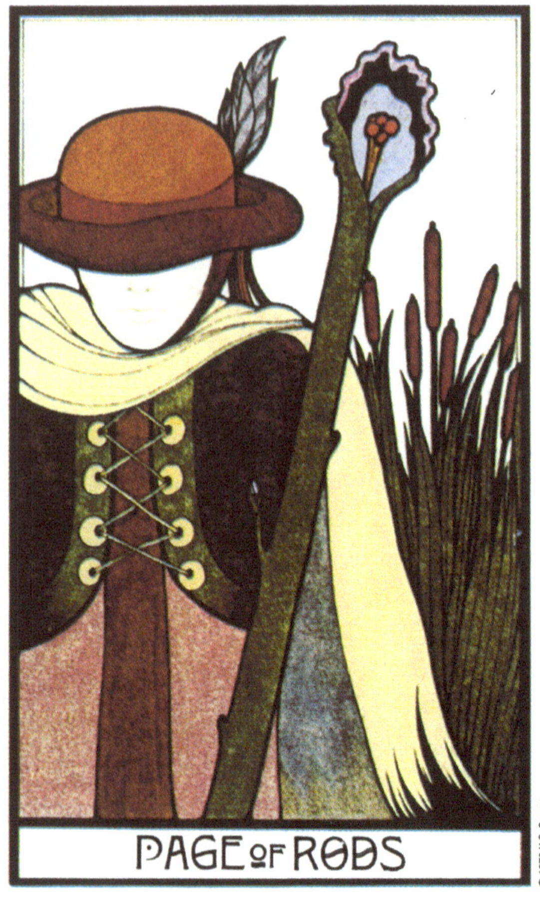

A young woman of simple origins. She wears a feather in her wide-brimmed hat. Her eyes are hidden. She brings secret messages and wise counsel.

The seven cattails echo the energy of the Chariot, which this Page needs to embody in order to discover and direct her will. At the moment, the Page seems unaware of her own will, her own ideas, her own potential.

The lack of specific physical characteristics makes it easier for us to see ourselves in this card. We are now aware that it is time to look up, look around, and learn to listen to our soul. As the earth element in the fire suit, the Page warns us against allowing ourselves to remain stuck in the current situation.

We have abilities and we have ideas. When we add our will to them by borrowing energy from the Chariot, we create a potent force to direct us toward our goal. We must take action, we must start, we must move forward.

A young man stands on a precipice, overlooking three golden pyramids. He wears the robes of a royal attendant of ancient Egypt. He holds the Staff of Authority, with which he announces royal visitors. His Rod is surmounted by a lotus blossom, the sacred flower of the Pharaohs. He is faithful and true, a messenger of Truth.

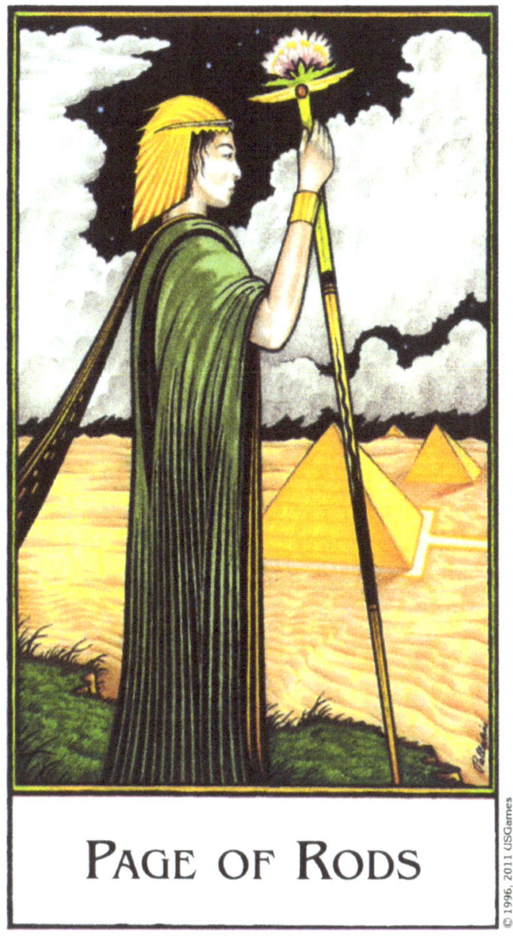

A young Egyptian court official surveys the desert. The pyramids show him that directed will, when focused and transmitted through a group, leads to achievements much larger than can be done by a single person.

Perhaps the Page is considering how he would have organized the construction, or altered the design, imagining what he will do when he moves into the role of authority.

The lush green of the grass on which he stands contrasts with the desert sands, reminding us that we need to nurture our physical selves in order to have the energy needed for effort and achievement. The Earth element of the Fire suit reminds us that having physical energy is needed to start—and finish—our projects and plans.

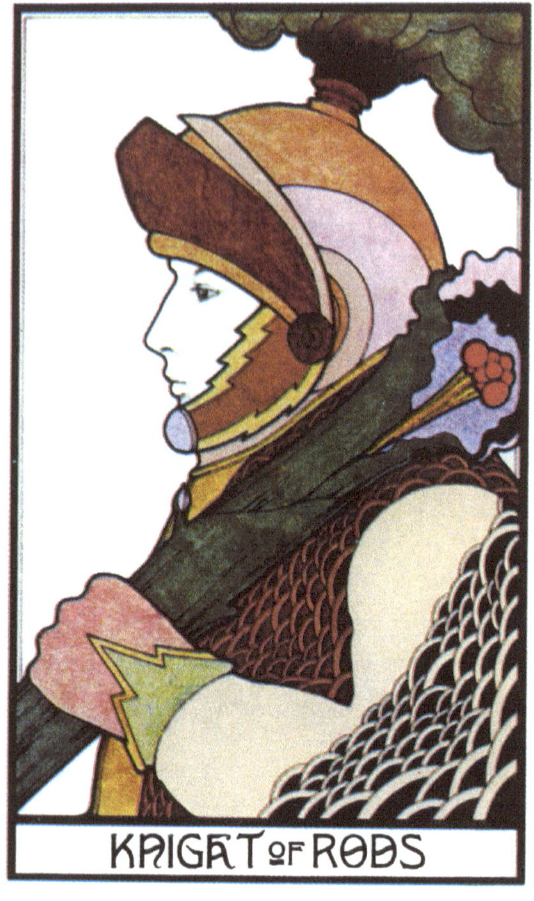

A handsome young Knight carries a flowering rod. It is his only weapon. He is strong, honest, and true. He goes out into the world searching for truth and beauty.

He is not a warrior—he seeks peace.

As the Fire element of the Fire suit, this Knight is the pure expression of dynamic will. The lightning shapes on his face guard and glove tell us of the quickness of his energy. The feathers arising from his helmet appear almost as plumes of smoke, reinforcing the fiery energy. The curves of his helmet mimic the shape of a ram's horn, tying this card to the Emperor and his vital energy.

The Knight holds his rod with confidence and assurance. The plan is made, the way is clear, and he moves forward with the boldness of clarity and awareness.

A horseman in golden armor rides his white stallion under the midnight sky. He is not preparing for battle, but rather is on a journey of self-discovery. He holds his flowering rod like a lance, ready for what may come. His horse is strong and resolute. Nothing will stop them on their search.

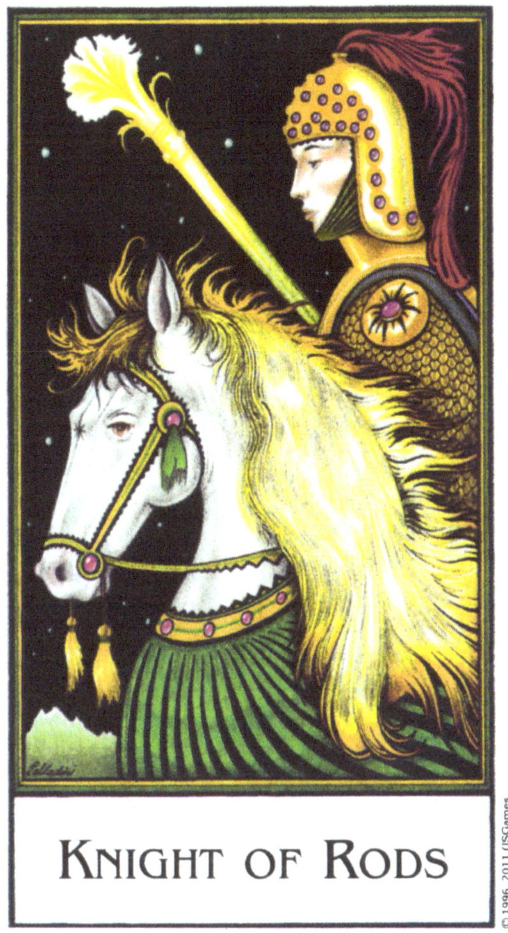

The Knight is mounted and ready to ride. He is focused and determined, calm and confident. His horse, too, embodies these energies.

His armor and headpiece recall those of the Emperor and Chariot, calling the qualities of those cards into this one.

Courage and wisdom direct the will to prompt, positive action.

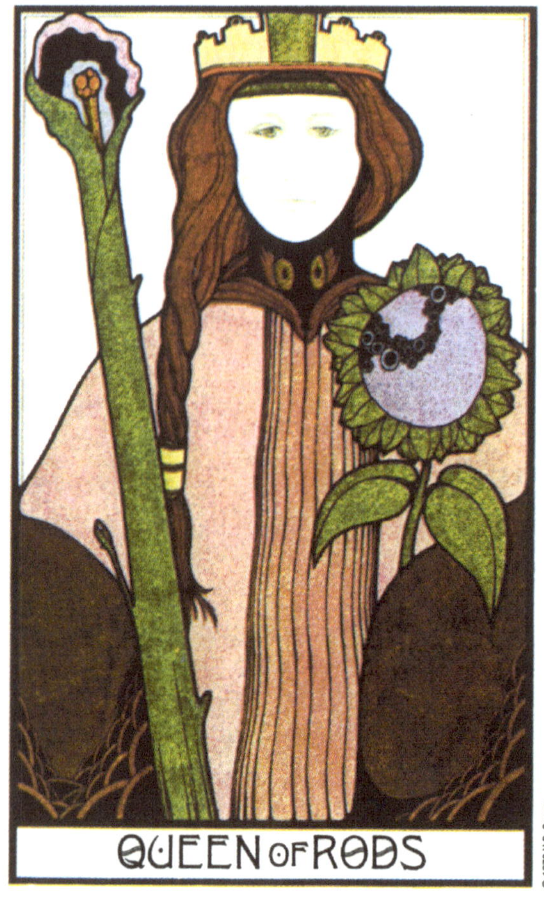

A warm, devoted woman. She has a kind face. She is an ideal companion for the King of Rods. A strange flower grows in her presence. She rules with wisdom and intelligence.

She is a rare woman.

Like the Empress, the Queen of Rods represents the female energy of creation. As the Water element of the Fire suit, she brings emotional and intuitive wisdom to the creative process in a perfect balance. Her emotional cool keeps creative passions in rein; her fiery passions keep the water from turning to ice and freezing the creative impulse.

The blue sunflower—the color of the Moon on the flower of the Sun—emphasizes this feminine energy and the subconscious elements of creation. The perfect balance of feminine and masculine energies multiplies her creative abilities. She flows in her creative process, directing her energy, emotions, and ambitions to achieve her goals.

She uses her physical energy from the Empress, and her spiritual energy from the Hanged Man, to create a harmonious, pleasant, and interesting world. She is complete in herself, and a perfect complement to her King.

A beautiful, strong Ruler, with wisdom and happiness upon her face. She wears a crown and headdress of gold and purple, the colors of royalty. A sliver of the crescent moon hangs in the starry night sky. She, like the King, carries her royal Scepter, which is in full bloom. Her rod is fertile, magical, and wondrous. From it grows harmony, happiness, and wealth. The Queen of Rods is chaste, loving, and honorable.

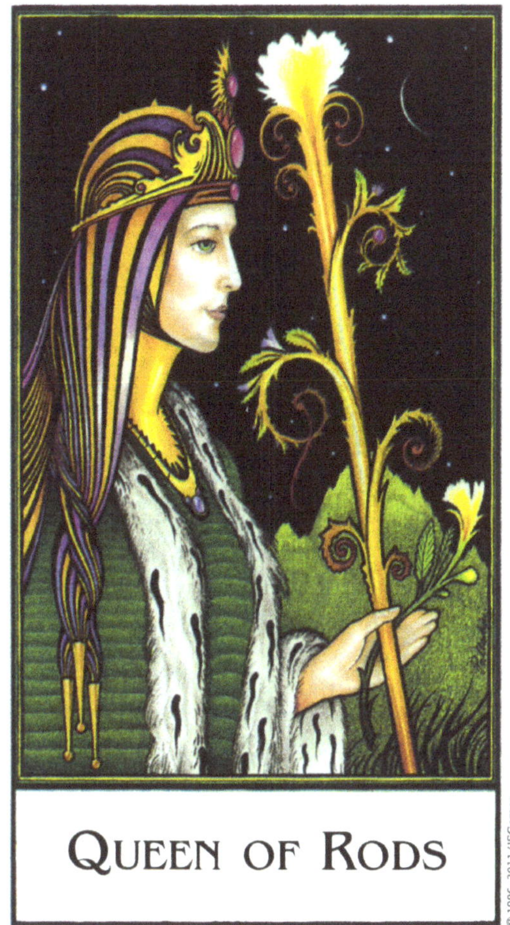

She faces to the right to engage directly with her King. Her sumptuous robe, matching the King's, also matches that of the Emperor—ermine, symbol of royalty, whose black splashes resemble the spermatozoa which fertilize the egg to create physical life. These symbols also connect her with the Empress, the perfect expression of the feminine power of creation.

She is calm and serene, emotionally grounded and confident in her will. She knows her abilities, learned from the Empress, and focuses them to fulfill her roles and responsibilities and achieve her goals and desires. She is creative, strong, and draws upon the infinite creative energy of the Universe to move through her days.

The crescent moon tells us that she has found the necessary balance of emotional and intellectual energies to access her full powers of creativity, making her a glorious Queen in her own right, and the perfect partner for her King.

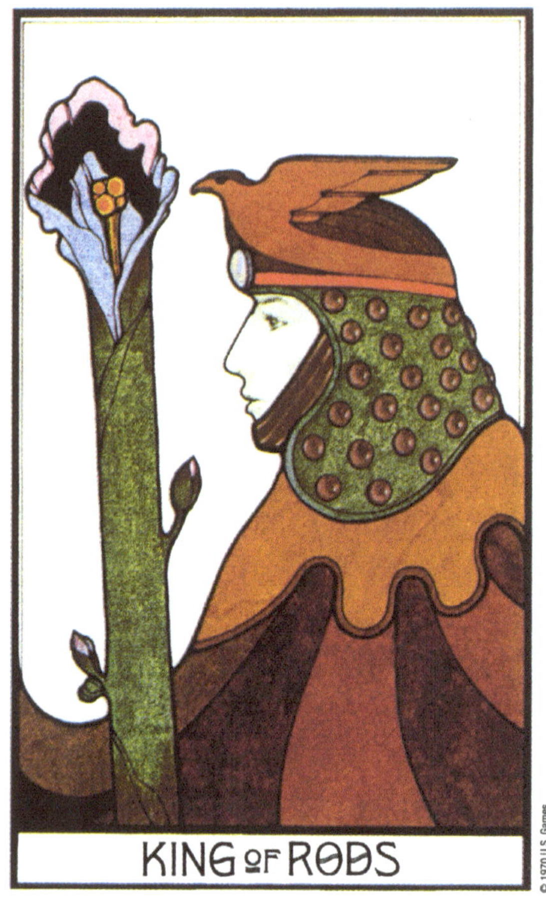

He is a ruler of great strength and power. His is garbed for battle… The unceasing battle of life itself. He wears the symbol of the hunting hawk—wise, swift, and deadly. His rod is flowering. It is a strange flower, a rare flower: the flower of new life. He is a warrior King—honest, conscientious, and just.

The bird on the King's helmet embodies the swiftness of his thoughts and ideas, and his ability to express them eloquently and clearly.

The lines on his cloak show the movement of energy as he disperses his ideas, whether engaging in earnest discussion or issuing absolute commands.

He is infused with the energy of fire, and, as the Air element, he displays and disseminates his directed will through directing the actions of others.

Like the Emperor, he is calm and resolute. He has learned much from his experiences, and he rules with authority and care.

A noble, impassioned, powerful Ruler. He wears the ermine-trimmed robes of State, bearing a rampant lion, the symbol of strength. He holds a jeweled scepter, which blooms in the light of the full moon. He believes in strength in battle and ardor in love.

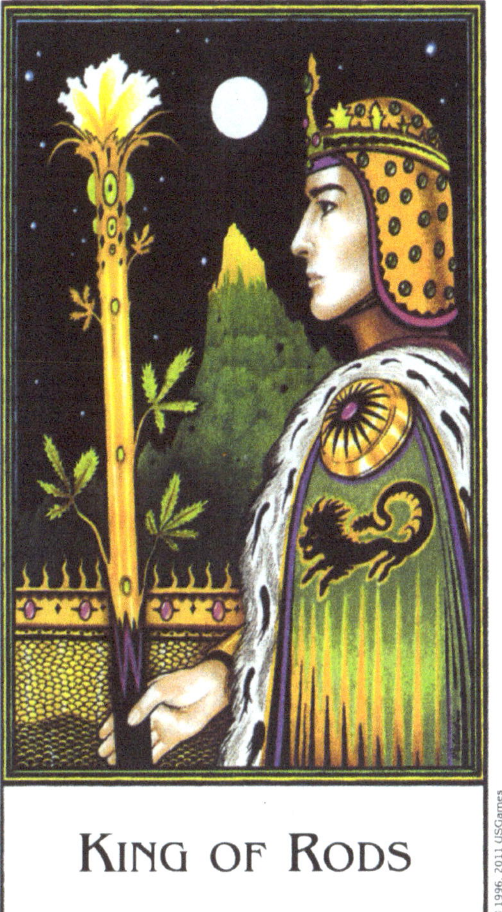

Here the King faces left, towards his Queen. They must work together to create their world. The King provides the thought from the Air element, while the Queen provides the emotional energy of the Water element.

The full moon indicates that, through his connection with the Queen, he is able to access his emotional reserves for his creative process. He is proud of his creative abilities, and appreciates the creative energy of his Queen.

The dragon embroidered on his cloak tells of his courage, his potency, and the incredible energies he brings to the process of creation. Like the Emperor, he is bold, strong, and wise, drawing upon his experience to create a dynamic, prosperous kingdom.

The Minor Arcana

The Suit of Swords

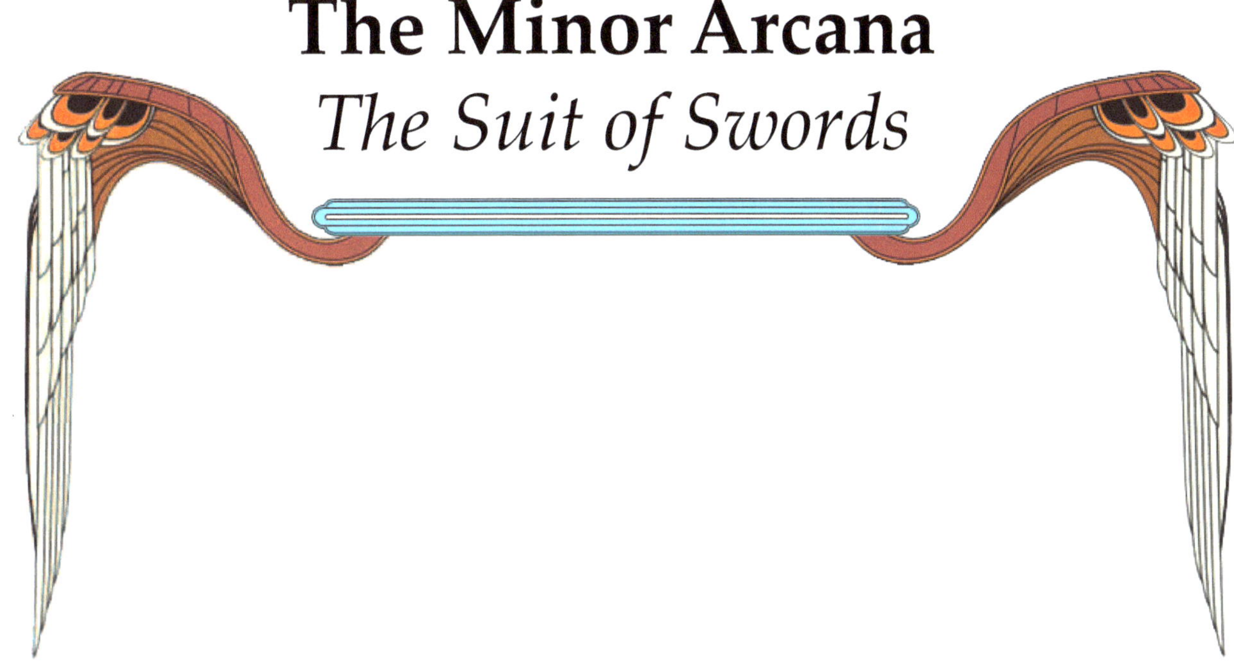

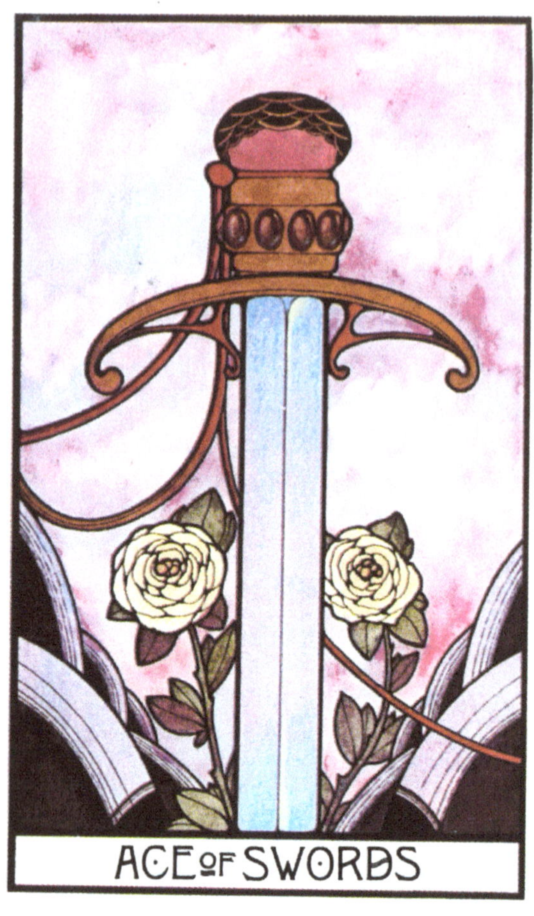

A strong, bejeweled Sword is set against an evening sky. The Sword is seen point down, having completed its battle against the forces of evil. Two white roses flank the blade, the roses of purity and the victory of good.

The combination of intellectual thought and imagination creates many ideas—more ideas than we can possibly ever take action on.

A new idea arises. You can see the end result in your mind's eye, even if you can't see the path. You're not sure how you'll get there, but you know exactly where you're going.

Waves of potential provide energy and encouragement. Draw on the Magician (1) energy for inspiration and clear thinking to manifest your ideas. Be prepared to find advantage in random events and encounters (Wheel of Fortune, Card 10). Visualize your accomplishment, see it clearly in your mind's eye, filled with the light and joy of the Sun (19). All of this One energy gives you singleness of thought and purpose to lead you to action.

A strong hand in golden armor emerges from storm clouds. It holds a Sword of pure gold, with a hilt of jewels and curved graceful decorations. The sharp blade is encircled by a flowering vine bearing blossoms of royal purple. At the tip of the Sword, set against a starry night sky with crescent moon, is a royal crown of delicate design. This is the Sword of a king, all-knowing and invincible. This is triumph.

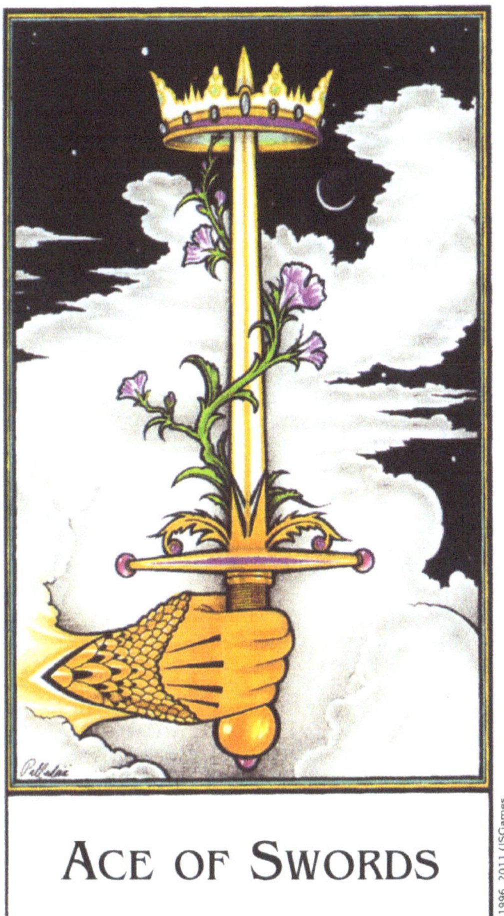

The waning crescent moon runs throughout the suit of Swords, and is also seen in the Ace of Pentacles. The clouds here are a backdrop to the symbol, whereas the clouds in the other Aces frame the other suit symbols. This Ace is the only one to show a gloved hand with the suit symbol.

The energy of this card feels more tied to the Magician, with its controlled energy, than its *Aquarian* equivalent, and therefore less subject to delay and detours from the miscellaneous circumstances created by the Wheel.

The gold of the gauntlet, sword, and crown reference the connection with the energy of the Sun card, despite the nocturnal setting of this image.

Alone among the Aces, the Ace of Swords features a crown in addition to its suit symbol, setting a majestic tone to the suit. As the suit progresses, however, the cards show us how the crown weighs heavily on those who wear it. The flowers represent life and growth, which are carefully controlled and centered on intellect. The clouds are almost shaped like a person with their left arm raised—the opposite of the Magician, whose right arm is raised and whose sword points down to earth.

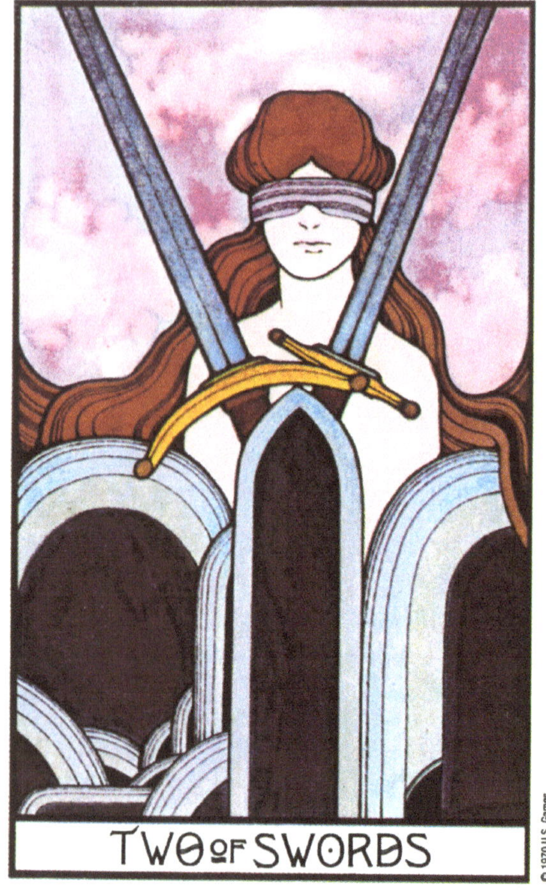

A young, long-haired woman holds two broadswords. She is blindfolded. She cannot see, but she senses all around her. None will get past her sharp Swords.

She is truth, and beauty, and art. She guards the path of knowledge, preventing evil from intruding.

The *Aquarian* Twos show us the Ace reflecting on itself: both the symbol mirroring itself, and the figure(s) in the cards turning inward for reflection. The Two of Swords takes this to the extreme—the blindfold ensures that the person cannot look outward for meaning, significance, or guidance.

The reflective energy of the Twos, shown in the careful balancing actions in each of the cards, requires that we look honestly at ourselves and our choices, much as the High Priestess requires of us. We must question ourselves as thoroughly as the High Priestess does, and answer ourselves with complete honesty.

Potential energy is still running high, expressed by the lines and curves of the shapes in front of the figure. We must shift our focus to our internal processes in order to reach the best decision; the blindfold allows us to shut out distractions so we are able to do so.

The time for asking advice and seeking counsel is over. We must think our own thoughts, take our own advice, hold our own counsel in the matter.

This card says that the decision is completely yours to make. You need to shut out the opinions and expectations of others and listen to what is true for you. We cannot move forward except by our own decision, our own volition.

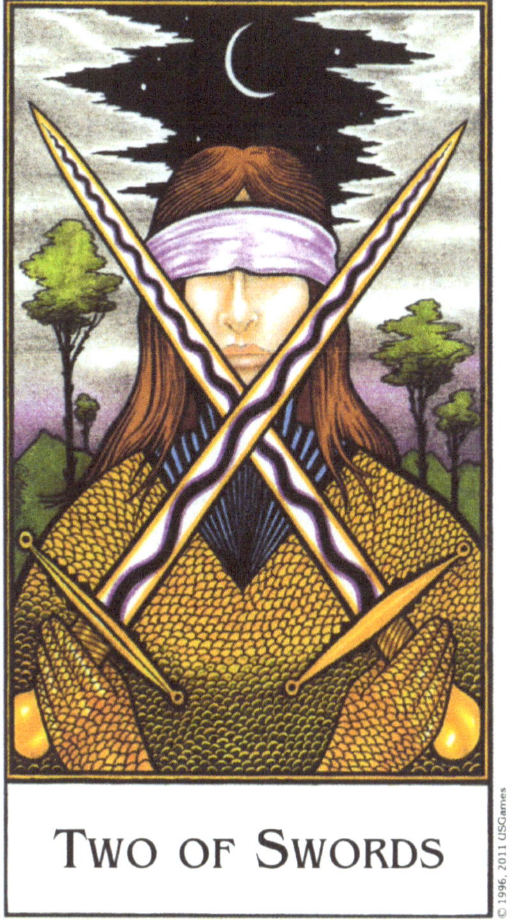

A female Knight in golden chain-mail holds two crossed Swords. She wears a silken blindfold. She guards the verdant land behind her.

Only the true of heart and spirit may enter.

The figure is clad entirely in mail, completely protected. The two swords create a protective barrier—but while nothing crosses in, nothing crosses out, either. Change requires movement, which the figure is unwilling to make.

The blindfold keeps the focus internal, echoing the reflective nature of the High Priestess. Unlike the High Priestess (2), however, nothing is given, no energy flows outward.

The lines on the swords indicate intellectual energy flowing from the general (hilt) to the specific (tip) and back again. The Knight is caught in a mental loop, repeating the same thoughts, holding the same internal conversations, playing out the same scenarios, over and over again in her head. She is protected from the influence of others, yet needs the mental discipline to channel her thoughts in a progression, rather than in a never-ending circle.

Overshadowed by the waning moon, she needs to draw upon the solar energy represented by her golden mail and gloves to clarify her thinking. The silver and gold metals combined in her swords give her this ability. She needs to uncross the swords to turn the closed loop of her thoughts into productive mental activity.

Sometimes we have a big idea and need to refine it; sometimes we have a spark of an idea and need to expand it.

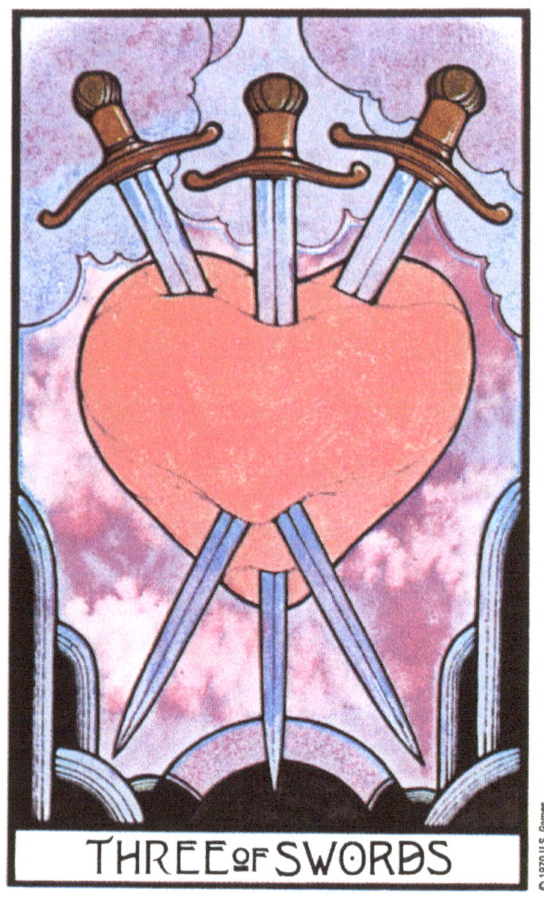

A heart is pierced by three Swords. Life penetrates our tender souls.

We must continue, despite the pain.

Our hearts are sick with regret over a choice not made, or unexpected results of a choice made.

When we encounter our first setback or disappointment when pursuing a dream, the heartbreak can feel unending. We wonder how we will survive the loss, the pain, the seemingly endless delay in realizing our dreams.

The potential is still there. The plans can be changed to account for the new circumstance. Much is different, but not all is lost.

View this as an opportunity to discard what does not work, to remove what limits you.

Acknowledge the pain, heal yourself, and move on.

Tears rain down from a clouded night sky. Each teardrop is a memory of pain, loss, missed chances, or forced changes. Three golden Swords pierce a living heart. All people know the pain of life.

Here, we feel the echoes of the Sacred Heart of Jesus and the lesson of the love and compassion Christ had for humanity in spite of his suffering.

We, too, can heal from our suffering and continue to love.

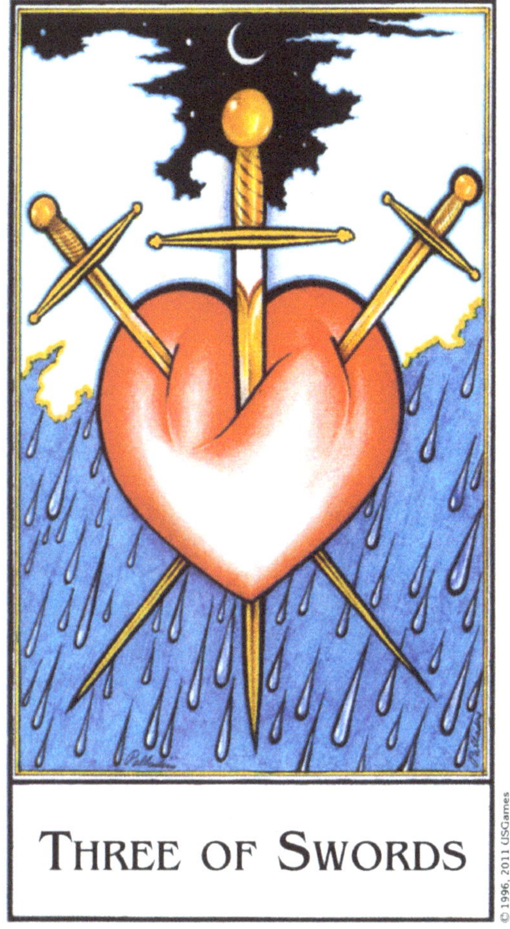

Pain, pain, and more pain, with the moon in wane. We are accustomed to functioning with swords piercing our heart.

Living with the pain of the swords embedded is familiar, but it is still pain. If we move the wrong way, the swords shift and re-injure us. We fear movement, but we must move on, or die from the pain.

Removing the Swords reopens the wounds, and we experience the pain anew.

Once the swords are removed, however, we can truly heal. Acknowledge the pain, feel the pain as you remove the swords—then let yourself heal.

The Empress energy of the Three helps us to heal. The surrender learned in the Hanged Man (12 = 1 + 2 = 3) gives us the spiritual strength to move through the pain and learn from the experience, taking us to the place of grace and wholeness exemplified by the World card (21 = 2 +1 = 3).

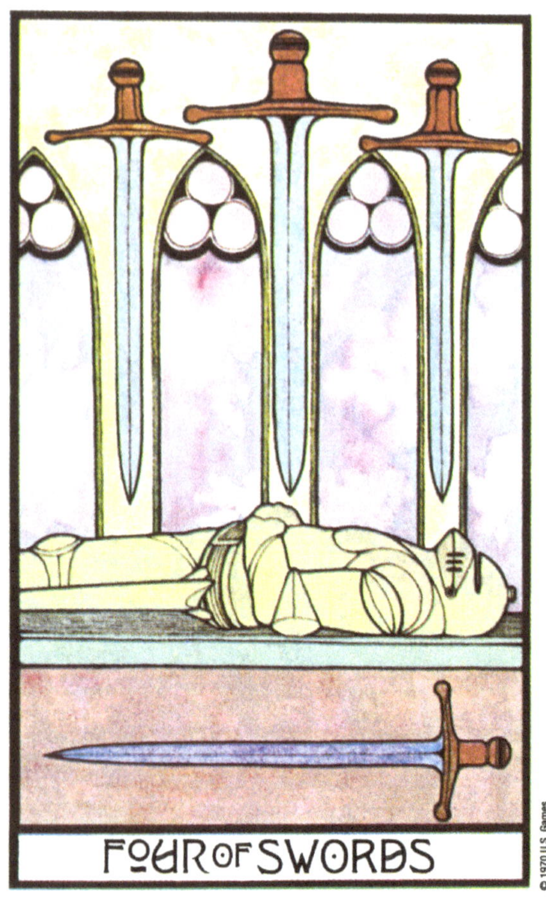

A Knight wearing a suit of armor lies on an altar. Three swords hang suspended between church windows. A fourth sword lies beneath the armor. The swords point down toward the Earth.

The Knight lies resting. He is not dead. He is in the repose of the exile, cut off from the world. Inside his iron helmet, he is recuperating from the battles of life.

Rest. Refine and re-define your dream based on prior events. Deep consideration and thoughtful choices are required before starting the next phase.

This card is linked numerologically with Death (13 = 1+ 3 = 4), and some people see this image as a knight's effigy on a tomb.

The Knight is undergoing a similar passage of deep rest and transformation, although, unlike Death, this is not a final passage; he will awake and return to his life. However, he will not be as he was before, and his life will likewise not be as it was before. His stillness and withdrawal from life make him like the Hanged Man, whose energies are dominant in this card.

The time for action will come; now is the time for rethinking priorities, revisitng old dreams, and revising plans to more closely align with your new self and new life when you emerge from this quiet time.

A Knight lies full length upon a golden table. Fantastic flowers are etched upon stone under him.

Three golden Swords float in the night sky. A fourth Sword lies upon his chest. His full suit of armor is bejeweled and shining. He is solitary and sleeping. He dreams of his exploits and the pain and suffering he has been through. Soon, he will rise again, refreshed and ready for battle.

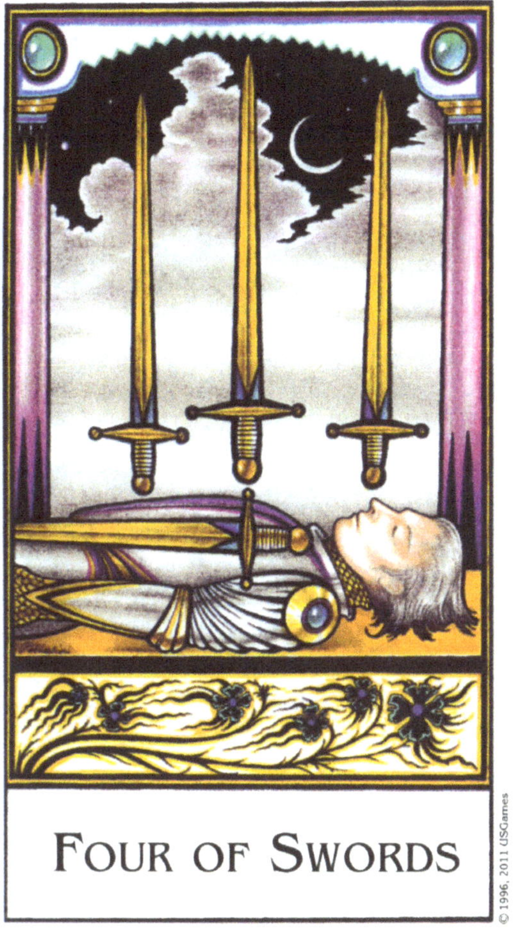

The Knight encourages us to rest and protection. The flowers on the base of the crypt suggest life and growth to come. The pillars echo those in the High Priestess, suggesting a rite of passage in a sacred space, an initiation on a deep level, also calling to mind the influence of the Hanged Man.

Old ways of thinking and believing must pass; new clarity arises. The death of old limits, limiting beliefs, limiting thought patterns, limited ways of seeing, allow us to live more freely and authentically.

Awake to see the world with new eyes, new mind, new soul. The wisdom of experience, combined with a new self born of the time in transition, will lead you stronger, wiser, and more prepared for the road head, and more easily to victory.

Like the Emperor (4), claim your power, establish your kingdom, and take your place on the throne.

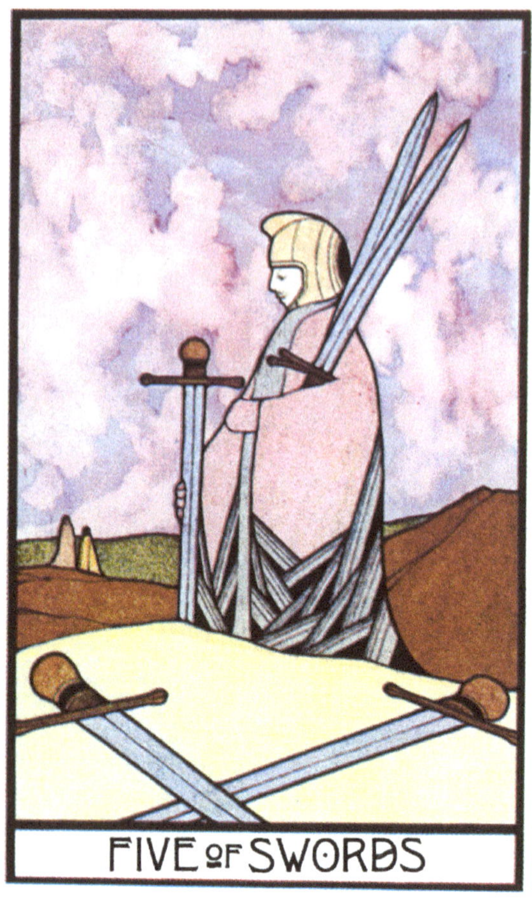

A man wanders the battlefield. He is collecting the Swords of fallen combatants. He carries two and is pulling one from the ground. The bodies of the warriors are gone. Loss and defeat can be felt. There is dishonor here.

Echoing the Hierophant, this card tells us to pay attention to what we have learned; it has cost us dearly. The original two swords (the old idea) are left behind. The swords being carried are the new vision of the original idea. Lighter, sharper, and more elegant, the new way of thinking incorporates what you have learned.

The woven pattern at the bottom of his cloak indicates that some crystallized thinking remains. We are still caught in unproductive thought patterns, which lead us to repetitive, self-defeating behaviors.

We must be willing to change our ideas about the world and our own self. These new ideas create discomfort as we are required to acknowledge external defeats and internal deficiencies. We must acknowledge how things are, and how we are, before we can think about new ways of living in the world and being a better version of our current self.

Do not let history, past mistakes, or old ideas slow you down. Take from your experience only what you need to move forward in the next phase.

A Knight in full armor wanders the empty battle field under a crescent moon. He is gathering Swords of the dead. He feels the humiliation of loss and defeat. We do not know whether his side was victorious or defeated. It does not matter. All war is useless. There are no victors in battle. Degradation and destruction are felt by both sides. He is remembering the time of peace and happiness, which is now gone.

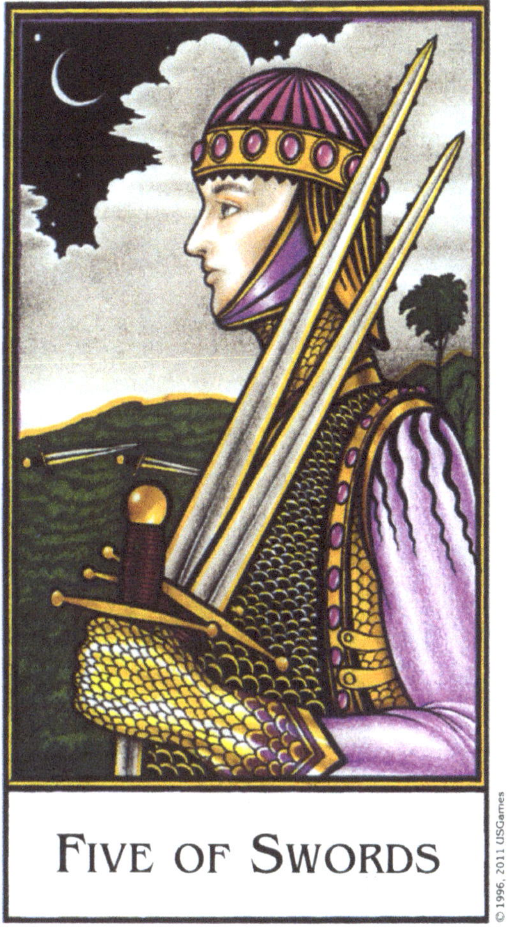

Having discarded limiting mental patterns (the two swords stuck in the ground), move forward with new knowledge, new perspective. As an echo of the Hierophant (5), this card represents lessons learned and empowerment through knowledge. Acceptance of the need for change, even if one is not fully reconciled to it, is required in order to move forward from the battle.

We cannot heal if we stay at the scene of the battle. We accept the experience, internalize it, allow it to strengthen us, much like the process of Temperance (14 = 1 + 4 = 5). As metal is tempered to make it strong and flexible, so we are tempered by our life experiences, especially those of pain and loss, to be more aware and more responsive to life.

This card tells us it is time to move forward calmly, eyes open, aware and alert. Fulfillment of duties and obligations through intellectual will, even if emotional will is not present, is our duty now. In performing this duty, we undergo the tempering of heart and soul. Now is our opportunity to rise to meet life, to withstand the tempering process and come out stronger.

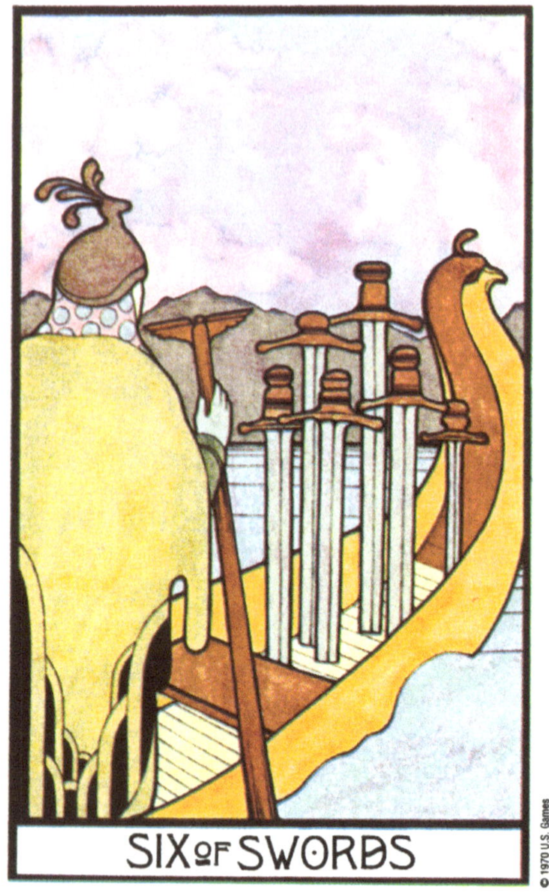

A hooded figure guides a boat holding a winged oar. Six Swords are thrust into the floorboards of the boat. The prow of the boat is carved into the head of a strong bird of prey. They are headed toward a mountainous shore.

The goal is a resolution of difficulties, achieving a noble end to the journey of life. The oarsman is resolute; the distant goal will be reached.

The time has come for movement forward in the second phase of the situation. You cannot stay where you are, no matter how familiar, no matter how comfortable.

The bird shape of the man's helmet mimics the prow of the boat, and connects with the wing-shaped oar handle. These symbols reinforce the air element of the suit in this watery image.

The orderly curves of the cloak hem tell us that his emotions and intellect are in dynamic balance. He is not run ragged by his emotions, nor is he acting only from cold logic. He has made his decision calmly and after suitable deliberation. He takes appropriate, timely action to advance his plans and his life.

Movement forward is required to complete the second phase. Renewal of potential is achieved by relinquishing regrets, mistakes, stuck energy. Hard lessons have been learned with much pain and loss. Remaining in the midst of the deserted battlefield denies life, denies growth, denies possibility.

Moving forward is the only choice.

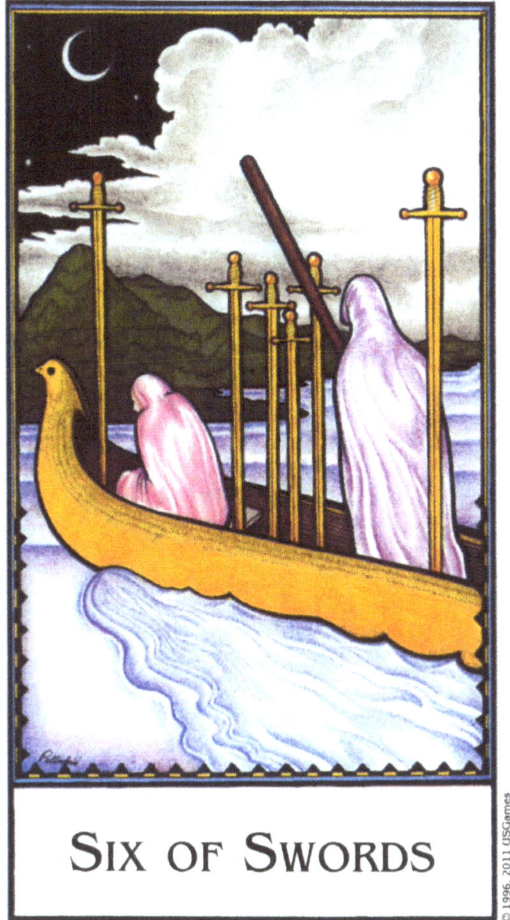

An oarsman guides his boat across a river toward a distant shore. He carries an unknown traveler and six Swords. This is a card of exploration, both internal and worldly.

The journey is uncertain. Adventure awaits. The outcome is unknown.

The silhouettes of the people in the boat echo the bird figure on the boat's prow. Birds migrate because they are compelled by survival; so, too, we must move on, move forward, despite fear, sorrow, or reluctance.

It is time—or past time—to move on. Our soul is guiding us, even if our mind is unwilling to go, and tries to frighten us by conjuring thoughts of hostile lands, evil monsters, and untold disasters waiting ahead.

Are you the person huddled in fear, or the stalwart guide? Which will help you move forward with calm and confidence? As with the Lovers card, being in right relationship with yourself is the path to growth and living fully.

These are also the first two un-armored figures in this suit, signifying emotional and intellectual vulnerability, further echoing the Lovers card.

The Devil (15 = 1 + 5 = 6) tempts us to stay where we are: familiar, even if hellish. However awful it is, it is what we known, and familiarity contains a small bit of comfort, even in the most dire circumstance.

We must look into our own souls, for there we shall find the courage to say "no" to the Devil, to say "no" to the repetitive, self-destructive behaviors the Devil encourages, and to say "yes" to what is healing and helpful to us.

The sword stand high, as tall as, or taller than, the people in the boat. The swords tell us that our true Self knows what is right. By listening to our soul, our clarity of thought and purpose will start us on our way, and see us through this journey.

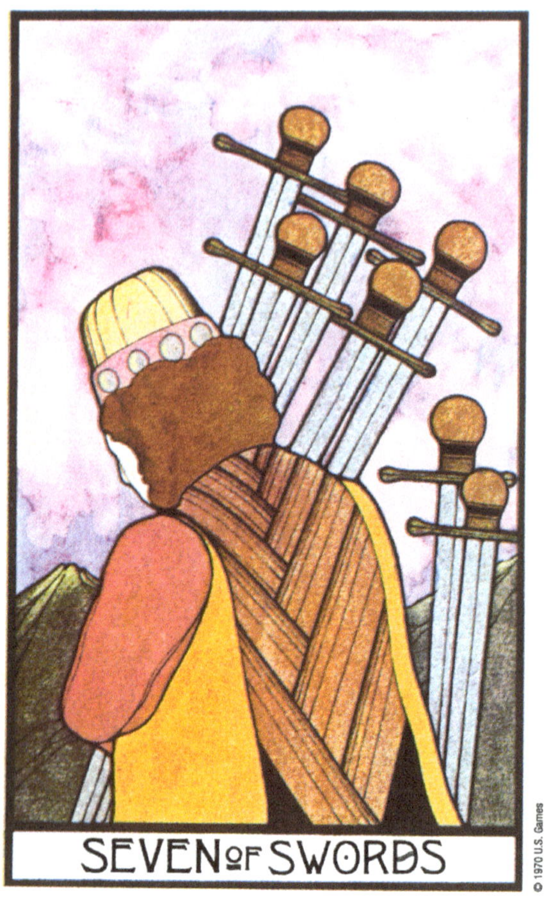

We see a figure in a conical turban and decorative cloak carrying five broadswords. Two more Swords are beside him. A mountainous landscape is all around. We cannot see the face of the person, who is neither male nor female. Where are the Swords being carried? And why?

This is a card of secret plans, expectations, and hopes. Perhaps a battle is coming or has just ended. Counsel is needed. Care must be taken. Plans must be precise and directed toward good.

Further refinement of ideas and ways of thinking creates a renewed awareness of what to leave behind. Ideas and actions which were not useful the first time around will prove no more helpful with repetition.

The geometric pattern on the cloak can represent the clarity of ordered thought, and yet also warn us against becoming stuck in unproductive mental processes. Crystallized thinking creates repeated failures and prolongs the pattern of the problem.

As with the Five of Swords, we are reminded to take with us only what is true, what is right, what is helpful and hopeful. We must be realistic about who we are, and where we are, and at the same time, remain calmly focused on our strategy for progress and victory.

Continue moving away from limiting factors, beliefs, and behaviors, and continue moving towards growth, progress, and wholeness.

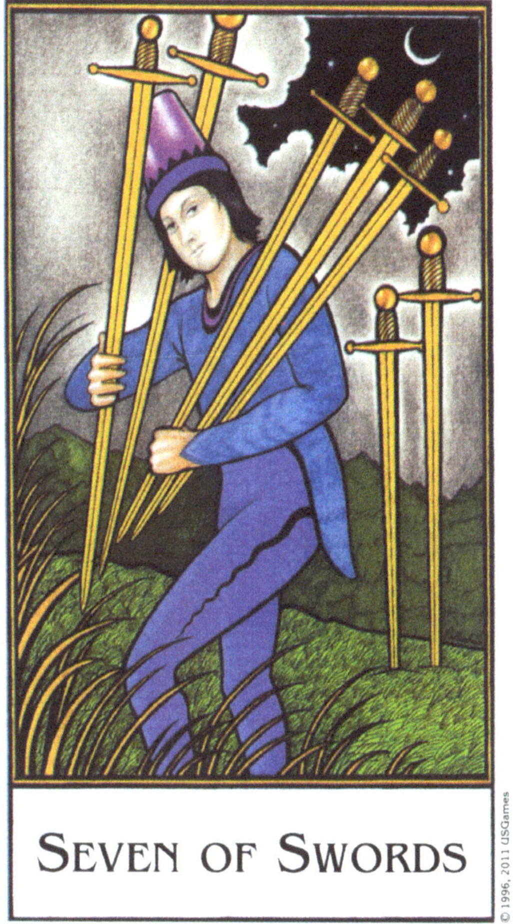

A man in bright bluish-purple clothing carries five golden Swords. Two more Swords are thrust into a grassy field behind him. He looks us confidently in the eye. A crescent moon shines in a clouded night sky. The Swords do not cut his hands.

He has secret plans, wishes, and hopes. His Swords will help him achieve those things.

Bare hands rashly grasp five swords by the blades, not the hilts, representing self-injury through unclear thinking. Muddled thoughts produce damaging actions. The card tells us we may also be over-thinking something, or thinking about too many things at once without real consideration or meaningful evaluation of any of the ideas.

The man seems unclear as to what he is going to do with the swords, or perhaps has a plan that he does not wish us to know. He seems to be taking them because they were left unguarded, an opportunity of a moment rather than a clear plan. He may not have any use for them himself; he may be planning to sell them to others who do have a use for them. Whatever his thoughts, he does not wish to share them, or the swords, with us. He is too absorbed in his impromptu plan to consider what he is doing, or the consequences if he is caught.

We need to re-ground the mental energy by re-staking the swords in the ground. Pick them up by the hilt, one at a time, and use your intellect to solve problems instead of creating problems through incomplete thoughts and half-formed plans. Not managing our thoughts creates harm for ourselves and others; we must think clearly and act with integrity in order to live a meaningful life.

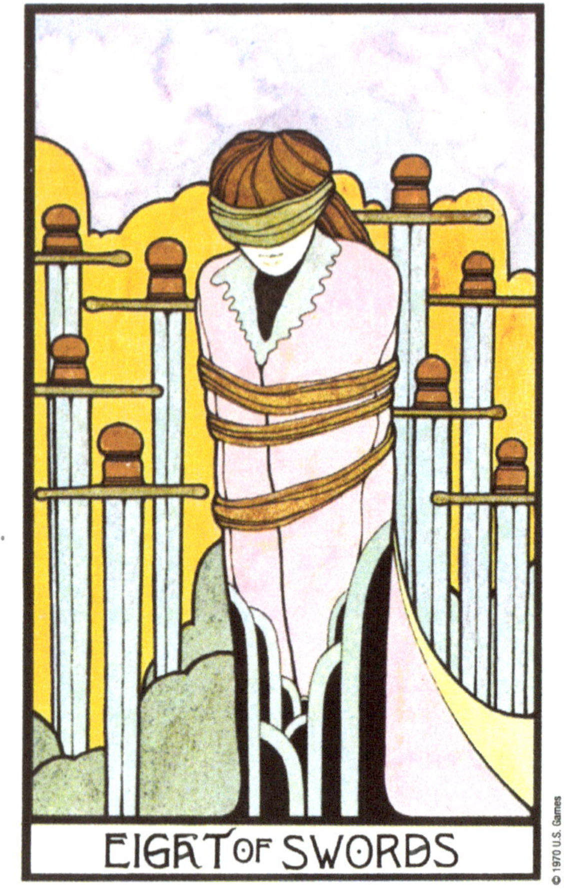

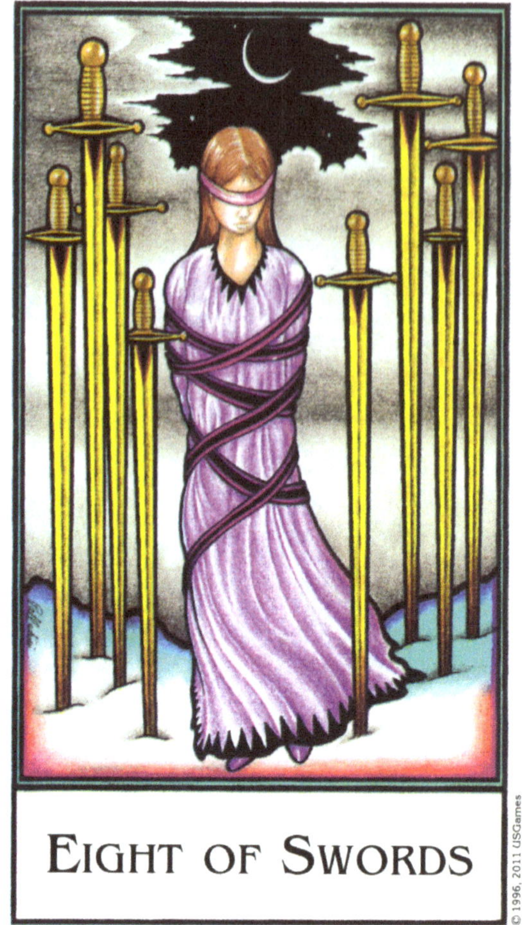

The two women are bound and blindfolded, like prisoners before execution. They are surrounded by Swords for protection against the danger the figures cannot see. Disaster is possible, but never death. Both night and day skies are clouded. Confusion and uncertainty bind and blind us. Choose a path. Follow it. Make no excuses.

The *Aquarian* images shows us that the illusion of entrapment falsely holds us back. The figure is rooted in potential, even as she is fenced in by her thoughts. Like the Seven of Swords, the geometric pattern on the cloak speaks to us of the balance of emotion and intellect. In this case, however, the balance is static rather than dynamic. She is unable to use her emotional energy to change her thinking, and her intellectual energy is too tightly bound in repetitive thinking to redirect her emotional state from fear to courage.

Limitations of our own creation are the real issue. Look within, as with the Two of Swords, to regain perspective and rediscover your true direction.

We need to recognize our strengths, our abilities, and our own brilliance in order to free ourselves of the loose bonds which seem to hold us so tightly.

The *New Palladini* card tells us that, bound by externally imposed expectations which we have internalized, we are trapped by our own confusion. Rather than helping us turn our focus inward to solve our problems, the blindfold keeps us from seeing that we can move out of the situation by taking one step forward.

We invoke the energy of the Strength card to give us courage to face our fears and see them for what they are—False Evidence Appearing Real.

We look to the Star (17 = 1 + 7 = 8) to give us hope to believe in our own best self, our own virtues and qualities of soul. We can then come to truly believe that we can shake the bonds, remove the blindfold, and walk forward bravely on our path, with hope in our soul.

Believing we can is half the work; believe, then achieve.

Set strong boundaries and reject others' expectations that do not align with your authentic purpose. Move forward in the direction your soul chooses, not along the path that others would have you walk.

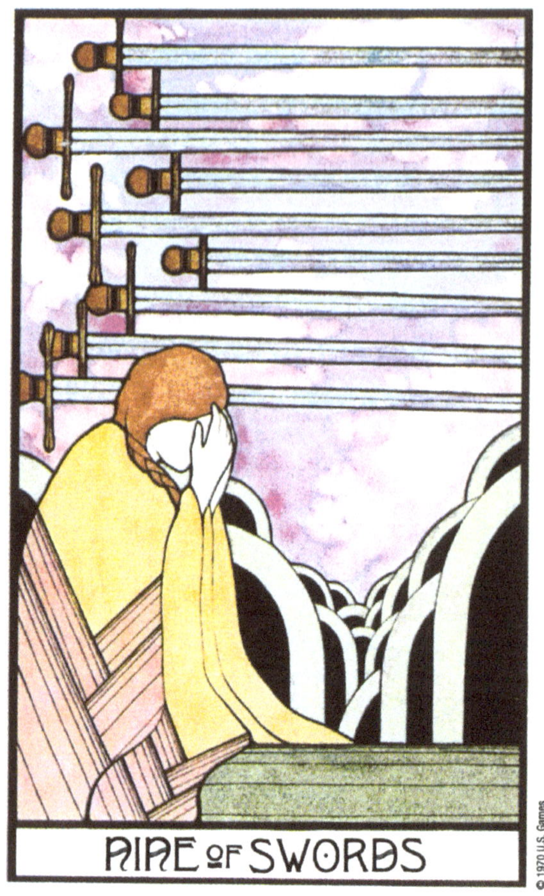

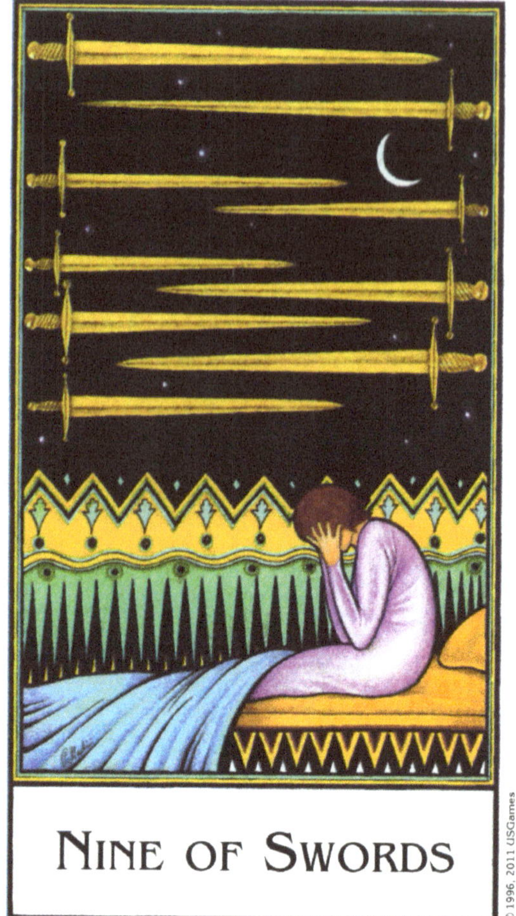

The two figures are weeping. Death, despair, disillusionment, delay, deception, and disappointment haunt them. Even in bed at night, the memories will not allow rest. Everyone suffers.

With time, the past fades. The pain is forgotten, the lessons remain.

The *Aquarian* figures is bound by seeming mountains of her static mental and emotional energies, the same pattern seen in the Eight of Swords. The geometric pattern on her robe reinforces the crystallized thinking with which she torments herself, replaying the same self-defeating scenes in her head, day and night.

She covers her eyes, unwilling and unable to believe that anything will ever be different. The swords floating over her head seem like a cage capping the mountains, but there is a way out in the space between the two, if she has the courage to open her eyes to see it.

The *New Palladini figure* likewise covers her eyes, unable to cope with the prospect of being held captive between the swords and the mountains. Like the swords, the mountains in this image are sharp, and their motif is painted on her bed frame to add to her distress.

She has no respite, no rest, and, unlike the *Aquarian* image, she seems to have no way out.

She must reconnect with her emotional self, as depleted as it is (reflected in the waning crescent moon above her), and gather her emotional strength with the waxing moon, to find her way out of her despair.

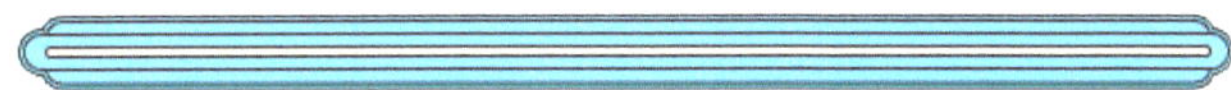

Overwhelmed by the potential for success as much as by the fear of failure, we are caught in endless worry. This card tells us to let go of self-doubt, to grow beyond prior limits. Shatter the illusions of limitation and move forward.

Self-doubt rules the day, undermining our lives. Questioning our choices and regretting our decisions prevents us from clearly seeing what is and what could be if we just believe in ourselves. We all make mistakes, we all have regrets.

We must ask ourselves which is harder to live with: regret from chances taken, or regret from chances not taken?

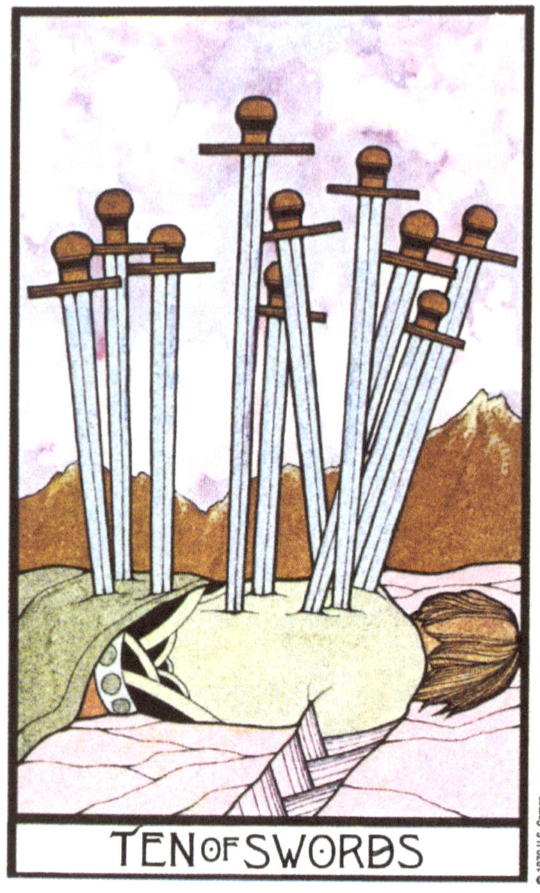

A card of suffering and affliction, but not of violent death. The Ten of Swords is a disturbing image: a man pierced by ten swords.

Each Sword brings pain, but also lessons. Sadness is necessary in order to value happiness. Tears will dry.

Our inability to manage our thoughts kills the dream, and with it, part of ourselves. The necessity of change is radical and urgent, and cannot be denied except at great personal cost. You simply cannot continue to stay stuck; things will only become worse.

We again see the curved pattern of emotional stasis on the tunic, paired with the crossed lines of stagnant thought on the sleeve.

The betrayal is unexpected, and yet inevitable. If we do not allow ourselves to grow, if we insist on remaining stuck in one thought, one viewpoint, one way of being, we sell ourselves short, and leave ourselves vulnerable to manipulation by those who seem to agree with our point of view. We become easy marks for those more clever and less scrupulous than ourselves, and thus become co-authors of our own ruin.

Some potential remains; tap into it to revive and rescue yourself. Draw upon the Magician (1) energy and be open to the surprises and unexpected events of the Universe (10) to move forward into the healing energy of the Sun (19).

A prostrate figure bleeding from ten wounds, inflicted by long, golden battle Swords. Under a starry sky with a crescent moon, the lessons of life are learned.

None of the wounds are fatal, only painful and deep—but the scars will be reminders.

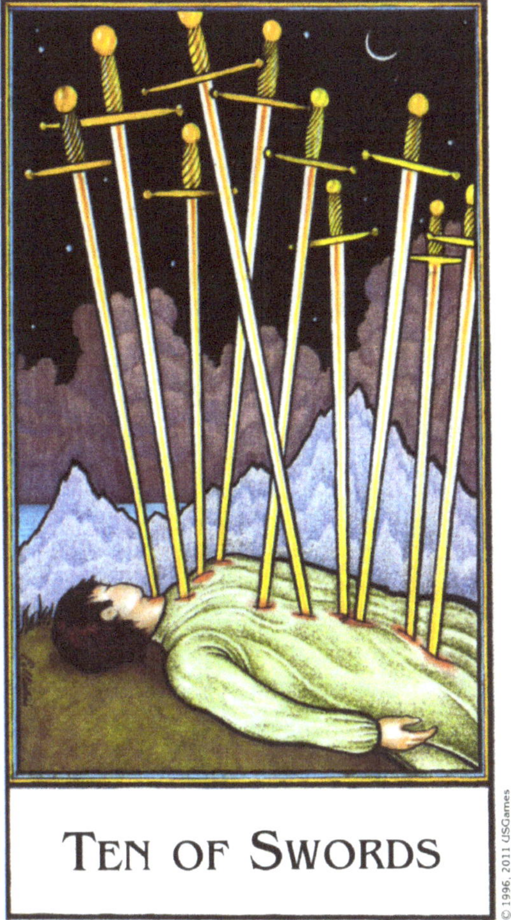

In contrast to the *Aquarian*, the figure here has been stabbed from the front. Choosing to believe what others tell us instead of listening to our own wisdom is the ultimate betrayal of self. We allow others' limiting beliefs and negative judgments to rob us of joy, of hope, and ultimately, of life.

Stop listening to the external negativity, start believing in yourself. You have wasted enough time giving others power over your life; reclaim your thoughts and reclaim your life.

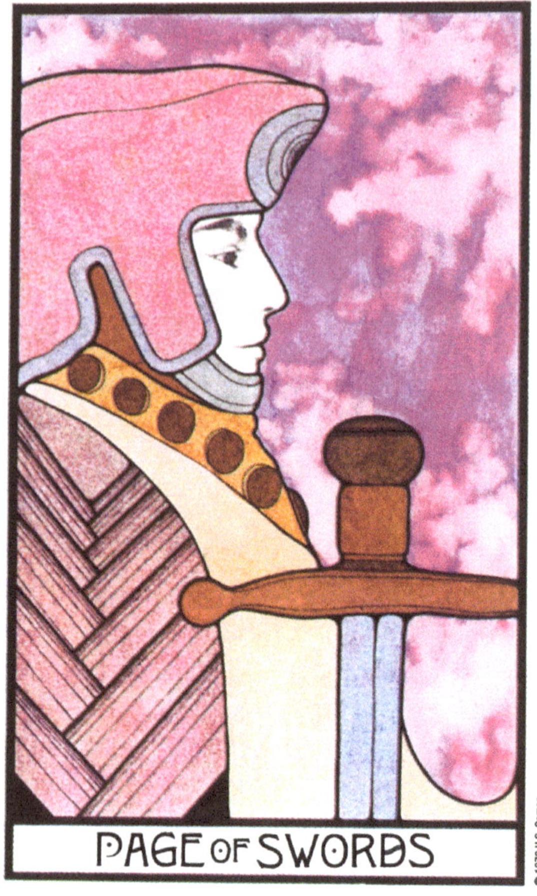

A young man who serves his Knight well. He is watchful and attentive. He aspires to be a Knight himself someday. He seems to be thinking about the future, of the day when he goes out into the world, dedicated to truth and freedom.

The geometric pattern of crystallized thinking is a carryover from the 10 of Swords. Some progress has been made, but the radical re-formation of ideas has not been completed.

As the earth element of the air suit, the Page is grounded and calm, perhaps too much so. He needs to shake off his restrictive mental patterns, shake himself out of his comfort zone, and move forward.

We must clear our heads of old ideas which are no longer valid or relevant, and discard information which is not true or useful.

Old problems require new solutions. You cannot use the same thinking that created the problem in order to solve the problem.

Repetitive thinking will only re-create the original situation and perpetuate the problem. Grasp the sword and cut the Gordian knot of tangled thoughts to create clarity and a new way forward.

A young man holds a golden sword upright in both hands. He wears his armor of golden scales. His face is still young, and his eyes are innocent. To be a Knight is a very great responsibility. He will soon have to prove himself.

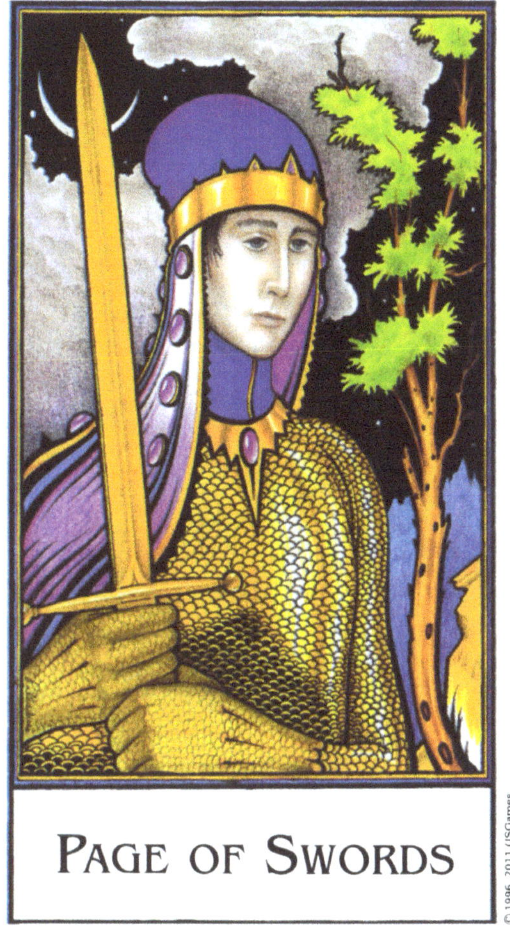

The figure from the Seven of Swords has learned the lesson and is now armored and gloved. He knows to handle the sword by the hilt.

The scales of his armor are like those we see on the High Priestess. From her, the Page learns the wisdom of self-reflection and the importance of clarity of thought. He is coming to realize that true knowledge is the most useful and versatile weapon. he learns to use this knowledge as he learns to use the sword which symbolizes it.

He serves his Knight well and with true devotion. In turn, the Knight serves his Queen and King with steadfast courage and deep loyalty. We all serve someone, we are served in turn.

The Page's growing awareness of his role in his society and his place in the cycle of life spurs him to greater service and a truer sense of self. Clear thinking helps us to see what is good; seeing what is good inspires us to be better.

Learning how to organize our thoughts is the first step; managing our thoughts, rather than allowing them to manage us, is the path to wisdom.

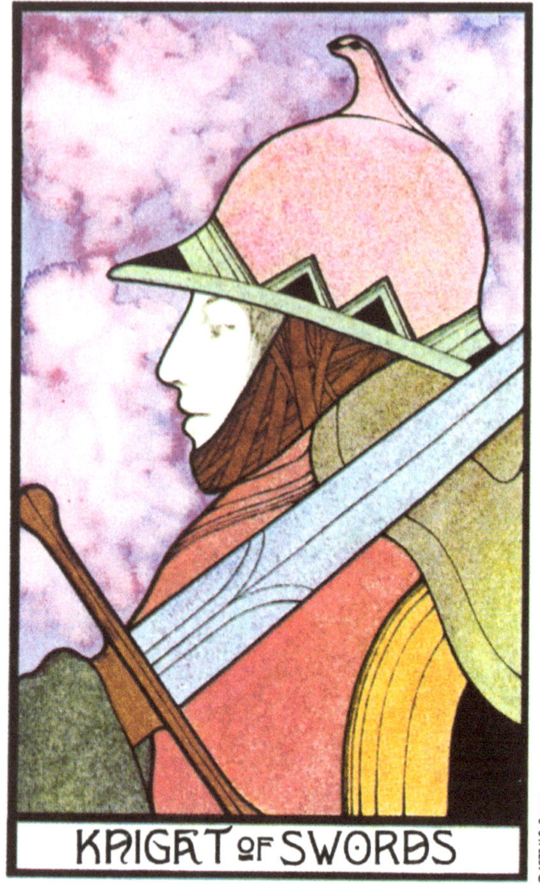

He is brave, skilled, and determined. He does not seek conflict, but if forced to, he will fight without regret.

Bringing the active energy of Fire to the contemplative energy of the Air suit, the Knight reminds us that it is not enough to create a plan; action is required to bring the plan into reality. A brilliant idea is only a concept if it is not carried out through positive action.

The geometric pattern on his helmet signifies his clear, orderly thinking and his knowledge of Life and Self. The bird shape on the helmet reinforces his connection to the air, the element of his suit.

He is served well by his Page, whom he teaches well. The Knight is thus able to serve his Queen and King well, defending the land from enemies and maintaining internal peace.

He acts from a place of calm confidence, sure of his abilities and secure in his role in the world.

The breakthrough has occurred. Unencumbered by self-doubt, fear, and negativity, you are able to move forward.

He rides a swift, silver stallion and brandishes his sword before his enemies. His armor is made of pure gold. Evil fears him, for he rides forth in the service of justice.

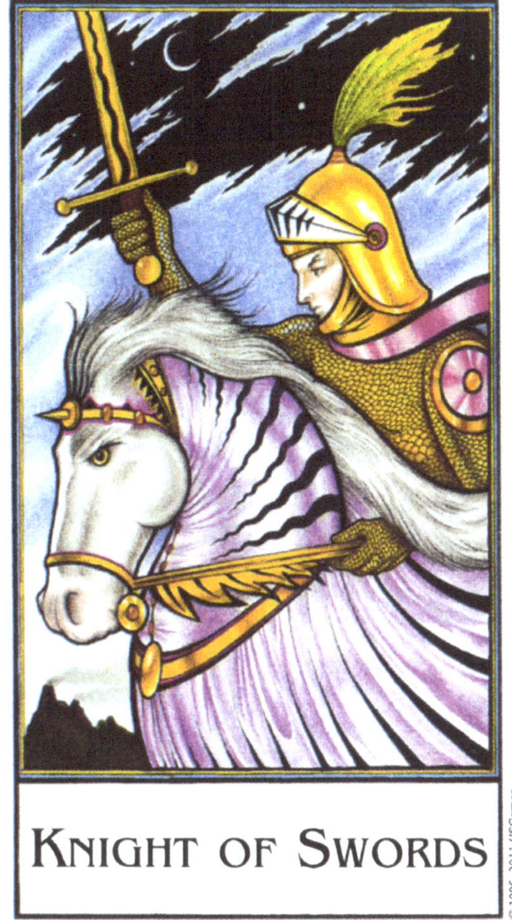

Now that we know how to organize our thoughts, we learn to direct them in order to accomplish our goals. Like the Page's service to him, the Knight's service and loyalty to his Queen and King is complete and strong.

The Knight's armor signifies the ability to manage thoughts; the sword, the ability to direct them; and the armored horse, the ability to establish and maintain boundaries and enact plans.

The more we can focus our intellect on our goals, the more likely our chance of success. Logic, order, and discipline are required to maintain order in the midst of battle, whether armed combat, or simply the day-to-day struggles of life. Our clear thinking and focused action reduce chaos and increase the likelihood of victory.

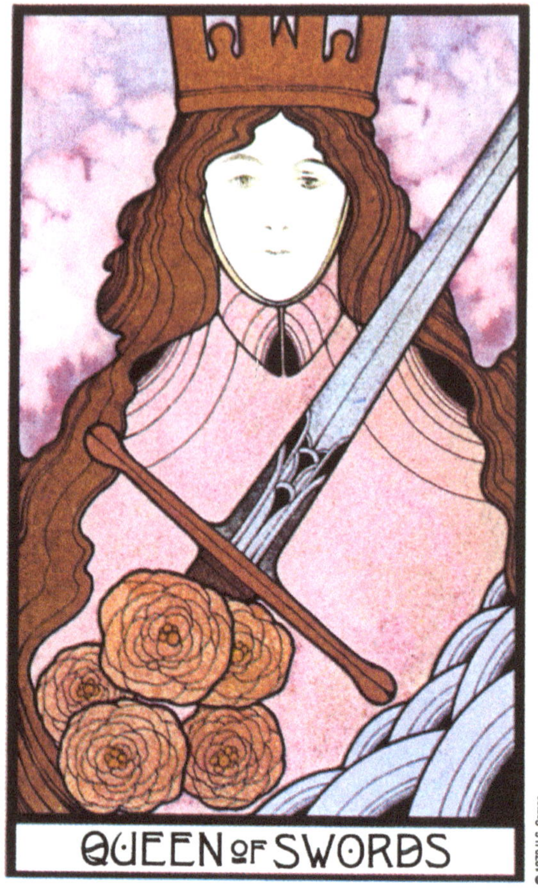

A beautiful woman wears a crown of the finest red gold. Her long dark hair flows around her. Five roses of a strange color surround the hilt of her royal Sword. She has sad eyes, for she has seen much—disappointment, disillusionment, and pain. She feels it all.

Emotional and intellectual energies are in balance. Energy moves freely, expressed in the complementary geometric and curved lines. The potential is realized, and the realization creates new potential in a self-perpetuating, virtuous cycle.

The roses, as living things from the earth, bring in the grounded energy of the suit of Pentacles to create stability. The outline of the city's towers on her crown lend further stabilizing energy to the image.

She has known pain, and pleasure; loss, and relationship; sorrow, and joy. She has experienced so much, and knows it is all part of life, and therefore she does not regret any of it. She understands the cyclical nature of life and living, and embraces it all from a place of intellectual focus and emotional groundedness.

The Water element of the Air suit, the Queen provides the emotional energy to guide the intellect in making wise decisions based on a whole approach to the situation, not simply on rational logic or limited reason. Her whole Self is awake and aware, and she lives fully through it all, regardless of what happens.

A strong, serious Queen holds her golden sword, which is encircled by a flowering vine. Her face is severe, perhaps angry. She knows too much. She has seen injustice and greed. She prepares to fight for good. Evil cannot defeat her golden sword.

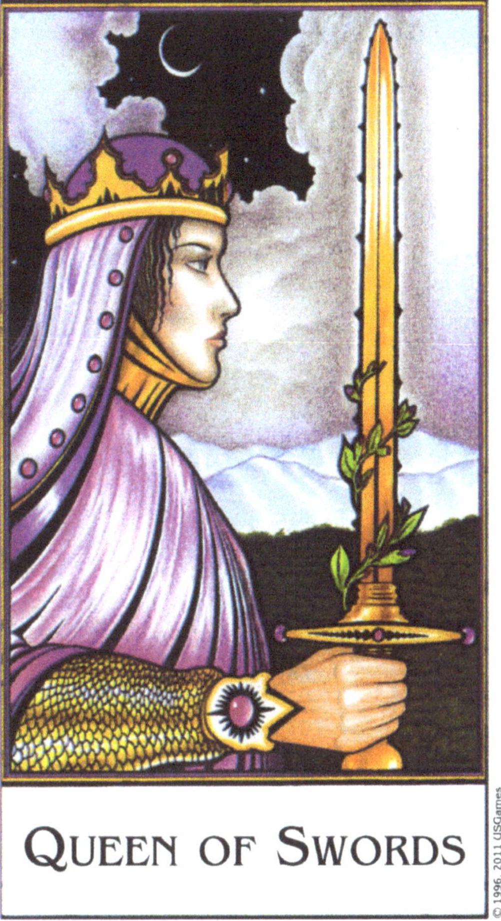

Wearing the crown of the suit, she holds the flower-entwined sword from the Ace. Her hand is bare, signifying mastery of, and unshielded contact with, her intellectual power. As the emotional anchor of the suit, the Queen embodies the ideal of emotional and intellectual balance; heart and mind work in unison to create mental and emotional honesty as the foundation of a balanced, complete life.

Like the Empress, she understands and values her connection to the natural world, symbolized by the flowers on her sword, which brings in grounding influence from the Pentacles. Like the mountains behind her, she is rooted in being, strong and resolute. She thinks, feels, and acts in accordance with her true nature.

The vine-wrapped weapon shows us that right thinking produces joy in the mind, just as right living creates joy in the heart.

The Queen, rather than the King, owns the symbols of the suit, emphasizing the necessity of the water of emotion to balance the aridity of the intellect in a mature life.

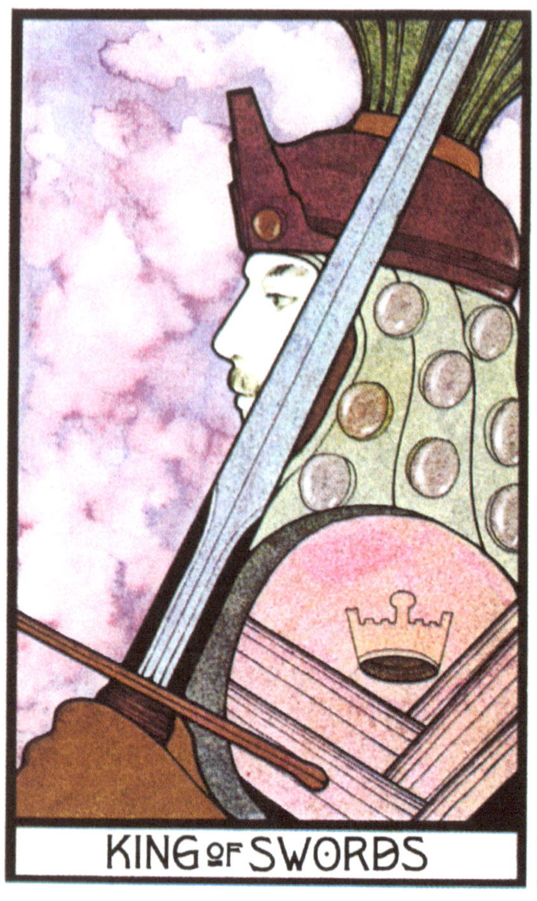

A strong, noble monarch is dressed for battle. His plumed helmet is his crown. He holds his sword. It is unadorned, simple, strong, and deadly. It is a sword of war, and ultimate victory.

As the air element in this suit of air, the King is the ultimate expression of the qualities of this suit. The orderly geometric lines on the card signify his mastery of his element, his intellect, and his Self.

All serve him with action, and he serves them with inspiration. He has learned, and through his exemplary speech and actions, teaches well what he knows.

The wisdom gained through prior experience serves as a shield to protect against repeating the same mistakes. The sword is etched with the waves of potential to indicate the new possibilities that spring from prior achievements. Move forward calmly and confidently, as does a King.

A young, crowned King holds his unsheathed sword. He is justice and virtue, and he holds the power of life and death. We see a crescent moon in the sky, a symbol of life that appears throughout this suit. In the coming hardships, the Moon will guide you.

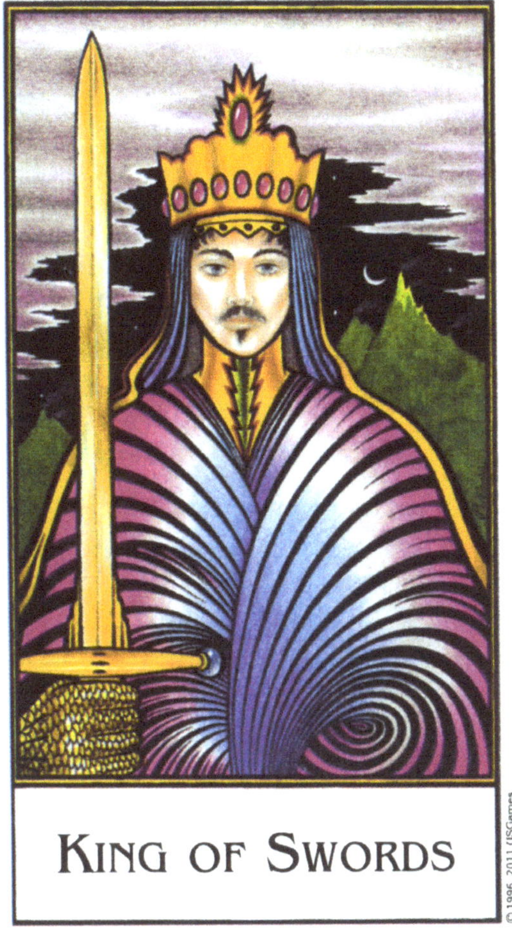

His crown is more elaborate, and his sword more simple, than those of the Queen. The glory of the intellectual life (the crown) is solid, as compared to the Queen's crown, which is open and leaves her head open to the emotional influence of the moon directly above her. The King's moon is off to the side, showing a weaker influence of the emotions on the intellect.

He, too, leads by example, with the wisdom of experience. He is also wise enough to listen to others, and to learn from them to deepen his own knowledge through indirect experience.

The intellect is a formidable defense and presence, and yet, as the Air card of the Air suit, the King requires armor and robes to anchor him. He shares the grounding Pentacles influence of forest and mountain with his Queen. Between the pair, they comprise all the natural elements and make a complete, balanced world.

Without the ability to ground and focus our intellect, all we have are ideas that are never brought to manifestation.

The Minor Arcana

The Suit of Cups

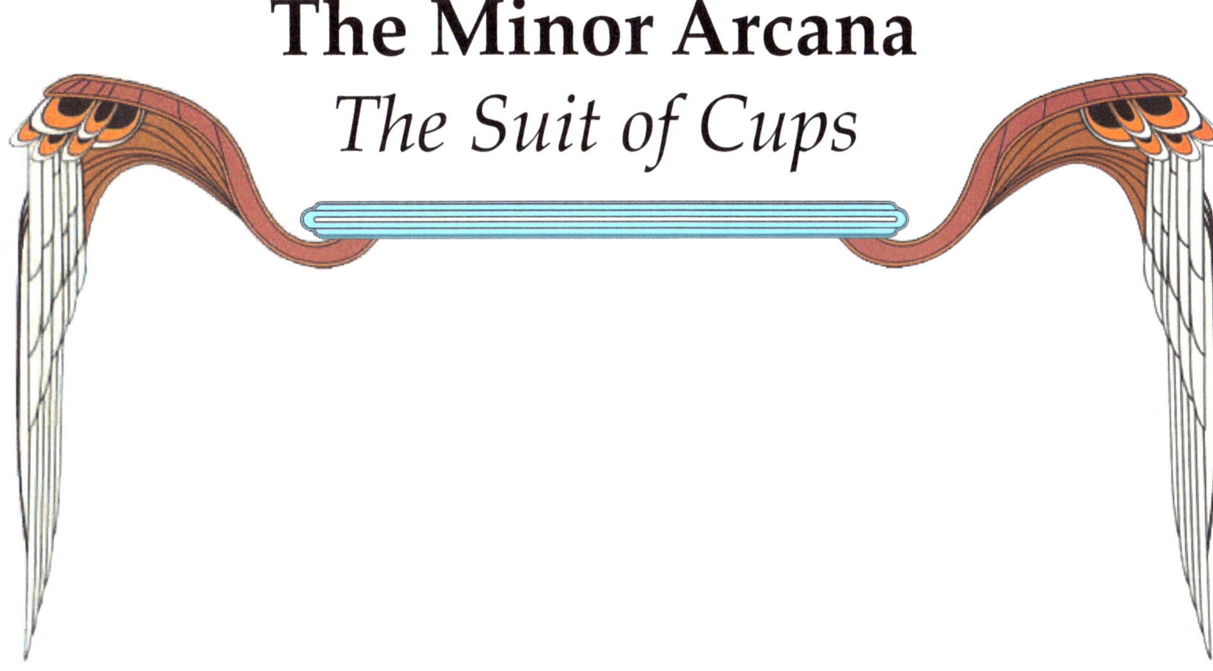

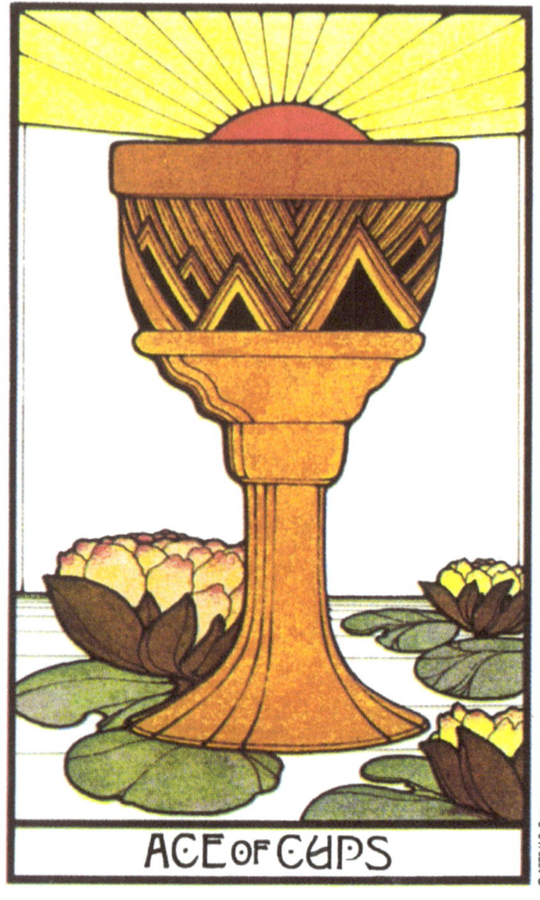

The Sun rises with a golden Cup. The Cup floats upon lotus blossoms. Fertility, abundance, tranquility, peace are all found here.

As the container of our fluid emotions, intuitions, and dreams, the Cups represent the element of water.

The *Aquarian* Ace floats amid water lilies, the sun rising from its rim. The emotional energy is contained—abundant, but nonetheless contained. The water of emotions is balanced by the open space of the sky, the intellect.

The rising sun represents the emotional energy of life. No matter what awful things may happen on any given day, the next day will bring sunrise, a new day, and a new opportunity to take action to manifest our dreams with renewed emotional energy and sense of purpose. Let your soul be your guide.

The lotus flowers show the beauty of emotional growth and fulfillment, telling us we can create such beauty in our hearts and souls, and in the hearts and souls of others through the bonds of friendship and love.

The Ace has transformed from the Aquarian Deck. The Cup is stronger and more beautiful. Its healing waters rain down onto the lotus pool. The hand of the Creator emerges from a storm cloud to hold aloft the Chalice.

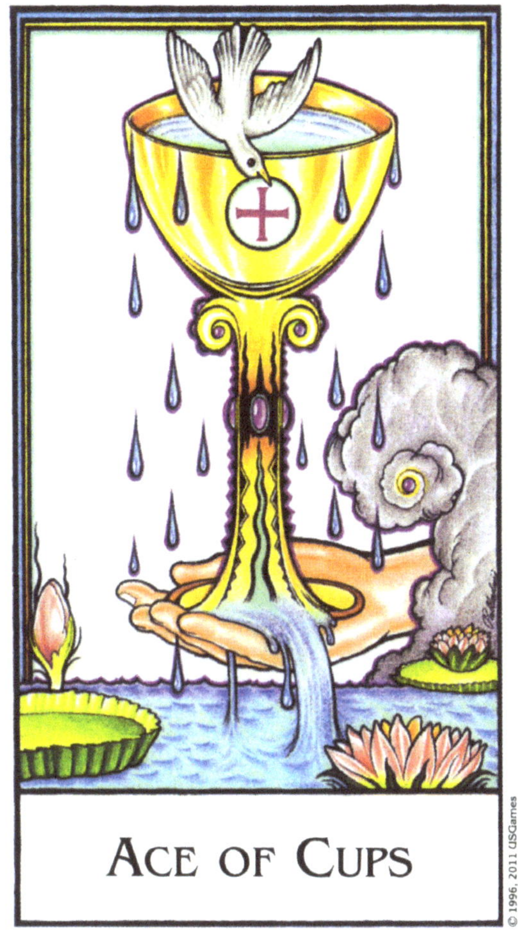

This Cup seems to rise from the water, raised by the hand in the cloud. The cup is full, drops of water fall from its rim, water pours forth from its base and returns to the lake. The emotional energy here is held but not contained—it flows in abundance, manifesting in the water lilies and lotus flowers floating on the lake.

The dove of peace brings a consecrated wafer (such as those used in Christian rites of Holy Communion), a reminder of our emotional connection to Nature and the Universe. We must draw on the power of our emotional connections with these to live fully.

As in the *Aquarian* image, the flowers remind us that inner beauty—the awareness and cultivation of our best Self—create outer beauty in all aspects of our lives. We must wholly love our own Self in order to be able to love others wholly, and, in loving them, help them learn to love as well.

Both Aces encourage us to tap into our emotional and intuitive wisdom to fully experience life and to love fully and fearlessly.

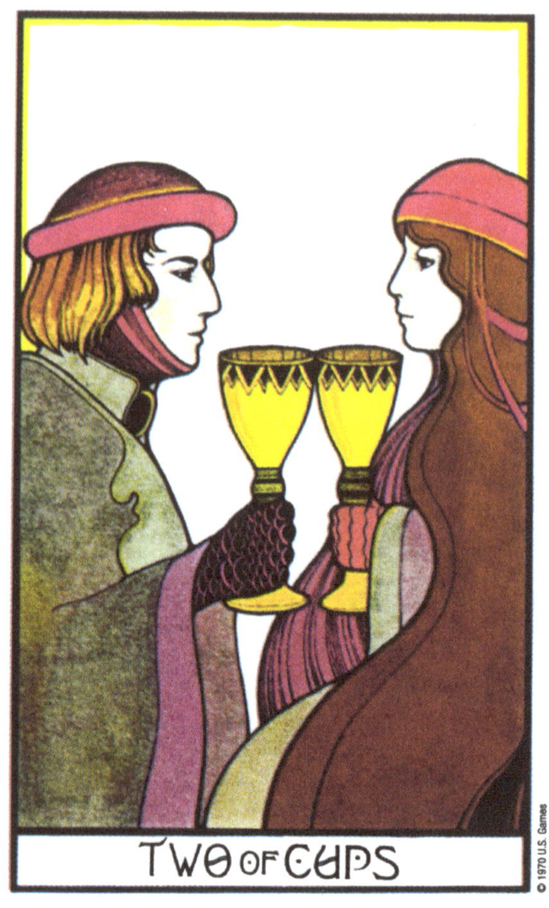

A young couple touches Cups in a toast to Love. They are joined by friendship and harmony. They respect each other and their union will be powerful. Their love is deep.

Numerologically related to the High Priestess, and symbolically linked to The Lovers, the Two of Cups is a rich read.

The reflective quality of the High Priestess has the figures in mirror to each other. Each reflects an image of the other back to that lover, while also looking to see themselves reflected back to them in their lover's eyes.

Do we like what we see of ourselves? How does our lover's image of us fit our own image? Do we feel diminished, disrespected, and unappreciated, or do we feel accepted and adored?

Does our lover see us as more than we feel we are? Do we believe we can be the person our lover thinks we are, or are we overcome with fear of failing to live up to their expectations?

How we see our loved ones, and how they see themselves, can be quite different images. An honest heart and wise soul reflect a truth the lover may not be able to accept, whether from vanity, fear, or an inability to see themselves in a positive light.

Although the cards depict what we assume is a couple in a romantic relationship, as with the Lovers card, it refers to all relationships, not just romance.

The Aquarian couple is fully clothed and even gloved, so their only contact is through their eyes, their words, and their cups. The must see clearly and speak the truth lovingly from within their wrappings.

A youth and maiden are pledging each other, and they wear purple and gold wreaths of victory on their heads. Above their Cups rises the Caduceus of Hermes. Two snakes intertwine between the wings. Above is the head of a lion. The Caduceus is the staff of the herald who proclaims the victory of love over all things.

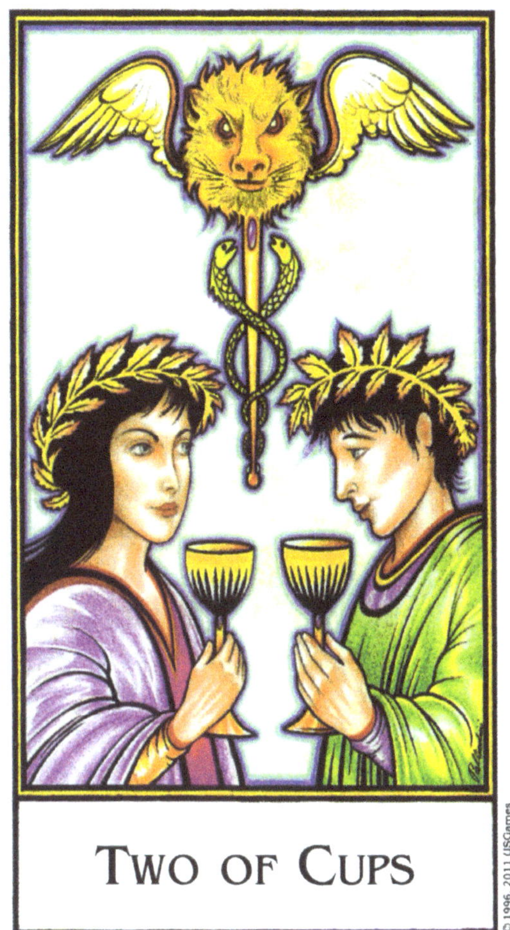

This couple is more open to each other visually, although they have no direct physical contact. They stand apart, their cups do not touch. The man looks at the woman, the woman looks up and to the side. She reflects not only his self back to him, but also reflects the world back to him.

The card also asks us to look at ourselves and our roles in all of our relationships. We may be a strong leader at work, and defer completely to our partner at home. We cannot define ourselves by one role, one relationship, one person's view of us.

It is important to see yourself clearly with your own eyes, and to see the world on your own terms, not just as a reflection of someone else's experience. Seeing through the eyes of others teaches us empathy and allows us to experience the world in new ways. We must also experience the world directly for ourselves in order to be a whole person in relationship, not half of a person who is incomplete without the other.

The winged, lion-headed caduceus reminds us of the healing power of love. We heal others by loving them, and heal ourselves as well by living a life based in love.

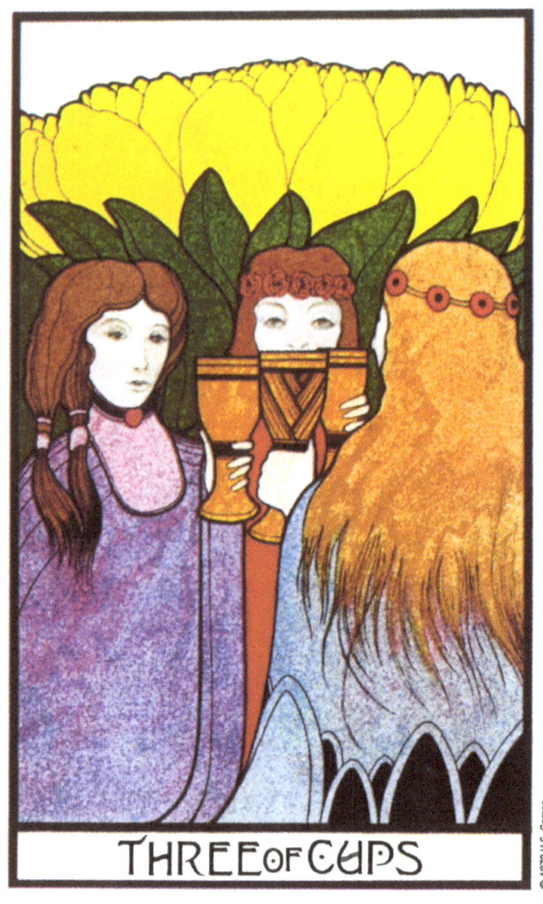

Three young maidens touch their Cups together in a toast to Life. They are celebrating joy, fulfillment, and love. A huge gold lotus blooms behind them, each petal of life unfolding, revealing the glorious gifts within.

Tapping into the Empress's capacity for creativity and joy, these cards show us scenes of shared celebration.

The women seem to be celebrating, although the expressions on the faces we can see are fairly neutral. They raise their cups in a toast with the third woman. The scene is dominated by a bright yellow flower, a physical manifestation of sunlight, which indicates a time of joy.

Many people consider youth as a happier time than adulthood, because youth is seen as a time of fewer responsibilities and more options. However, if we are honest, we know that we can be just as happy—or even happier—as we move through our adult lives. While adults have more responsibilities than children, we also have more freedom to choose how and where we live, who we love, and what we do with our time.

In adulthood, we learn to better cope with sorrows and setbacks, and we learn to take great joy in small things as well as major events. As adults, we understand that each day is a gift of 24 precious hours to live, learn, love, and revel in the wonders of the life we share with our family and friends—a gift that we know we will not receive forever.

The future is uncertain. We make the most of today, and share our blessings with all around us with an open heart and a joyful spirit.

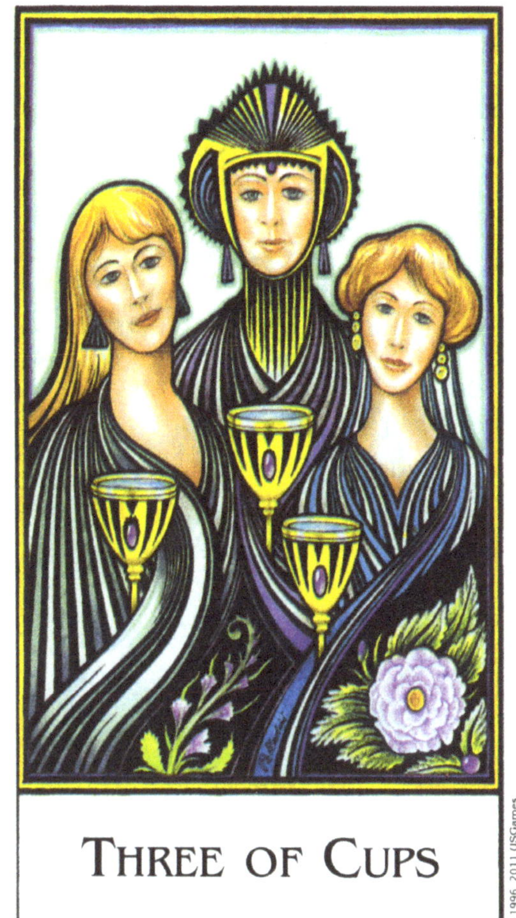

Three mature women look intently at us. In the folds of their flowing garments are three magic Cups, filled with the waters of Life. They are asking us: Are you happy? Are you fulfilled? They offer the healing waters of happiness to us.

Drink from the Cups!

The women here are clearly relaxed and joyful. As mother, daughter, and granddaughter, they also represent the phases of a woman's life, and the concept of the Triple Goddess—Maiden, Mother, and Crone. Their robes are the same woven pattern in different colors, underscoring their connectedness and similarities while expressing their individual personalities.

The blooming flowers echo the creative energy of the Empress, which the women channel in their lives. Like the Empress, this card speaks of female power and creativity; not just fertility and childbearing, but generativity of all kinds, creation and manifestation in its infinite variety.

Their appreciation of life and their joy in living is not overshadowed by their times of sorrow, pain, and loss. They have learned from those experiences, and the lessons have given them a richer connection to love and joy. Each woman knows in a deep way what is truly important for her, here and now, and each woman makes the most of each day to create a better life tomorrow.

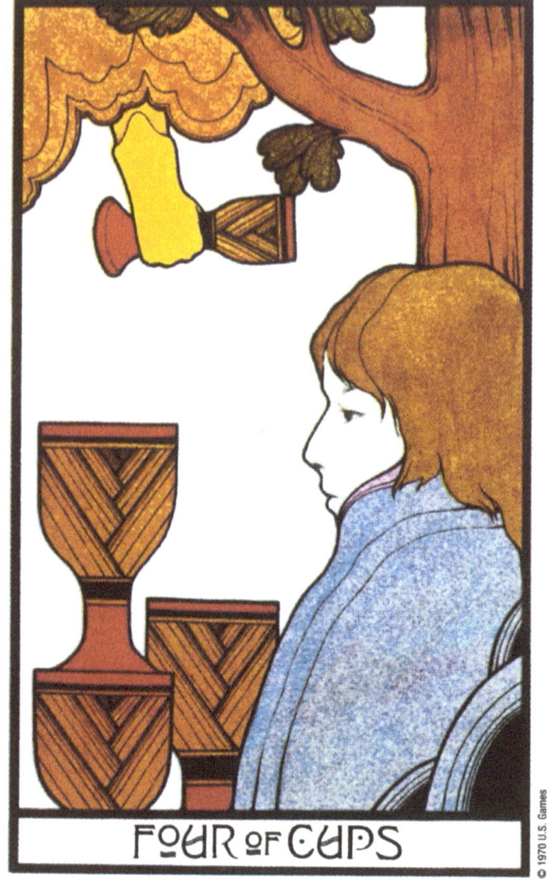

She is thinking. She knows it is time for a change. A gloved hand emerges from a cloud above, holding an empty Cup. There are still three Cups filled with many future things. Yes, it is time for change. Life is short.

Where the 3 of Cups reflects the emotion of the Empress, the Four expresses the energy of the Emperor. The Four typically carries a sense of completion, but both of these cards emphasize the lack of fulfillment one might expect an Emperor to experience once he has conquered his empire and there are no new lands to acquire.

The *Aquarian* figure stares ahead, perhaps at the three cups stacked in front of her. She wishes for a fourth, that is, for completion and fulfillment, but does not see the gloved hand from the sky offering the cup.

She needs to look up, to see beyond the immediate moment, to look outside the present circumstance. She is stuck and unable to make use of the opportunity until she allows herself to recognize the opportunity.

The cup is empty because the recipient must choose how to fill it, just as we must choose how we fill our days and our lives.

Each day carries a certain amount of tedious but necessary tasks, such as laundry and paperwork. Each day carries a certain number of tedious and useless activities, such as waiting in line or sitting in traffic. The more efficiently we can deal with those things, the more time we have to fill with things we willingly choose.

Do we choose something pleasant, refreshing, and fulfilling, or do we choose whatever is easy and quick?

We can fill our days with joy, friendship, and rewarding activities, or we can fill them with worry, self-created problems, and pointless activities.

What do you choose to fill the Cup of your life?

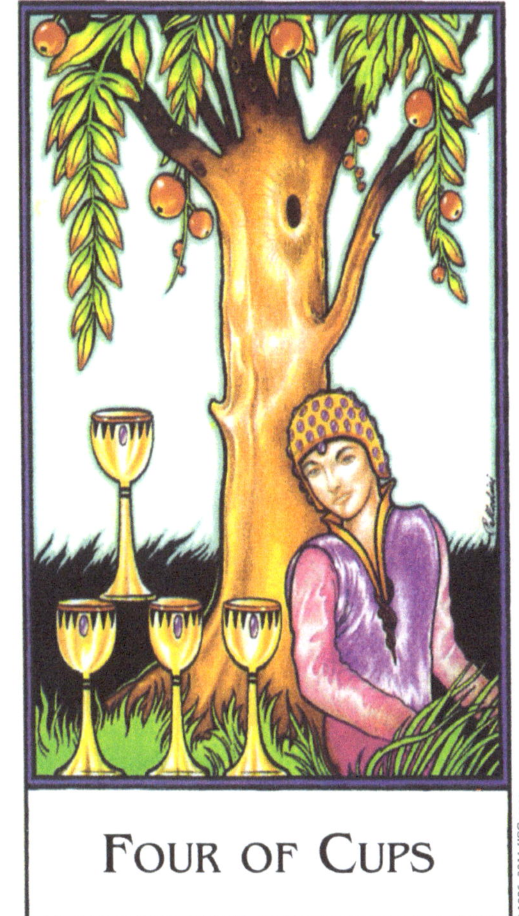

An androgynous figure sits beneath a fruiting tree and contemplates four bejeweled golden Cups. The figure wears an expression of confusion, and, perhaps, discontent. If a change is made, other things must change too. All life is interconnected.

Change must come. Choose wisely.

The four cups are arranged in such a way as to indicate that a fifth cup is missing. The figure stares at them, aware of the missing cup, but continues to sit under the apple tree rather than seek the cup. Change is required, but the person seems unable or unwilling to contemplate the change.

Sometimes, change is easy. We know what to do, we take action, and everything comes together just as planned.

Other times, we have difficulty deciding what the right thing is, or the best option is. Or, we know what we need to do about one thing, but we are uncertain about how to handle the other aspects the change will bring.

We may feel so overwhelmed by the idea of changing everything that we become paralyzed by the thought, and do nothing.

You have four cups. You have what you need to find the fifth cup. Stop thinking and take action to achieve what is truly important.

Both images speak to us of the need for awareness—awareness of what we feel is missing, and awareness of how to fill that need. Whether it is being handed to us, or whether we must actively seek the fifth Cup, our fulfillment and completion of our lives is our own responsibility.

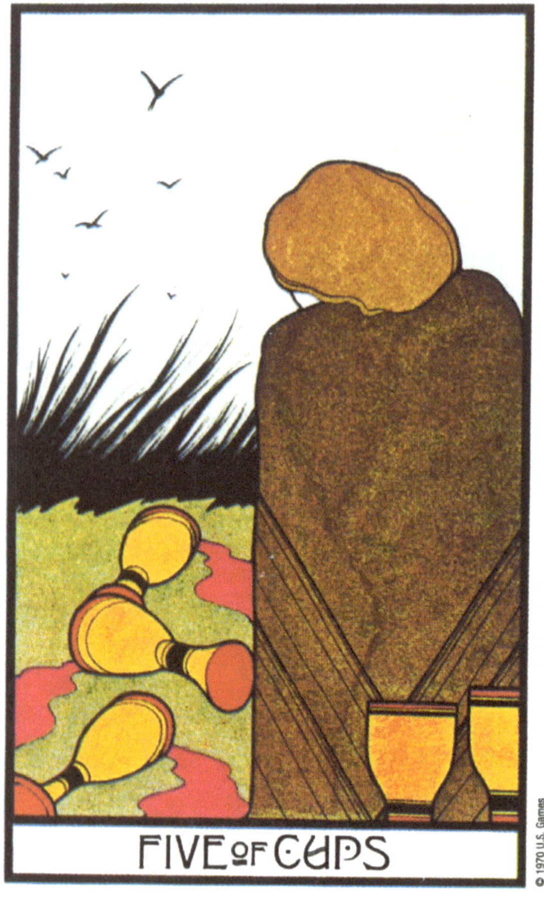

This is the card of loss, but something remains. A loved one dies, but we hold on to the memories. We lose our innocence, but we gain wisdom. The cloaked figure stares at three fallen Cups. Blood flows from them: the blood of hard work, the pain of love, the bitter disappointments and harsh realities of human life.

Two Cups remain standing and filled. Life goes on. New love awaits.

Both images tie directly to the RWS version of the card. A cloaked figure stands looking at three goblets which have been knocked over and emptied of their contents. Two goblets remain upright behind the figure.

The cards speak of sadness for what has been lost, regrets for missed or misused opportunities. While it is important to acknowledge and mourn our losses, we must have the emotional discipline (learned from the Hierophant, who shares this number) to move on from the situation once we have healed.

This card is also tied numerologically to Temperance (14 = 1 + 4 = 5). Temperance is needed her, to regain our emotional equilibrium and to return to our center. We must process the pain of the experience and temper it to become emotional wisdom.

The figure clothed in purple feels the pain of great loss. He is in a harsh, thorny place. A golden tower stands high upon a rocky crag. Two jeweled Cups stand behind him. They are filled with life waiting to be lived. Lost material things can be replaced. The spirit lives on after death.

Pain leads to introspection, and loss makes us value all the more the things we still have.

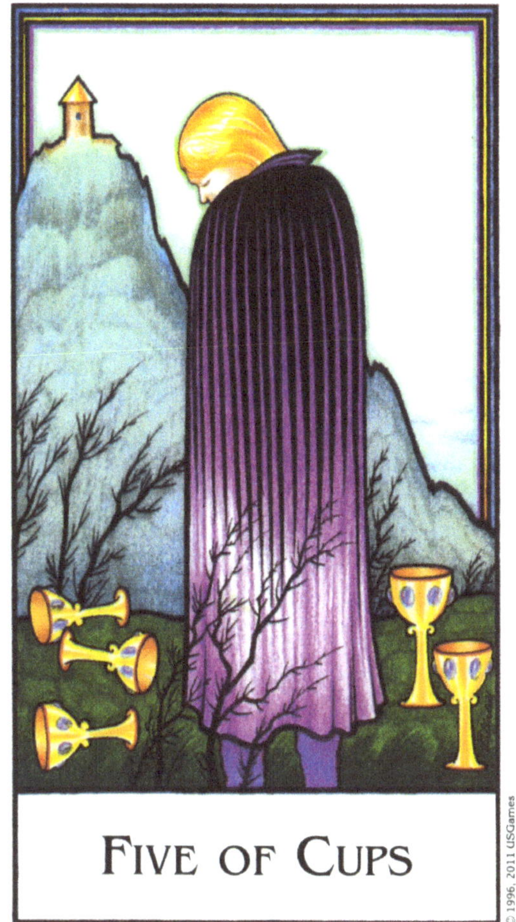

The image reminds us to open up, to see things from a wider perspective instead of staying wrapped in our misery. Yes, three cups are empty, but they are not broken; they can be refilled.

As with the Four of Cups, we must make choices about how we fill the cups, and how we fill ourselves emotionally.

We cannot change what happened, or what did not happen. We cannot change what we did or did not do. The wine is spilled, the time has passed, the loss has occurred.

We can learn the lessons of loss and move on. We do not know what will happen when we move on, but we can be certain that nothing will happen as long as we allow ourselves to remain stuck where we are.

The figures also have two cups remaining—reserves and unused resources—to sustain them. Whether the figures are prudently guarding their reserves, or blindly refusing to shift focus to see them, is in the eye of the beholder and varies depending on the question, the client, and the other cards in the spread.

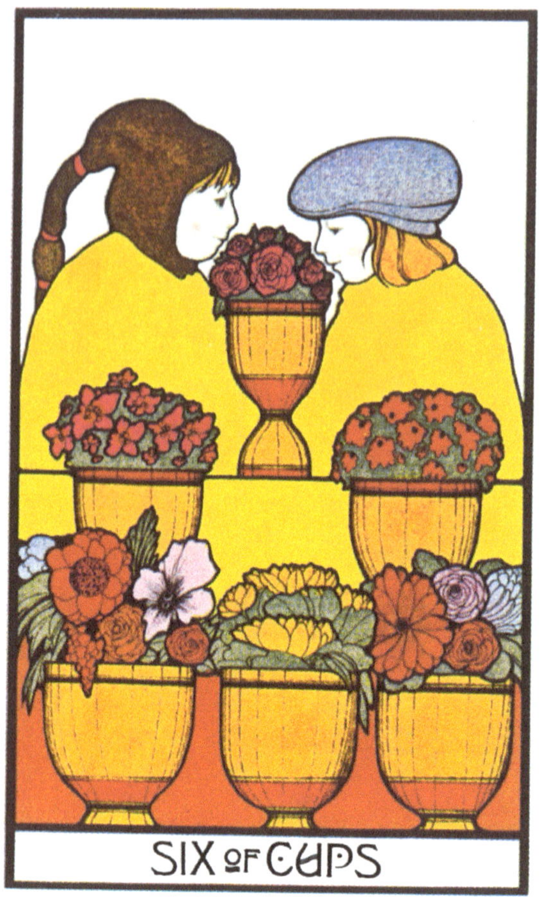

The constant renewal of Nature, the renewal of all things. The flowers bloom, go to seed, and then re-bloom. Two young children smell the floral perfume, and gaze into the heart of the blossoms. There, hidden, lie the male and female parts by which the blooms will procreate and carry on Life.

We can easily see how the *Aquarian* image ties to the Lovers card (its numerological reflection). Two children of unspecified gender converse as they enjoy the abundance of flowers. A card of sharing what is good, of appreciating the pleasure of the shared moment, makes this a card of pleasant emotions, associations, and memories.

Connected numerologically with the Devil as well, the card can carry a darker meaning when it is surrounded by other challenging cards.

Remaining stuck in memories prevents us from living fully in the current moment, and keeps us from participating fully in our present life.

Happy memories can help us through difficult times, but excessive nostalgia simply provides an unhealthy escape from the present if we do not exercise some Lovers balance in our feelings and thoughts. Let the happy memories sustain you, not detain you, as you walk your path.

Abundance and fertility spring from the jeweled Cups, Nature in full glory. Irrepressible Nature is bursting forth. The energy flows on forever.

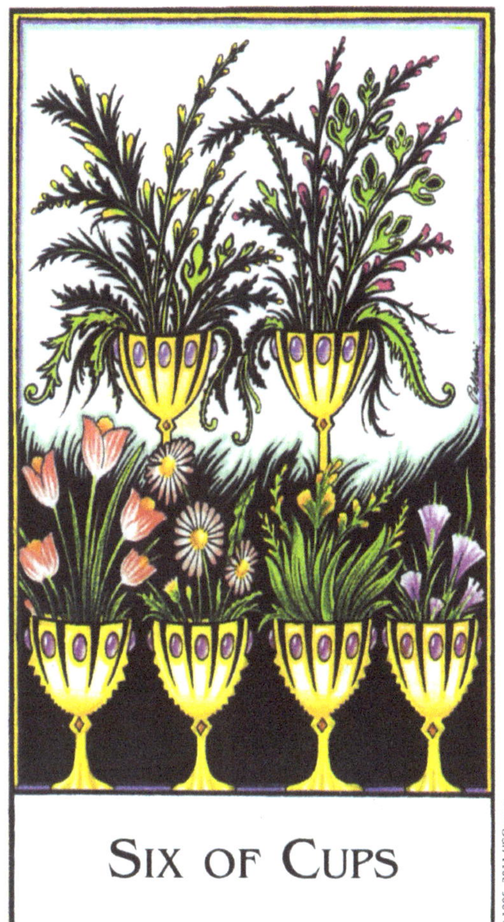

This image is more abstract, and does not have any people in it. We are presented with six goblets filled with lush blooms and greenery. If we think of the Lovers, we might consider this a manifestation of loving energy. The loving care lavished on the flowers by the gardener is made manifest in the rich variety and luxurious growth of the plants.

This card, too, carries a caution. While many plants are beneficial, some of the prettiest ones are also dangerous to our health. Belladonna, which means "beautiful lady", is enticing, and has some beneficial uses. It also known as Deadly Nightshade, and is quite poisonous.

Some are helpful in small doses, or from certain parts of the plant, but larger amounts, or the wrong part of the plant, can be toxic. Foxglove contains digitalis. A little can help regulate an erratic heartbeat; too much brings death.

We must make informed choices and understand what we are choosing. We choose wisely, and put forth our best efforts to have it turn out well.

When we love fully and devote ourselves with an open heart, beautiful changes are possible. Our joy increases when we share it with another loving heart; love creates joy, joy creates love, a happily self-sustaining cycle of sharing and fulfillment.

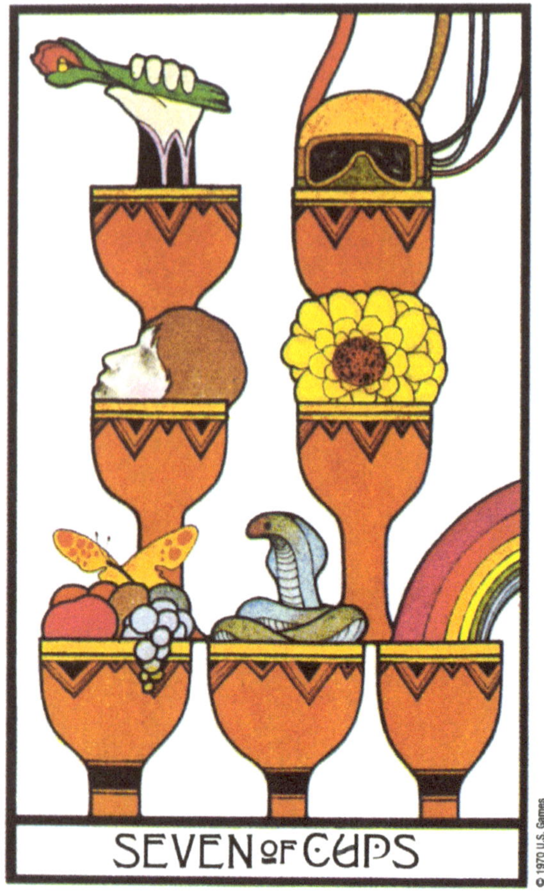

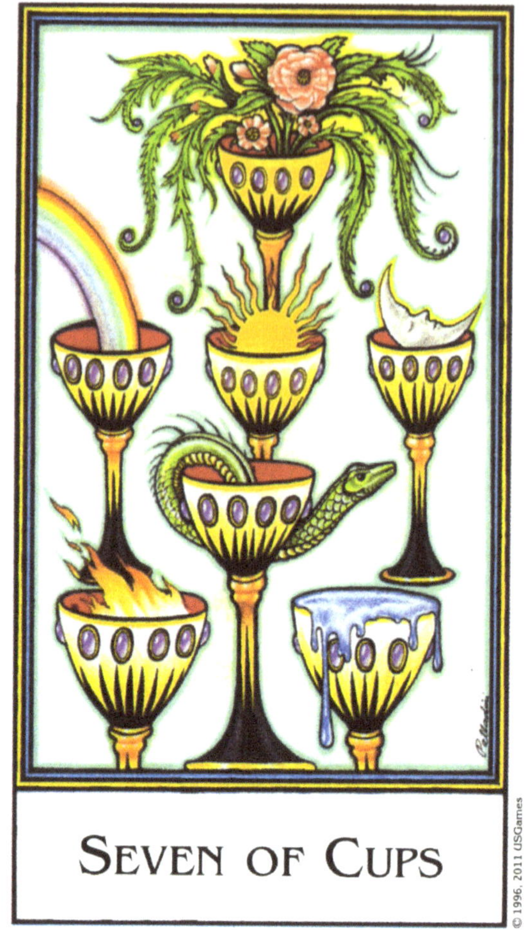

The seven Cups hold all the elements of Life: Earth, Air, Fire, Water, nature, the sun and the moon, evil and danger, man, and technology. Abundance and variety are all-important. This is a card of plenty and hope, and the full scope of the human experience.

From the simple pleasures of the 6 of Cups we move to the complex and contradictory emotions of this card. When we remember that this card links to the Chariot and its ambitious energy, we are able to access its meaning more directly.

Both decks depict seven cups containing a variety of objects, most of which are not typically found in a cup.

The specific meanings of the objects will differ depending on who is doing the looking.

The rose may symbolize love, or may be seen as a goal which stirs great passion.

The diving helmet could be taken as a possible career probing the depths of the sea as an oceanographer, or the depths of the human soul as a psychologist.

Perhaps the snake is an invitation to wisdom, or is a warning against unwise actions.

The rainbow is a promise of success, or a warning that we are chasing an impossible dream.

Do we need fire to inspire? Water to cool overheated passions?

Each symbol can be read as an encouragement, a warning, or a suggestion.

More important than any one meaning for each object is the overall message: We all have desires, we all have ambitions, and we all experience conflict about this. We judge ourselves for wanting something that no one else values, or for not wanting what everyone else wants.

We judge ourselves for being too ambitious, or not ambitious enough. We are rarely comfortable with ambition. To manage our discomfort, we may dilute our ambitions so much they cease to carry meaning for us, or give into them in the extreme and sacrifice important parts of ourselves and our lives to achieve inflated and inauthentic goals.

The cards requires us to balance the “go for it!” energy of the Chariot (7) with the “be careful out there!” energy of the Tower (16 = 1 + 6 = 7). Over-confidence and over-caution are the two extremes, and we must find the right combination of capability and possibility to aim towards success.

Applying the lesson of the Chariot, we are encouraged to be honest with ourselves about our goals and wishes, and to focus the energy of our desires to their positive accomplishment.

Dare, decide, and do!

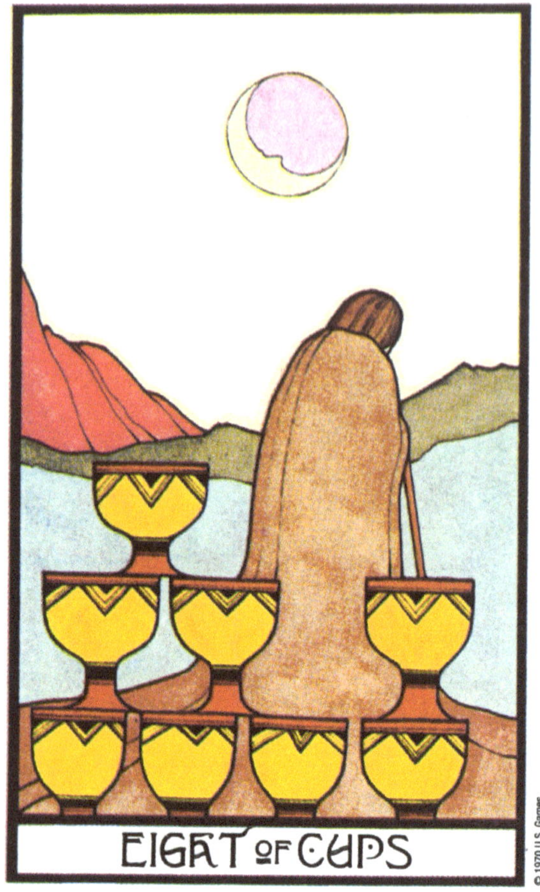

A sad man leans on his cane. He has turned away from his golden Cups. Perhaps he has rejected what they contain, or perhaps they are empty.

The cups are stacked unevenly and are off balance. Similarly, the man in the card is emotionally off balance, and adjustments are needed in both the arrangement of the cups and the arrangement of his life to restore his emotional balance.

By moving the far right cup into place, the empty space in the middle row is filled and balance is restored to that row. Doing so also creates a space for the ninth cup to be added to the top row, which then creates a space for a tenth cup at the top to complete the pyramid.

The ninth cup must be found, filled, and positioned with care, reflecting the man's emotional challenges. Perhaps he needs to heal from something in his family history, or recover from a broken heart, or simply realizes he has outgrown his current situation and needs to move on to a place where he can grow into wholeness.

Whether the viewer feels the man will be able to tap into the hope and the healing energies of the Star (17 = 1 + 7 = 8) to give him the emotional strength (Strength card = 8) to locate the missing cup and to repair his emotional being will say much about the viewer's own emotional state.

We must figure out what the missing cup represents, and then figure out how to create that missing piece to restore ourselves to emotional wholeness. The journey may take longer than we want, and take us unexpected places, but we have Strength and the Star to sustain us we heal and grow into brighter and better versions of our Self.

A dejected man walks toward the sea. He has left his jeweled Cups behind. A full moon lights the man's way. Behind the mountains, a huge storm approaches; now, he must prepare.

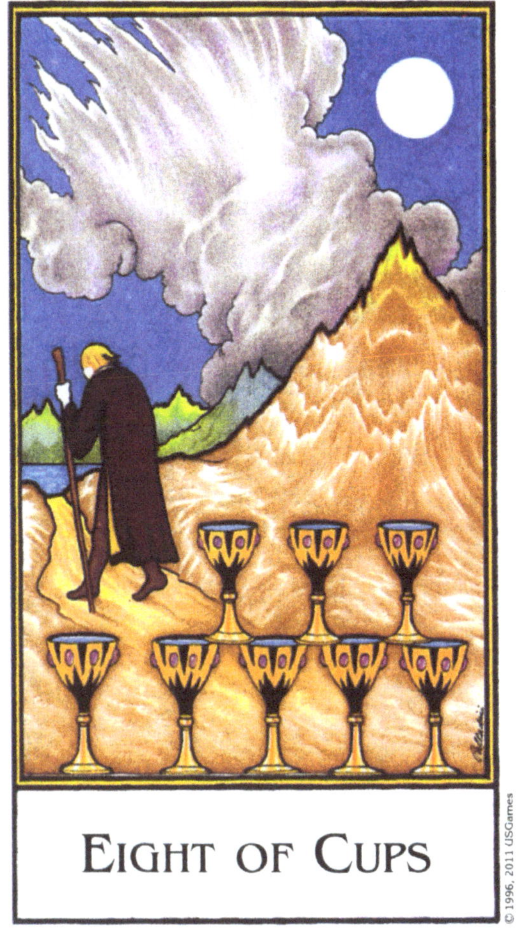

As with the *New Palladini* 5 of Cups, this card shows an orderly arrangement of cups with space for an additional, missing cup needed to complete the pattern. The image carries a feeling that the person in the *New Palladini* 5 has managed to pull his emotions together, restore a sense of self, and experience real emotional growth.

Having reached a certain level of emotional strength (an echo of the Strength card), the man is now able to see what is missing. Knowing it will not be found in the present circumstance, the person sets forth to find the missing element. Whether a continued internal exploration of emotional growth, or an external quest carried over from the Chariot energy of the 7, the character has the resources to undertake the search with a realistic chance of success. He is aided by the hope in the Star card, and inspired by its promise of healing and peace after this time of emptiness and uncertainty.

We can rely on the energies of both the Strength and the Star cards to provide the focus and inspiration to recognize what we need to do, and to take the required actions with calm confidence.

The card clearly tells us that our current situation requires emotional maturity to see things as they are, and encourages us to take positive action to make necessary changes and move forward towards wholeness and peace.

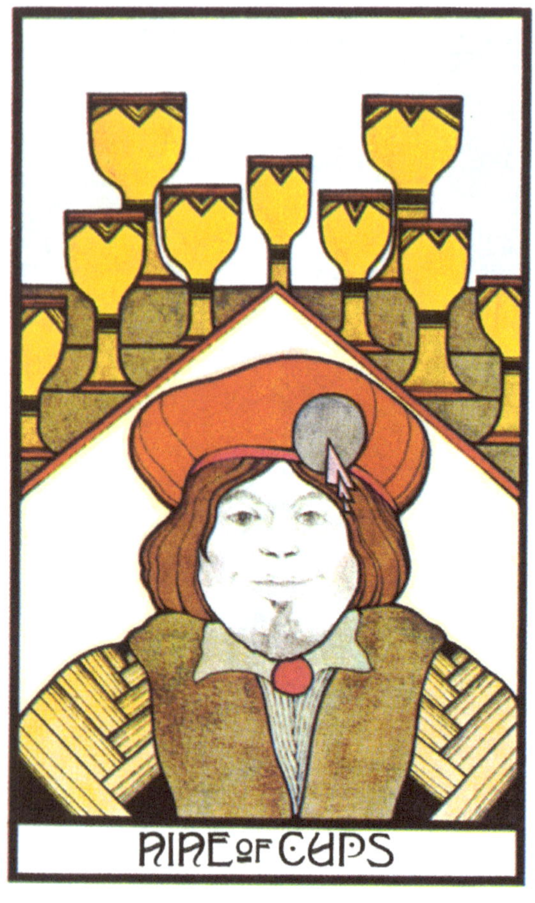

We see a happy man. He has everything he needs spiritually, materially, and physically. The Cups provide all he requires. They contain all the riches of life.

Success! The missing Cup has been found; the missing element of our emotional satisfaction has become part of our lives. We experience contentment, a sense of comfort and well-being which allows us to experience the abundance of life on all levels.

We have learned enough about ourselves from the emotional aspect of the Hermit (9), and worked through the doubts and ambiguities of the Moon (18 = 1 + 8 = 9) to have become fully aware of our true emotional gifts and strengths, and to recognize our roles in the web of family, friends, and community. Healed and whole after our quest, we joyfully fulfill our roles and responsibilities.

As with the Six of Cups, the energy creates a self-perpetuating positive cycle of emotional energy.

We have enough—joy, love, fulfillment, wonder—to enjoy for ourselves, and to share with others. We enjoy our own satisfaction, and sharing our emotional and material abundance with others allows us to take pleasure in their joy and contentment as well.

A man who loves to eat is surrounded by a feast. Nine golden goblets of wine are behind him. His smile is pure happiness and satisfaction. He has succeeded, and is content.

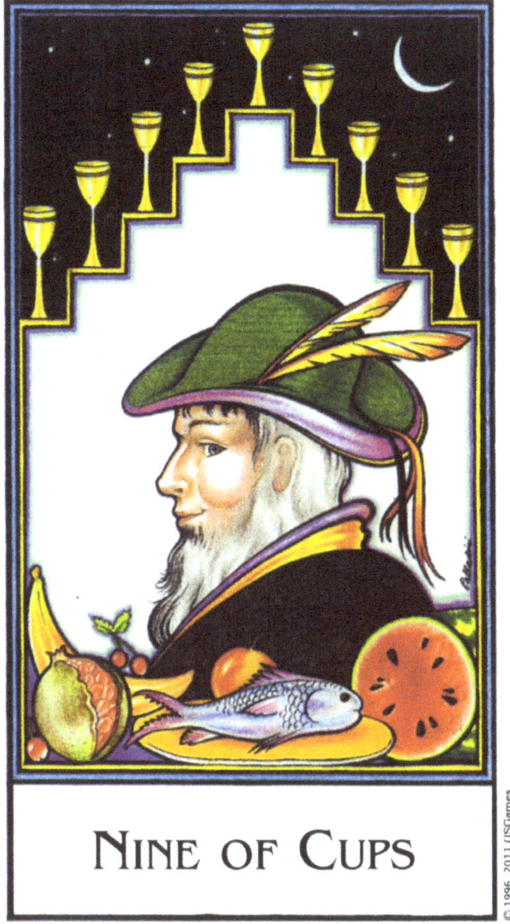

We have learned the lesson of joy from the Hermit, and now endeavor to pass the lesson to others. We are ready and able to share with those around us; what remains to be seen is whether they are ready and able to accept what we offer, and whether we can trust in our good fortune to be able to enjoy it and share it.

The shadowy influence of the Moon (18 = 1 + 8 = 9) is reinforced by the crescent moon on this card. There may be shadows of fear and doubt which threaten to diminish our joy. Perhaps we secretly fear losing our abundance, or we feel undeserving of our blessings.

These shadows of worry and doubt undermine our contentment, and prevent us from truly enjoying our emotional and material good fortune. In extreme, these feelings will take us back to a Four of Pentacles situation as shown in the *Aquarian* deck, unable to enjoy what we have earned, and hoarding our wealth for fear of losing it.

We have worked hard to earn this reward, so we can remind ourselves of this as reassurance that we are capable of maintaining and building upon our work. We can likewise feel reassured that we deserve no less than full enjoyment of what we have created, whether our creation is a solid financial foundation for our family, or a strong support network of friends to give us a sense of belonging and security.

We can choose to focus on the positive and the possible, and enjoy the life we have created.

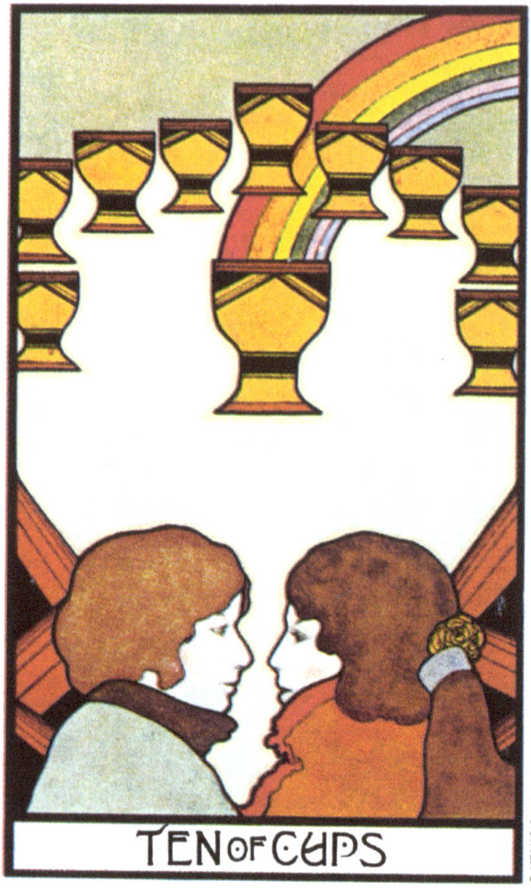

True love is crowned by a rainbow. All the full Cups of life await.

Love is the answer.

This is the "happily ever after" card. The 10 completes the numerical cycle of the suit; we have progressed from the potential to the realization of emotional maturity and right relationship with ourselves and others.

The *Aquarian* 10 of Cups is the maturation of the Two of Cups. The couple closes the distance seen in the Two, connecting directly on the emotional level, no longer needing the symbol to create their bond.

The variety of emotional experience in their relationship, and their ability to express this experience, is reflected in the array of cups in the sky. The geometric border shows us the orderly growth and expression of emotion resulting in the rainbow above. The rainbow itself is the expression of the full range of emotional experience in life which creates each of us as the individuals we are when entering into a relationship.

Each of the Cups bears a jewel of a different color of the rainbow. The rainbow arches high over a golden castle by a lake. Happy lovers live there.

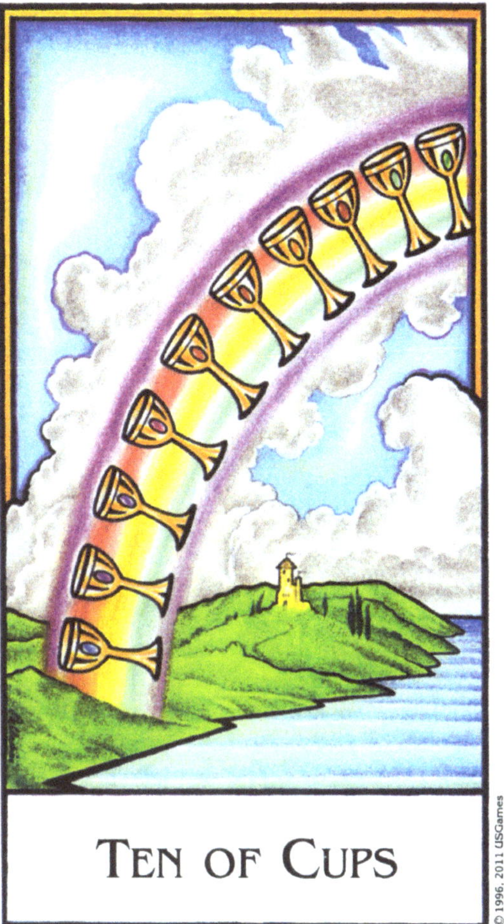

This image is more abstract. A castle sits in a green landscape next to the water; no people are depicted. We can read this card as a situation instead of a specific relationship. Whichever it is, we have reached fulfillment and are in a joyful time.

The cycle of the seasons in nature mirrors our own emotional seasons. We can use this card and the Sun (19 = 1+ 9 = 10) to give us hope when we feel caught in a dark time. Just as the darkness of winter follows the golden hues of autumn, the green and warmth of spring will follow the cold of bleak winter, both in nature and in our souls.

The rainbow goes from earth to sky and back to earth, half a cycle of the Wheel of Fortune (10). Things are looking up, things are looking good; we enjoy this period, and we also know that things can—and will—change. The rainbow appears in the sky when the Sun comes out after a rainstorm. We enjoy the rainbow and the Sun's light, knowing that the rain will come again.

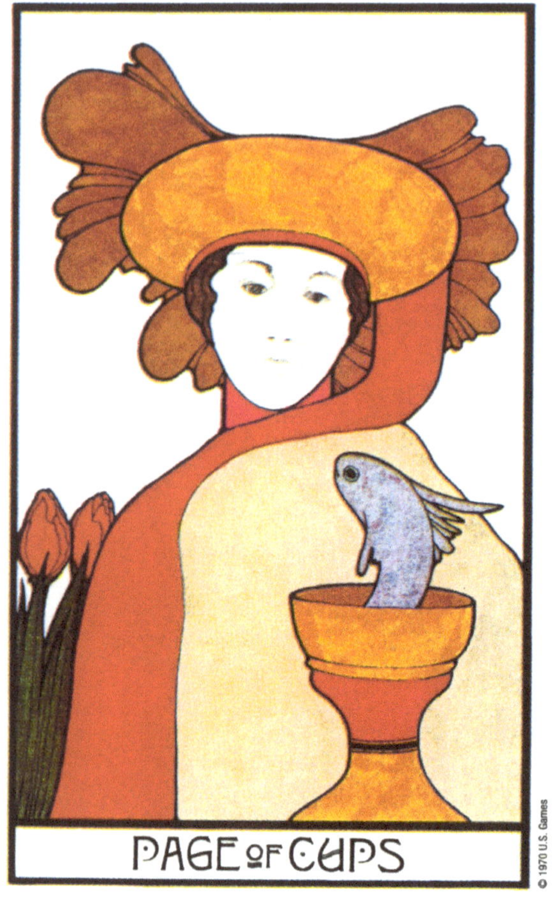

A thoughtful young person contemplates a fish emerging from a golden Cup. The waters of Life have given birth to a new creature: an expression of fertility and life.

The Page serves the Knight, preparing her for battle. Although sensitive, strength and loyalty are the most notable attributes of the Page.

Both Pages look intently at their Cups, from which rises a fish. The Pages seem unsurprised, as though a fish in one's goblet is an everyday occurrence—which, for the emotionally aware individual, it is, at least on the symbolic level.

The fish is our emotional wisdom, our intuitive voice, the watery part of our subconscious that rises to the surface in the form of advice, insight, and, when needed, warning. Listen to the fish—the fish *knows*.

The *Aquarian* page has two red roses of desire, grown but not yet in bloom, suggestive of her growing emotional awareness—growing strong, but not yet fully developed. The potential is becoming manifest, but more emotional growth and self-awareness are required to become her better Self.

The young Page is listening to a fish. His plumed hat blows in the wind. He is learning much. The fish is telling him secrets of how the universe works, how mankind works, of the power of love and the secrets of the human heart.

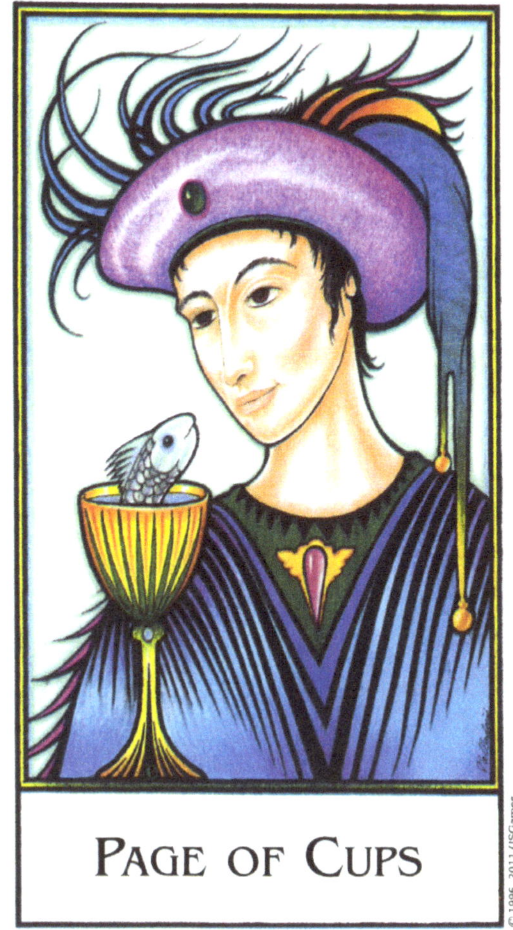

As the Earth element of the Water suit, both of these Pages tell us that a solid emotional core is necessary for growth into emotional maturity. Too much Earth, and we become stuck in the mud, unable to change and grow. Too little Earth, and we are unable to root ourselves emotionally. Either way, we are unable to mature into our roles in family and society, and remain stuck in an emotionally underdeveloped and unsatisfying position.

We must ground ourselves in a stable and flexible emotional reality to be able to grow into our true selves. We must listen to our own intuition to guide us to our emotionally authentic way of being, to live fully and with great joy.

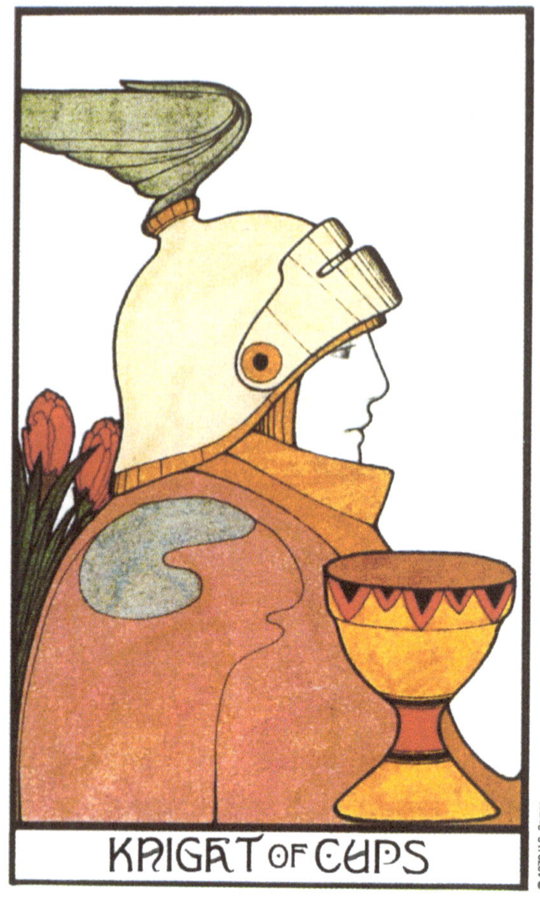

A young woman waits. She wears her jousting helmet, crowned by the wing of a raven. She looks apprehensive. A contest is coming—always.

The Page's roses have opened and are blooming for the Knight, signifying the growth which moves us to a new level of maturity. Her Cup is next to her, keeping her aware of, but not solely focused on, her emotional state. She is able to incorporate her emotions into her life without letting them run her life. The winged helmet shows her ability to balance feelings with thought before taking action.

The silhouette of the ram on her cloak links her to the Emperor, emphasizing that action is required to take the emotional impulse from idea to reality.

Whereas the Emperor often succeeds by suppressing his emotions, the Knight is learning to manage her emotions. Her self-awareness allows her to use the energy in a positive way moving her towards mature fulfillment of her responsibilities, rather than diverting energy needed for growth into simply suppressing her emotions.

With this awareness, she can become a perfect commingling of the creative emotional energy of the Empress and the disciplined intellectual influence of the Emperor—a whole person, fulfilling her role calmly and confidently as she serves her Queen and her King.

This Knight of Cups is a woman. She has just completed her joust. She lifts her Cup in triumph. She wears a plume upon her winged helmet. Flowers celebrate her victory.

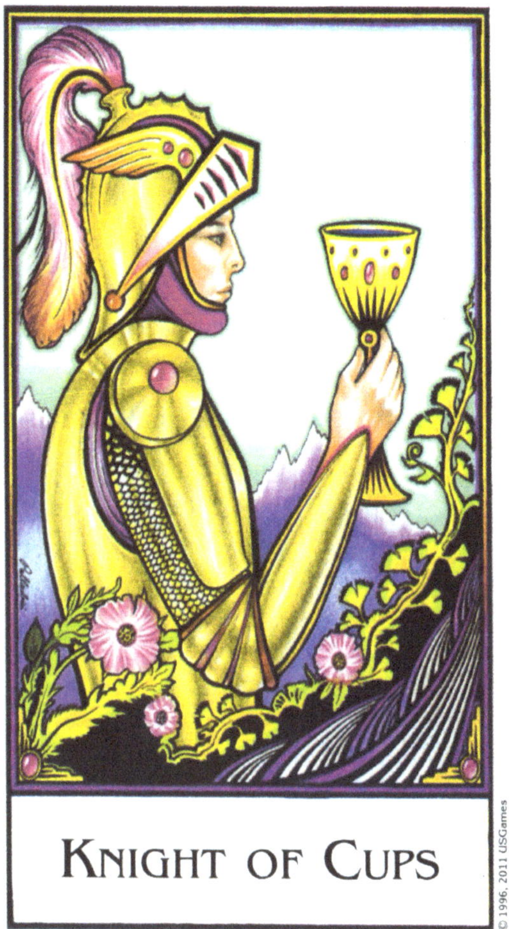

This Knight seems to be more in a state of contemplation. She holds her Cup and focuses intently, her winged helmet lending mental energy to the emotional process. The blooming flowers indicate growth, although perhaps a slower and more organic process than the calculated plan of the *Aquarian* Knight.

As the Fire element of the Water suit, the Knights remind us of the need for action—we must dare, decide, and then do something for anything to change. Wishing is not enough; we must act on our desires and plans for them to become reality.

The Chariot energy of doing, governed by the intellectual energy of the Emperor, gives this Knight the tools she needs to achieve her goals. Her ability to combine both the emotional Empress and intellectual Emperor energies gives her the same potential as her Aquarian counterpart to become a whole person, responsible to herself and her community, calmly and confidently fulfilling her purpose and creating her world.

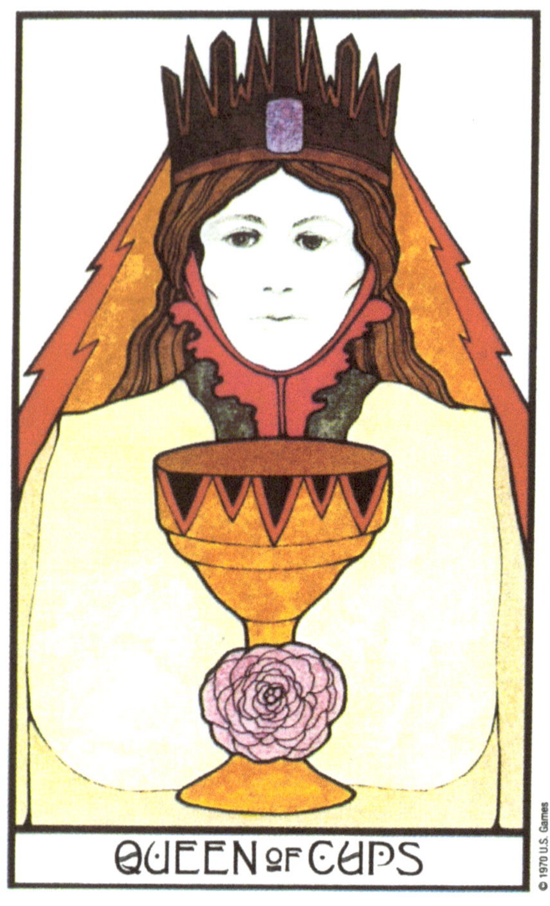

The Queen of Cups is filled with power. Lightning strikes her crown. She has loving eyes. A pink rose wraps around her golden Cup. The Cup is very large in order to hold the waters of life. Fertility, intelligence, and strength are combined in Queen of Cups.

As the Water element in the Water suit, the Queen of Cups is pure emotion, pure intuition, pure vision. She is perceived as unusually psychic, which she undoubtedly is. Her highly developed emotional intelligence and deep intuitive wisdom give her the ability to see and sense others' emotions and motivations more keenly than they themselves can often see and sense.

Strong in the power of her suit, neither Queen needs to hold her cup. It stands before her, symbol and repository of energy, to replenish and refresh both the Queen and those to whom she offers her wisdom.

The *Aquarian* Queen gazes directly at us, questioning us, leading us to question ourselves. Lightning radiates from her crown, enveloping her like the veil around the High Priestess.

Like the High Priestess, the Queen challenges us, questions us, and leads us to learn our own truth. Where the High Priestess, as a spiritual authority, withdraws from the world, the Queen, as a temporal authority, does not need to set herself apart physically. She is in and of the world, and her vibrant energy transforms wherever she is into safe and sacred soul space. She creates her own temple of wisdom for all to enter, wherever she is.

She is beautiful. She is dreaming. She is thinking of visions in her golden Cup. It brims with sacred waters of fecundity and fertility. A fine jewel covers her third eye. She is strong, yet gentle, fair, and honest. An ideal Queen and perfect ruler.

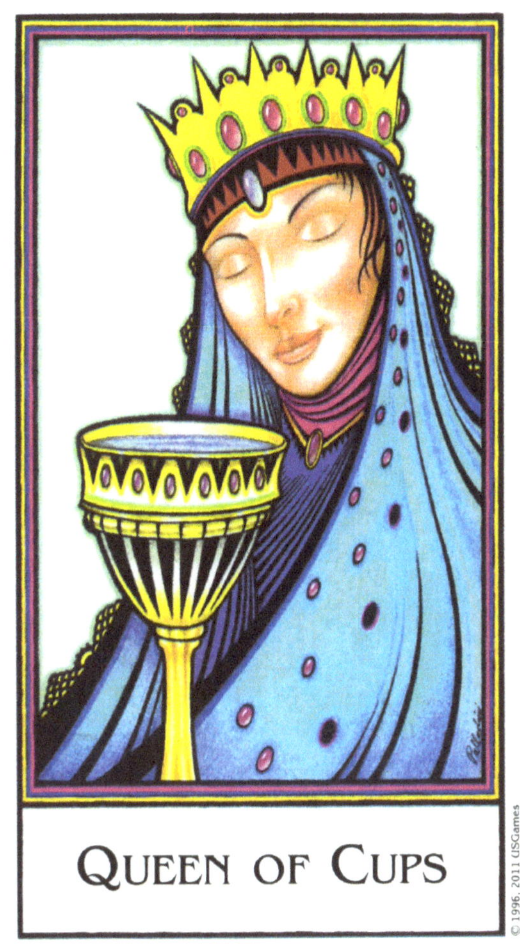

The *New Palladini* Queen wears an actual veil, and meditates with closed eyes. She does not have to use her physical eyes to see us, to see who and what we are. She sees us as we truly are, and, if we are honest, we see what she shows us without defense or denial. We must accept who and what we are, and allow ourselves to imagine who we can become, before we can make any meaningful changes in ourselves and our lives.

Like the High Priestess, the Queen of Cups knows when we are in need of guidance and can challenge us with her wisdom and insight to discover the truth in our own souls. She will challenge us to become better, to reach within ourselves to make contact with, and to bring forth, our emotional gifts and soul wisdom to heal ourselves and others. Being in her presence is enlightening, but not always easy.

The Queen likewise knows when we are in need of emotional nurturing and healing; like the Empress, she can personify the Great Mother, and help us to heal ourselves, and thus to heal others. The gifts we learn to accept from her become gifts we can learn to give to others.

The Queen knows what we need; listen and heed her words, and take action accordingly.

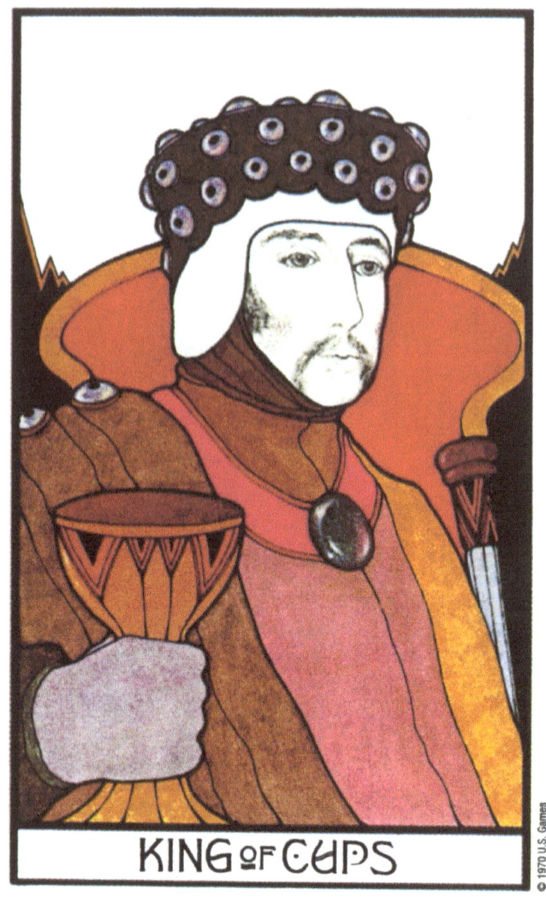

A strong Warrior King. His Scepter and Cup are signs of Power. He is deep in thought, thinking of ways to help his people prosper and grow ever more joyous. He is a good King; an enlightened ruler.

Where the Queen allows us complete immersion in our emotional experience, the King, as the Air element of the suit, tempers our emotional immersion with mental engagement.

Both Kings hold their cups, directly controlling (or trying to control) the emotional energies by focused thought. The warning here is that too much control over our emotions stifles our humanity and cuts our connections with those around us. Similarly, too little control over our emotions causes others to withdraw from us because our instability creates an unsafe environment.

The head of the *Aquarian* King's scepter is tipped by a knob with a geometric pattern matching that on his Cup, further underscoring the mental effort of channeling the emotional energies. His scepter rests at his side, ready for use, directing his will, channeling his emotions, and focusing his thoughts on productive actions and positive results.

The King of Cups is able to manage his emotions in service to his intellect, rather than having one predominate in his personality and behavior. This ability allows him to be a just and fair monarch, and earns him the respect of his people.

A kind intelligent ruler, half male and half female, holds a jeweled scepter in one hand and a golden Cup in the other. The Cup is filled with water, as the sign of the Cup refers to water. Behind the King, we see a dolphin leaping from the sea as a ship in full sail passes by.

The King is the ruler of a prosperous and happy land. There is wealth, commerce, and abundance. Guided by the King's wisdom, the kingdom will prosper in happiness.

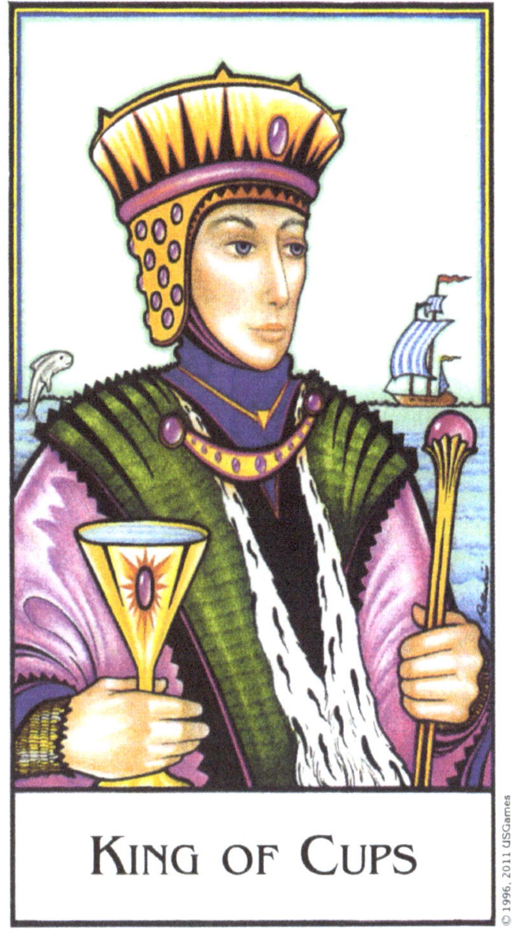

The *New Palladini* King holds a scepter, its jeweled knob also matching the cup, balancing the intellectual and emotional energies. The friendly fish from the Page of Cups reappears here; the King, despite an airy inclination towards the rational intellect, maintains the strong connection with emotions and intuition.

The sperm-like pattern on the robe, the same as the Emperor's, emphasizes the masculine energy of this King. The colors of the clothing and the facial features are similar to those of the High Priestess, calling forth the feminine side of this King.

The gender mix intentionally introduced into this card reinforces its message of the balance between water and air, emotion and intellect, feminine and masculine energies.

The ship, representing action, once again completes the triad of Dare (fish), Decide (King), and Do (ship).

The Kings remind us that the combination of intellect and emotion is powerful alchemy. The will desires, the mind inspires, and events transpire. To achieve success, the will must be managed by emotional awareness and intellectual rationality; to move from an idea from theory to reality, the mind must be moved by will and the force of emotion.

www.ingramcontent.com/pod-product-compliance
Lightning Source LLC
LaVergne TN
LVHW070120110826
845147LV00002B/161
9780983302407